ATTACK WITH

THE **STACK**

CHANGE YOUR STORY
CHANGE YOUR LIFE
TODAY!

GARRETT J WHITE

Attack with the Stack: Change Your Story, Change Your Life Today!

Copyright ©2019 by Garrett J White

Wake Up Warrior™

www.wakeupwarrior.com

Published by Brand Elevate

ISBN: 978-0-9834724-2-1

Published in the United States of America

TABLE OF CONTENTS

SECTION TWO: THE ANGRY STACK

SECTION THREE: THE HAPPY STACK

SECTION FOUR: THE GRATITUDE STACK

SECTION FIVE: CONCLUSION

DEDICATION PAGE

No man arrives at a place publishing a book of this magnitude without a wake of powerful men & women who mentored, guided, coached and inspired him.

I dedicate this book to my original spiritual mentors that taught me via books, audios, events, small group masterminds and transformative one-on-one sessions:

Byron Katie
The late Debbie Ford
Deepak Chopra
The late Dr. Wayne Dyer
Eckhart Tolle
Neale Donald Walsch
Esther & Jerry Hicks
Tony Robbins
Brad Blanton
Jesse Elder

Your example set me free and inspired my pursuit of THE VOICE and the uncovering of the version of the Universal Curriculum of Awakening that I was called to broadcast to the world via the spiritual weapons know as the Stack.

To Natalie Martin

For keeping me focused, encouraged and on fire through the process, assuring that the message I truly wanted out to the world was being delivered through your writing, editing and curating of my message.

To Jeff McGregor

For staying constant and stabilizing the operations and systems of the Wake Up Warrior Movement that allowed me the time, energy and space to write this book and still maintain all of my business interests.

To My Best Friend, Sam Falsafi

Your courage to run into the NIGHT with me as we built Wake Up Warrior these past 6 years has been life altering for both of us.

Thank you for your courage, your example and your commitment.

To The Men Of Wake Up Warrior *(Past & Present)*

Thank you for believing long before it was popular to believe.

Thank you for trusting me as I was inspired to bring the CORE 4 and STACK GAMES to life real-time with you.

Your willingness to test and perfect these weapons with me will impact MILLIONS.

And Finally To My Queen, Danielle.

The greatest single mentor in my life.

The woman I love to loathe and who at times I loathe to love.

The woman who has taught me more about life than all of my mentors over a lifetime.

I love you deeply.

The End.

HOW TO READ THIS BOOK

The Warrior Game has been in full effect since 2012, but there are still men every day that have never heard of the Warrior's Way that were handed this book, so if that's the case for YOU, Brother, you're starting your journey SPICY with this book on The Stack.

Make sure that you read through the Preface for the backstory on Wake Up Warrior™ which was taken directly from the first few chapters inside of the WarriorBook tome. For those that are familiar with my origins as the Founder of the Warrior's Way, feel free to skip the Preface and head right into the Introduction, written by the lead trainer and one of my closest friends, Sam Falsafi.

Regardless of where you start, just know that this isn't going to be your typical business book. The focus is to get you to consistently desire writing and journaling in what is known as The Stack on a regular basis, so I've provided examples from my own personal Stack Library for each section. They are unedited and probably full of a bunch of spelling and grammatical errors, but the point of the Stack is to get the words OUT, rather than creating an edited version of life.

Each section is broken down according to the Stack in which they represent. You will be reading allegorical conversations that I had in creating each one of these Stacks, inspired by actual events that were occurring in my life at pivotal moments. In June of 2016, the birth of the MEGA STACK occurred, and consecutively each year after came the ANGRY STACK, then the HAPPY STACK and finally the GRATITUDE STACK in the beginning of 2019. You'll join into the conversation on their origin before learning each Stack's content, reading my examples and then having the opportunity to create Stacks of your own.

This is meant to be an interactive book where the inaugural Stacks within each section, and therefore the most poignant will be in texting format…as if you were scrolling through a text conversation that I had between myself and The Voice. If you have no idea what I mean by that, you'll soon be fully immersed in what this conversation looks like.

Something else to keep in mind is that as Warrior is continually evolving, so too are our weapons. The Stack is one that continually updates and improves, so some of the examples from my previous years of Stacking won't have all of the answers that are in the current Attack with the Stack Software.

The overall questions within the MEGA, ANGRY, HAPPY and GRATITUDE Stacks are presented in their entirety at the end of each section as well to help you with easy referencing for what that Stack specifically covers.

This book consists of sacred text and scripture from within my own life and is not meant to be taken lightly. I am inviting you to embark on this journey with me, Brother, and I want you to know that I had to go to a very vulnerable place in order for the content within this book and the Attack with the Stack Software to come about. This book provides insight into the passion and drive behind the whole Wake Up Warrior Movement.

THE PREFACE

WARRIORBOOK

Chapters One-Three

THE PREFACE
PART ONE:

THE PIT

> "Through me you go into a city of weeping; through me
> you go into eternal pain; through me you go amongst
> the lost people."
>
> **— Dante Alighieri**
>
> *The Inferno* excerpt from *The Divine Comedy*
> [Late Middle Ages Italian Poet, 1265-1321]

New Year's Eve, 2007.

As the rest of the world went about celebrating the dawn of a
New Year heading into 2008, I lay in my bed, inside my large
home that we had acquired not two years before. My wife sat up
next to me and I can still remember the current of wind from the
ceiling fan that I had become so addicted to, blowing down upon
us.

We had these huge shutters over the left side of some giant
windows that filled the master bedroom. I could see the moon
reflecting through these giant shades off my wife's face. She
turned and looked at me, with tears pouring down her cheeks: "I
did not sign up for this. How are you going to fix it?"

I lay down and put my hands back behind my head, closing my
eyes. My mind raced back to the summer, six months before, of

me sharing the stage with Tony Robbins at the Mortgage Planner Summit in Las Vegas, Nevada. My mortgage empire was expanding and we were dominating, and yet, here I lay, heading into 2008, with everything crumbling around me.

My Marriage Was About To Be Exposed For The Shell That It Was.

What's interesting about the tide is that when it begins to go out, it exposes everything that was hidden. At low tide, it exposes realities like rocks that you can't see when the tide is high; they're always there, whether you can see them or not.

When the financial tide in my life began to roll out, it exposed a painful reality inside of my life within my marriage, spiritual truth, physical body and business that I had been ignoring for years.

That reality was simply this: my life was not working, but because the money had been so good for so long I was able to simply ignore the painful issues.

The fact was that no matter how much I hustled every single day, my life had become a Sedation Game filled with quicksand that was constantly filling in every single hole that I attempted to dig.

No matter how much I tried to wrap my mind around what was happening, wanting to blame my wife for the pain I was feeling, the loss of all three of my businesses, and the implosion of my entire life, I wouldn't have had my rebirth without it.

Even if you've never heard of me or Wake Up Warrior™ before you picked up this book, understanding this journey of my life becomes crucial in seeing WHY the Stack was created in the first place: there was 1) a Pit that I started into and 2) the Systematic Sedation of men, which started a global movement with over 50,000 men in 37 countries and counting.

Yet you never hear people shout,

"Hey, you know what? I'm so glad that my life is burning down to the ground right now because eventually it's going to lead to a world-wide movement."

No, that's not the part of the story anybody actually wants to experience, or even acknowledge, let alone write in a book that matters. They don't want to experience the reality of me sitting in the basement with a bottle of vodka in one hand, drinking myself stupid every afternoon, trying to figure out how in the hell I got here, and how in the hell I was going to get out.

Reality Bites Hardcore
When In The Pit.

I reached out to many people while I was in the Pit but most of them simply thought the answer was, "Read this scripture, pray, and life will just work itself out." Although I could appreciate where they were coming from, at the same time it was not assisting me at all. Day after day, the Darkness of Uncertainty filled my veins, slowly killing all creativity and confidence I had.

Inside that pain, the drinking continued and the drugs soon followed. Because of the stories I lived in at the time, I felt that I couldn't truly expose my reality to anyone and so the cover-ups began.

I would button these exposing parts of myself up every single day as I put my suit jacket on, and I would go out into the world and pretend. Pretend that my life itself hadn't faded into oblivion; that I wasn't hurting. What I didn't realize at the time was that I was slowly committing suicide.

I couldn't see that what I was creating were even greater problems stacked upon the problems I was already facing. Perhaps as you are reading this book of Warrior Scripture you might be sitting there with the thought, "Garrett, I don't drink, I don't have marriage problems, my life is really good;

I just want *more*."

Or

"Garrett, my life is good, maybe even great, but I'm bored out of my mind and feel like I am about to burn it all to the ground."

There Was No Thinking Outside of the Burning Box.

There are two ends of the same burning wick. You see, your kingdom can be destroyed equally from one of two directions.

    1-Boredom

    2-Burn Out

I know it sounds ridiculous to some, but I have watched more men burn their lives to the ground out of boredom when life was good than I have seen men over the years destroy everything because of burnout.

In my life I have experienced both and 2008 was not a Boredom game; it was a Burn Out Game.

As My World Was Burning To The Ground...

I Was Left With The Greatest Challenge That A Man Faces When Shit Is Not Working: Shift.

You would think that shifting would be easy when something is not working at the level you know it could and should, but the challenge is the fact pointed out by Albert Einstein,

"A man's mind lacks the capacity to solve the problems it has created at the same level of thinking that originally created the problem."

I was stuck. My mind was closed and I was stuck in a suicide mission of thoughts. I wanted out of my burning world but I had no idea how to do that, and the possibility of accessing my own liberation based on where my mind was, sat at about zero.

I Was Stuck; I Felt Like A Slave To My Own Mind.

I tried religion, fitness, marriage counseling, talking to my parents; none of it was working. It seemed to me that I was doomed to a painful death, convinced that I was fast on my path to becoming another Entrepreneurial Statistic of Failure.

When I fell, everyone disappeared and I was alone. The hundreds of people I had employed, all of the individuals I had supported over the years, gone. There I sat, alone, trying to find the answers in my own insane mind. Why does my life hurt so much? Why am I so angry? Why do I feel so helpless? Why do I have all these questions? What are all these desires that I am feeling? There was no one to ask; nowhere I could go to find these answers.

I Started Searching Desperately, Trying To Find An Answer...

...(any answer) that would give me some kind of direction. After hundreds of conversations with the leaders at church, the individuals in my neighborhood, the people who were supposedly my friends;

I started to realize that they were also stuck in many of the same problems that I was, but they lied and suppressed and weren't willing to acknowledge them yet, so our conversations would end up fruitless.

I was so sick of the flat, shallow conversations I was having. Nobody, it seemed, was willing to talk about *real* Shit: The Panic, the Pain or the Problems they were facing.

See, I was looking for Support in all the wrong places.

"How do I fix this painful reality called my life?" I asked myself.

Unable to find freedom through this internal conversation, I began to blame my wife for everything. The Blame Game became the easiest move making my wife a target. I blamed her for my pain. I blamed her for my confusion. I told myself a seductive story that supported me in casting her as the character of my destruction.

As I assaulted my wife with my verbal venom, I had become completely ignorant to my role in my own pain. I ignored the fact that I had shown up like an idiot for almost a decade in our relationship; the more I told myself this insane story that it was all her fault, the more I believed it.

In My Darkest Pain, I Was Alone.

I had no Brotherhood. I had no Warrior's Way to Having It All. There was no CODE to live by. No Stack to use. I was alone, frustrated, hurt and deeply confused.

By the end of 2009 I was weighing it at 172 pounds because my solution to all of this pain was to start running every single day. For most people this would mean a 3-5 mile jog. But for me, this meant 20-30 miles every single morning. I was literally, physically, running myself to death. I looked sick and unhealthy. I would run and run and drink and drink, trying to find some connection inside of this pain.

Fueled by the story that my wife was the problem and the cause of my pain, I began to search for emotional support from other women in my life since I didn't feel I could get it from her. I was convinced that another woman was what I needed: one who could love, embrace, and accept me as I was.

This led me to an affair, and that's when I finally hit rock bottom. The day after the Affair, I stood in front of the bathroom mirror, looking into my sunken eyes after returning from a 32 mile run exhausted and ready to go back to bed. I could not recognize the man that stood in front of me. What had happened to me in less than 18 months? Where was Garrett?

I Wanted To Die.

Some men speak of their affairs as this glorious experience that they learned a lot from and even enjoyed. Not me. Mine was a one-time event, and it was the opposite of everything that my fantasies had told me it would be. After that experience, I felt more alone than I had ever felt in my entire life. I felt like God had left me just as my wife and family were leaving me. I was going to fucking lose everything, and for what? A one-night fling trying to escape who I was.

I was convinced that I had become cursed, and that God and the Universe had conspired against me, set out to destroy this shell of a man that I had become because somehow I had missed the turn in the road. That is, until I heard something. At the bottom of that painful Pit, all alone, there was a Voice that entered into my experience. It wasn't loud; it just simply said,

"Will you listen to me now?"

I don't know what your Pit looks like: it could be a small one, or it could be a massive crater like mine was. You could be in a situation in which life is painful, or you could be in a situation in which life is just numb.

You could be in a situation in which life is filled solely with pleasure but you know there's something more out there, and guess what?

Inside of all of that is going to come the same experience for you that I had; at some point, you will need to become humble enough, beaten-down enough, to listen to the Voice inside of you.

On that day, mine said,

"Are you ready to listen? Are you ready to hear what I have to say?"

As I rose from that place, I was very aware that I would likely lose my wife, my family; everything. I would become the second-time divorced man, children with two ex-wives, and a walking billboard for "*How To Fuck Up Your Life*, now playing in the douche bag next to you." The craziest part of these years? On the outside, everyone thought at some level I was just fine.

I knew I could no longer sustain the lies or the façade. I refused to continue to maintain the energetic resource necessary to mask, suppress and pretend that I actually believed what I believed in church; that I felt what I felt in life.

I Was Tired Of Pretending And Believing The Lies Inside My Own Mind.

I was sick of being a believer in God; I wanted to Know Him. I wanted to find and discover my Divinity, but the only way to do this was to have the courage to put my entire life on the line, and in that place, say, "If I lose it all, that is fine, because I am going to start from a foundation that is built upon Truth."

There's A Necessary Difficulty In Building A Foundation On Truth

Little did I realize how difficult this would be, and how much society does not support men like you and I to tell the truth. Not in business, not in marriage, not in life. We are surrounded by people every day who truly can't handle the full truth we have to share with them. These same people have told us to calm down, relax, or tone it down. They have asked us to be quiet. They have told us to shut up. They have demanded that we not share everything even if it means we die. The world is so politically correct these days that it's almost impossible for a human being to actually express what they are feeling.

For powerful men like you and I, this becomes our downfall. It becomes our casket. My life went to the place it went to, my affair happened, all because I couldn't tell the truth to my wife. I couldn't speak about how much I was hurting and about how big of a failure I felt like I was. I couldn't be honest with her or colleagues in business. Literally, the Truth would have set me free but I was unable and unwilling to speak it.

How Do You "Be The Man?"

One night, deep inside another fight with my wife, with tears pouring down her cheeks she screamed, "Just be the man!" It was the same fight we had every night about the same topics: sex, money, the kids...take your pick.

But in that night's fight, for some reason the phrase she screamed echoed in my soul:

"Just be the man."

The Problem arose in me for the very first time:

"I don't even know what the fuck 'Be The Man' means."

Here is the reality: My dad was never around to teach me how to be a man. He was gone all of the time providing for the family, and I appreciate his commitment to make sure that we had food and shelter. But because my Dad was gone all the time, do you know who was teaching me to be a man? My mom.

My mom is a total badass and I love her to death. I love my dad as well and know he did the very best he could, but he was not an example of what it was to be a whole man in our home. He was an example of what it was to be a sedated one, a one-dimensional father who could make some money but was not emotionally and physically around. I didn't grow up with mentors and guides and examples who truly taught me, "Garrett, this is what it means to be a man."

So, I Started Looking.

I thought maybe there was somebody who was doing this. Maybe there could be someone who had figured out how to train me to be a man.

I Googled "how to be a man" (true story) and all kinds of crazy shit came up, none of which had any semblance of what I was truly seeking.

Inside of that, I started searching and reading, going to events and programs, and figured out that part of my problem was that I had not been able to actually see the truth inside of me. I could fundamentally not answer what should seem like the simplest questions in life:

Who am I beyond the roles of husband, father?

Who am I beyond the experience of this religion?

Who am I beyond this political system?

Beyond all my labels, who was Garrett?

Who am I?

I had no answer for this. I didn't know.

But I began searching...for a Key...*something* that worked.

Then I started to have these other conversations enter into my mind. I went to a workshop where this guy was talking about these 12 categories of life. I looked at him: fit with a really beautiful wife. I'm hearing how they talk about sex and intimacy, while I'm sitting in this disconnected relationship in which things are not working out at all with my wife.

I'm looking at them as a couple. They're making money, they're fit, and all of this shit seems to be working in their life. They've got great kids. I'm like, "Oh my God, they must be full of shit. There's no way, no way possible, that these 12 areas they talk about could actually be real for them." And yet, they were.

I wanted to say, "Bullshit," because it seemed so impossible in my own life. Much like it might have seemed impossible to you to Have It All before the Stack. I couldn't believe it, yet deeply wanted it to be true for me also.

You might be having the same thoughts.

"Dude, I don't even know if this is possible. Can I truly have it all in my Body, Being, Balance, and Business, Garrett? I don't know. It seems like a concept that resonates as truth for me at the Core, but I don't know if that's possible."

If you're like I was, there's likely a part in you that is scrutinizing and part of your mind is listening, just searching for a reason to tell me to fuck off. I wouldn't be upset with you, because guess what my mind would have done? The exact same thing, because when I was in that state of wanting, it seemed so unreal, improbable, and impossible, that I could have it all.

The Blinders Were Painfully Small Through Which I Saw The World.

After searching and searching to find this, it came down to one simple truth; there was no training for what I was seeking. There was no comprehensive program on what it was to be a man, let alone a four-dimensional modern man facing modern problems in a modern society. The best that could be delivered up was a series of one-dimensional men who could train you on one, maybe two dimensions.

Most men that I had ever worked with, been in business with, or had as clients, were very good at two things: making the money and maintaining their body for the most part. When it came to spirituality, parenting and marriage, it was a nightmare. Occasionally I would meet men who were very, very good as fathers and amazing husbands, but they couldn't bring home the money; they struggled financially.

Or maybe they could make the money and they were very good at being a parent, but they were physically falling apart with diabetes, having to give themselves injections every day because their body was fat and had become a cage instead of a weapon.

I found some who were very, very spiritual, but the rest of their world was in complete disarray. They would sit and meditate all day, yet not be able to pay their cell phone bills let alone fund anything that would really change the world.

There Has Been A Systematic Sedation Of The Modern Man.

It was confusing to me, because inside of each one of their specific focuses they were amazing, but the moment it went comprehensive, they were left wanting. In the end, like myself, I recognized they were nothing more than one-dimensional douchebags that knew how to be good at one thing only.

Good for you, you're powerful inside a meditation room. Good for you, you're powerful inside a conference room at a meeting. Good for you, you're beautiful, amazing, and powerful with the weights inside the gym. Good for you, you're amazing when it comes to your kids. Good for you.

I was like, "Dude, how is it possible that we have defined being a man as a guy who just makes the money?" That seemed to be the only conversation that was consistent, that the role and goal of "being a man" was to make money. As long as that happened, sex should follow, and everything else should just take care of itself. Yet this was not my experience because I had made the money and still was left wanting: I knew that was a lie.

So I Went On A Journey
To Figure Out Why.

Along the way, I uncovered something so massive it was hard to believe at first. My reality, which was what most modern men were facing, had been manufactured over 100 years ago to systematically destroy mankind by sedating the Kings.

The results of living we were experiencing today had come on the wake of a series of world-altering shifts over a century that made it almost impossible for men like you and I to ever have it all.

My Brother,

All great revolutions began with a simple question.

My question was,

"How in the hell did we get here as men?"

The answer that I found I now call the Systematic Sedation of a Modern Man, but you're going to have to read on to the next chapter to learn how it all came to be.

THE PREFACE
PART TWO:
___
THE PAINFUL PROBLEM

> "The Industrial Revolution has two phases: one material, the other social; one concerning the making of things, the other concerning the making of men."
>
> **-Charles A. Beard**
>
> [Influential American historian in first half of 20th century, 1874-1948]

As much as I wanted to blame my dad for not raising me to be a man, the truth was, my father (like me) had been born into a Game of Sedation that had been gaining momentum for generations before he was born.

The Sedation Game was created long before my father and I were born, spinning out of control, taking men from a place of power and thrusting them in a place of powerlessness. This dark system was literally destroying kings and turning them into peasants.

By the time my father was born, this was all the men around him knew. He didn't understand the disconnect behind why, how, or what he was experiencing and feeling. The last thing in the world he was able to do was to actually talk with anybody about it. Why had this happened? See, I wanted to know and understand how we as men had gotten here. Every man I looked around at, and came into conversation with, far and few between were those who were willing to beat the drum the way that I believe a four-dimensional modern man living the Warrior's Way should.

Living in Power as a man these days is almost impossible with the current set up of rules and guidelines that we are supposed to follow according to what society has dictated.

There is an epidemic[1] of disconnected teenagers and men in their 20's and 30's who are literally becoming dysfunctional at everyday living of the most basic human skills.

This problem is not only apparent in the younger generations, but is showing itself in massive ways for men who are in their 40's and 50's, with suicide rates that have gone through the roof for men in their 60's.

Divorce Rates Are Running Rampant As Men Scramble To Try To Figure Out *"How to Be the Man,"*

while women grow tired of the pussies their husbands have become and would rather raise their children alone *and* fulfill both roles as Mother and Father than to be married to dead wood. There's an alarming rise of divorces[2] that we're experiencing inside of the United States being filed by women in

---

[1]This has been referred to as extended adolescence, see Additional Resources for more information and later further into Part Two: The Painful Problem

[2]"Divorce After 50 Grows More Common" internet article by Sam Roberts from *The New York Times*. Retrieved 11 February 2016: http://www.nytimes.com/2013/09/22/fashion/weddings/divorce-after-50-grows-more-common.html?_r=0

their 50's: the moment the kids graduate from high school and move out, they look at the man they have tolerated for nearly three decades and say,

"Forget you, my kids are out of the house so I'm out of here to finally live my life."

Men are left hollow and alone, and don't know why because they were acting like what they thought a man was supposed to act like. The truth is, there are tons of programs that help women, but when was the last time you saw one to help men? It didn't exist. I couldn't find one, which is why I launched Wake Up Warrior in 2012 and began building online platforms since 2015. Within the last decade, I uncovered the facts about the Systematic Sedation of Men including the *why* and *how* it happened. I discovered that history can teach us more about our own lives and how to course correct them when things are off than what I ever imagined.

In order to understand how my dad and I got to this place (and how you did too), we've got to go back to the late 1800s and early 1900s, on into the beginning of what became known as the Industrial Revolution. There was a fundamental shift in the way that living occurred here inside the United States and around the world at this time.

The Shift Would Affect Everyone And Literally Change The Way The World Worked.

Before the Industrial Revolution, the majority of society existed in what has been labeled an agrarian existence. This way of living occurred in the following reality: Dad, mom, and child co-creating together. They were feminine and masculine equals, yet at the same time distinct and different in their roles with the man as the head of the household. A typical day for Dad would be waking up in the morning then going to work on the farm minutes from the house and at the core of his Community. Guess who also got to watch and participate in this same work every single day?

Johnny. Little Johnny would go to work with his dad side by side, literally, every single day. Little Johnny was seeing through example on how being a man worked. Dad didn't disappear for the day and then return home to guide the children at night. From breakfast to lunch to dinner, dad was actively role modeling to children respect, education, hard work, fear of God, connection to the queen, respect and responsibility. Every single day, dad was demonstrating to his sons the answer to the question, "How Do I Be A Man?"

That Same Question Is Still Asked Today, Yet A Massive Shift In Mentality Led To A Different Answer.

What does this have to do with the Industrial Revolution? Everything, my friends. Until the 1800s, the majority of society lived in self-sufficiency this way. There was a co-parenting relationship: Dad was not sent away; mom was not sent away.

There was this home-base Core Connection where family mattered and was valued, where each individual knew his and her role in running a household and land.

This way of thinking and living had been a part of society for centuries, so surely a cataclysmic event caused this great shift in thinking, right? It did, a plague came about, but not as a natural disaster.

The promise of more caused us as a Society to shift from this agrarian age in which Mom and Dad co-parented and co-raised the Children to one of seemingly limitless possibilities.

The Industrial Age offered up a Big Promise. The promise itself was an interesting one, very appealing to Mom and Dad. How do we know? Because it changed the entire world from what it was to the way that we know it now. Some people feel it was a bad, horrible, and an awful promise that caused the rich to grow richer and the poor to grow poorer. Although the rapid growth of industrialization did have its upsides in building a powerhouse nation in America, the downside as to what this did to the family was hard to ignore. The Industrial Revolution wasn't seen as a problem; it was a Solution to a Problem. With that solution came a "cost" many were willing to pay, which also brought with it a new series of problems that we could not have anticipated. This is the crazy Catch-22 part of all blessings: we can't have them without the downside curse of natural consequences.

So, What Was The Solution To The Problem?

The Industrial Pitch was essentially this: Move in order to progress forward. Literally, let go of the Farm and move your family from the country to the city. No more blood, sweat and tears with the back-breaking work of the farm. No seasonal issues with weather, or dealing with a starving family if the crops failed. Men were enticed to venture forth into the new possibilities awaiting them within the city with more certainty in the future there for what? More money. All at the low cost of simply leaving the home during the day for the factory and office.

Instead of Dad working side by side with little Johnny, he would be required to leave the home every morning, travel miles away to and go to work in the factory, a place that Little Johnny would not be allowed to work side by side with his father[3]. It was no longer a possibility to have hands-on schooling side by side while performing chores and working on the farm with dad, but that felt like a justifiable loss in order to give the family more, right?

What had not been considered along with this commute was the distance between this separate place of work and home, and that's where several other things began to shift in men. Before the Industrial Game, Dad was rewarded for playing the Game of Life on the farm by using his creativity, innovation, and ability to solve problems. This game play was worked out of a man with rote actions specific for one job. Men were punished in the marketplace for innovation because there was a systematic way

---

[3]Child Labor Laws came about during the Progressive Era in which children were also sent to work in factories, resulting in a whole generation of children uneducated as well as extremely unsafe working conditions. See Walter Trattner, *Crusade for the Children: A History of the National Child Labor Committee and Child Labor Reform in America* (1970) in Appendix Resources: Progressive Era.

of doing things that were not to be disrupted. He was required to sell his Crown for cash, taken from his position as a king and compelled to become a cog in a machine.

A significant percentage of males in society went from being a king in the home, praised in admiration by his children and his wife, where the family unit all worked alongside each other, to a disposable tool. Sometimes he would not even see the sun as he would leave for work early in the morning, enter the office while it was still dark, returning home late after long factory hours and commuting after sunset.

Men Were Facing An Exhausting Reality

On the odd nights that this industrial man got home before Little Johnny was asleep, he was so exhausted from the relentless grind that any attempt to fulfill a role as a father was mediocre at best in such a fatigued state. He still wanted to be there for his kids, but little by little as he started to climb the corporate ladder towards the Industrial Revolution's American Dream, priorities shifted more and more from the influence he once had while on the farm.

All of this was justified under the belief that the money was the most important gift he could offer his children: a future brighter than his own with opportunity to experience a "better" and easier life. What didn't he account for, however? The time he was gone from little Johnny and the impact of having mom fulfill both the Father and Mother roles meant that little Johnny wasn't learning how to be a man *by* a man.

Dad thought in his mind that at least they weren't living in tenements like some of the immigrants that had come over from the Mother Land where the whole family had to work[4]. There was more money, so mom and the kids were actually having the opportunity within the city to experience some things they didn't get to experience out on the ranch and on the farm. They wore better tailored clothes made from textile mills, and eventually moved up into a better house, therefore gaining more social networks and friends.

Dad looked at this overall experience as good. "This was beautiful," he decided. Slowly, though, the game was different, and Mom shifted as well, saying, "It's okay, Love. I know you're tired. You're doing everything you can to provide for this family."

Over One Generation Boys Were No Longer Working Side By Side With Their Father's Anymore.

They were no longer being raised by both parents. They had a father who only saw them for 1 hour, maybe 2, at night; this is what they saw and so they figured that's how it's to be done. It became the norm to be raised by Mother. This may not seem like a big deal, but just like all journeys that we take, if we shift just one degree, we split in a completely different direction. Look how quickly thousands of years of fatherhood had shifted within

---

[4]Refer to Additional Resources in back of book which talks about Child Labor

just one to two generations as the agrarian life was replaced by the factory and office life.

In the beginning, it doesn't really look like too much. After all, our whole purpose in life is supposed to be progress and expansion, right? And that's exactly what the Industrial Age and Progressive Era consisted of.

This simple shift declared, "Fathers, your job is to be a cog and bring home the bacon. Become a tool of production by being a cog in a system, inside the factory of the Industrial Revolution; that's how you hunt the buffalo now." Not a king with council to provide for your family the emotional, financial, social, spiritual support that you were once required to live and teach. That's outdated. Now we just need you to go produce in the office: "Go, make the money." The Progressive Era[5] then came in to rectify the unsafe and unlawful working conditions, but any thought on the mental progress of the working man became even more sedated.

We Were Progressing Towards World Wars

Part of that was due to outside events, when the world experienced a Great War[6] to end all wars, which further solidified this mentality that man serves society best by being away from the home. We had all of these boys that saw their Dad working in the factory and office become men as soldiers in World War I, learning firsthand in the trenches further 'progress'

---

[5]The Progressive Era was a period of widespread social activism and political reform across the United States, from the 1890s to 1920s.

[6]The Great War occurred from 1914-1918. See also The Great War in Additional Resources

that war brings. A nation-wide Depression[7] occurred as we were slowly reminded that it requires hard work to bring in the paycheck within an office or factory, but because jobs were so few, men didn't know what to do. Countries were invaded and declared war on others as World War II[8] then ensued, providing drafts and opportunities for men to continue to go out and not only provide for their family, but for their nation's freedoms and liberties.

In The Military, There Is No Room For Feelings.

We needed to take those feelings and suppress them because they'll get in the way of killing another man. Now, men have been killing each other since Cain found a rock, so none of that was new; what was new was that war had been created with industrial strength, and it required industrial men to execute it. To defend the truths that we hold self-evident here in the United States of America, men declared, "We've all got to go fight the wars of old men."

So, Johnny who was disconnected from Dad already has now learned to shut his feelings down. Entire generations of men were taught that their role was to not only hunt the buffalo, but at the same time, to not even feel. Feeling was not safe because you

---

[7]A time of great economic hardship in America between 1929-1939, but many countries were also facing economic hardships as well post WWI. Many other parts of the world also faced troubling times within their government, such as Germany electing a nationalist named Adolf Hitler to make their war-torn and depressed nation great again.

[8]WWII: 1939-1945. America joined the war after the bombing of Pearl Harbor, December 7, 1941, known as a "Day which will live in infamy" according to President Franklin D Roosevelt.

could die if you did, and so this global lie became truth. The message became: Feeling + showing emotion = death, so if you want to live, operate like a machine and act on what you're told, not how you feel.

This created what we have come to know in society as the Greatest Generation[9].

While the men were gone to War, the women were back on the home front, trying to figure out their new place in this new Age[10]. Society still had to continue, after all. For the first time inside the United States, we began to see a significant rise inside the capacity of employment for women. Women replaced the men who were called out to war in the factories AND were still required to raise the children. I'm going to have you consider that these events could have gone a different way in bringing the family structure back to where it was less than 50 years earlier, but instead, this then led to its own movement for women, shifting roles within society which we will discuss in a few moments.

Mixing The Industrial Mindset With The War Mindset, Entire Generations Of Men Were Told To Stop Feeling...

[9]A term phrased by Tom Brokaw in describing the men and women that grew up during the Depression and faced further hardships in the form of World War II and the resiliency that came from those events within human nature. See Additional Resources: World War II

[10]http://www.history.com/topics/world-war-ii/american-women-in-world-war-ii

...stay disconnected and don't you dare show any feelings or fucking bitch about how you might feel inside. Just get the job done. Don't talk about your feelings, don't talk about your emotions: men were taught to not feel. That being a man means you go get shit done regardless of how you're feeling at the time. You come home, and you don't bitch about it. You don't talk about it and you don't get emotional about it. You hold this stoic position of Emotionless Power. In doing that, you are a great man.

That was my grandfather, Colonel in the Air Force for 30 years. Beautiful, powerful man. However, in the final years of his life here on this planet, the truth started to come out about the pain of what is was to be him; how hard it was for him to be the Man society told him to be.

And yet, for his entire life he had been taught, trained, and educated not to be real, raw and emotional with his wife, his kids or his grandchildren. He literally stayed in the Game of War that feelings could get him killed. When he came back for his last 30 years, he didn't know how to operate any other way but Focused Fire on the outside with a Chaotic Emotional Circus occurring on the inside.

Twisted Feminism Only Led To More Confusion And A Painful Depolarization Of Couples.

And then during the 1960s things inside the United States began to take another massive shift. From finally gaining the right to vote in 1920, women created a small door and opened it slightly during World War II as men who were fighting in the war were replaced by women in the workforce, but it was the 60s and 70s that this Feminist Movement door fully swung open. Inside was a twisted, bastardized version of the feminist suffragists which declared: "We don't need men. We're not just equal, we're superior and they are unnecessary. We can do for ourselves anything that a man can do for us."

What started inside of feminism with votes for women and this first declaration at the door that said, "We want to have a voice" then shifted to the twisted feminist version which threw that door off its hinges with "We want our voice to scream out the equality we demand because we are the same." Equality became: we are the same, and in being the same we don't need you.

This became the Giant Rift, a depolarization of couples; men who were now having to compete with masculine energy with their women and intimacy was slowly being replaced with Competition.

Thoughts in Dad's mind started to become "It's hard enough that I have to go fight these assholes all day at the office. I then have to come home and battle for a voice inside my own home. I can't talk about my feelings anywhere because society told me I'm not supposed to in order to be a man.

If I'm completely honest, I already feel slightly castrated because I'm married to a feminist. I'm not sure what I'm supposed to do."Let's clarify what it means to be the same by recognizing what isn't.

A Penis And A Vagina Will Never Be The Same Thing.

A woman and a man are not the same thing. They never will be.

I don't care if you are gay or you are straight or whatever the hell your fucking sexual orientation is: There Is Woman And There Is Man. They Are Not The Same.

They can be equal, but they will never fucking be the same. One is not superior to the other.

This became another subtle insertion of a lie into our society as masculine traits of hunting buffalo began to rise in women and men began to get confused at levels they'd never been confused in before.

How do I actually show up as the man when I'm confused about what being the man means? I'm looking at this woman but she's kind of being the man, showing up like a dude right now. Confusion is running rampant for men because it's completely misidentified.

We don't even know what being a man *is* anymore because everywhere we turn men are being disappointed, disjointed, and disconnected. They're being told, "Shut up, go get the money, don't talk about your feelings, and just so you know, we don't need you because we're the same."

What quantifies this at an even bigger level? The Information Age[11]. This technological boom began in the late 1990s and then took off into warp drive after the early 2000s. For the first time ever, information proliferated globally through the World Wide Web, where information was no longer only found in books but at the ease of our fingertips.

Men and women began to search out insight through the onslaught of information as it became mobile through cell phones and various electronic devices within a few short years. And yet, all of this unlimited access to information was drowning us. Men and women were searching for answers only to receive contradictory opinions masked as fact; that if it's posted on the internet, it *must* be true. We think that information will actually liberate us, when it has enslaved us. We are becoming robots, plugged in to various electronic devices day in and out.

5 to 6 generations later from the men that left the agrarian lifestyle, boys are being born into a world that makes no sense. The lessons from these past generations of men and information doesn't liberate us, nor does it address the fact that we now have 75 plus years of patterns being built and ingrained.

Boys Are No Longer Becoming Men.

This confusion has become something known by psychiatrists as 'extended adolescence.' Divorce rates are running rampant (if a couple even chooses to marry) and we have more single moms with children than we have ever had in our planet's history. As

---

[11]See Information Age in Bibliography & Additional Resources

we've been able to vaccinate certain diseases that plagued society, we now have super viruses, more physical dis-ease and dysfunction than we have ever had. More disappointment and exodus from religion than we have ever experienced. More governments being toppled and confusion inside of political regimes than we have ever seen. Information has not made all things better, despite what the marketing claims. Information has merely accelerated the inevitability of the implosion in the world as we know it.

Inside of all of this there's this exposed reality of boys who are staying boys long into their 30's and 40's now, never leaving home. They're saying, "You know what? I don't know how to even play this Game called adulthood let alone know how to win. I don't know what it is to be a man. Nobody is teaching me. The men I see on reality television, YouTube, and social media are not teaching me. Governments and political officers aren't teaching me how to be a man. Everyone's getting divorced. Nobody is staying married. Families are becoming smaller. The entire landscape of making money is changing.

This Game Called "Being A Man" Is A Goddamn Nightmare.

Inside this confusion, single and divorced men simply choose to Not Grow Up. And why would they? What incentive is there except the miserable life that they saw their fathers live? "Eat, drink and be merry for tomorrow we die" has become the mantra of the Modern Boy Man who has forgotten he is a King.

Hell, at 30-40 years old, if you can still run around like a 22-year old frat boy, play *World of Warcraft®* every single night and *Call of Duty®* on your gaming system, get laid with girls that are 10 years younger than you, and consume an unlimited amount of porn, why in the world would you want to grow up and move out of your parent's basement?!

The foundation of our society is driven by kings and men, and the way they lead nations comes down to how they lead from the inside of their own families, and that family dichotomy is being destroyed. The boys that are being born into the Game have been given no clear path and so they choose to remain boys. Where does this lead?

A society that no longer wants to raise families. Pornography and quick promises of sex on social media platforms like Tinder have replaced any attempt to work on any form of lasting relationships, because that requires work. A lot of it. Over 35 percent of all content consumed on the web is pornographic in nature by men, so why are they buying porn? Why are they masturbating daily? Why is this occurring? Because men are lost without a road map. They have no idea what it is to truly be a man. And it is not their fault.

The Message Has Become So Confused With The Only Maps Women Have To Offer Titled "Read My Mind"

Or "Be the Man" which when opened has no Key to decipher the content inside.

Women are not to blame in all of this either. They are simply playing the Game they were also taught. Trying to play two sides of the equation, the first as the old school tactic of being a woman which says "Be the man" to their masculine counterparts yet even they don't know what that fucking means; they just know it's what they need. And then there's the other side of the equation, in which most of these women have become just as confused as men about what it actually means to be feminine resulting in a daily emotional castration of is it on or of? with the man they are with.

Nobody In Society Seems To Have The KEY To The MAP.

This is why my marriage was plummeting to divorce. Some people were like, "Well, that's because you cheated, dumb ass" which is definitely part of the equation in my own life. My Life was plummeting to divorce because neither one of us had an answer on what it meant to "Be the Man." Do you think my dad had an answer? No. Do you think my church leaders had an answer? No. Their answer was, "Pray to God." Nice. Fuck off. I appreciate your little Sunday School answer but it's not cutting it. It's not cutting it with me nor with any of the thousands of men that I'm engaged with on this topic every single week.

We needed something *more*. What even is the definition of a man pursuing a life of having it all? We knew what the one-dimensional man looked like: go make some money and workout. Hopefully inside of that you can get laid a couple of times so you feel good about yourselves. If your wife doesn't want to put out, no problem. Porn is just a few mouse clicks away and you can just jack off for free without making any deposits. If that doesn't cut it, then you'll cheat.

Inside Of This, Men Were Left With No Guidance System At All.

This isn't about women attacking, being wrong, or doing something stupid. Women were just as oblivious in the Game as we were (though we'd never tell them that).

Our entire society is plummeting into Chaos because kings— men—are not leading. Men are not standing. How is terrorism running rampant? Because even our political systems are not being led by kings anymore. Sedated jerks hold the seats. What runs rampant inside our body when it is not healthy?

A virus. Cancer cells become activated and begin to build without us even realizing it. We are getting destroyed from the inside out, both male and female. It's happening everywhere. *Everywhere*.

When I saw this, I realized it wasn't even our fault. I was sharing this information with a friend one day and I was like, "Dude, we're all messed up. I don't even know what we are supposed to do with this. How do we fix this?"

My friend responded, "Dude, why don't *you* fix it?"

"Pffft."

I Felt Like Most Leaders Feel When It Comes To Attacking A Giant Problem...

I questioned my capabilities and capacities: Who am *I* to do this? Who am I to be great and lead this Movement? Who am I to start this conversation and define what a man is? What a Modern Warrior Man is?

That's when I heard deep inside: *If Not You, Then Who?*

Long before society started questioning the validity of who I am, and whether or not I'm qualified, I was asking myself those questions. Who am I to lead? I've burned a lot of shit to the ground.

Why not somebody who at least has their shit together? Pick one of the clean cut guys. I'm a bit of a maniac. Why me? Why me?!

"Listen dude, if it's not you, then who?"

If not you, then who?

"Who is more qualified than a guy who has genuinely fucked everything up, to build the map on the way out of the Gates of Hell to the Place of Power? You speak about this 'have it all' situation, but you don't have it. So why don't you figure out how to build it?"

The Birth of The Warrior's Revolution all began with one idea...

This one idea began a Revolution. When I looked around at the results in our society on one dimensionality training, what I saw were men who were alone, depressed, hiding, sick, suffering, struggling, hurting, confused, frustrated, suicidal, homicidal, addicted, dying, and alone.

I knew what it was like because I have felt all of those things as well. I took that on and said, "If it's not me, then who? I don't know who else it could be, so I'm going to give it a shot. Not to lead other's lives. No. I just want to liberate mine."

And the desire for discovering that within me which would eventually become the Stack began.

THE PREFACE
PART THREE:

THE POSSIBILITY

> "But when a long train of abuses and usurpations, pursuing invariably the same Object evinces a design to reduce them under absolute Despotism, it is their right it is their duty, to throw off such Government, and to provide new Guards for their future security."
>
> **-Declaration of Independence**
>
> 4 July 1776

A worldview is nothing more than the world that we believe is real to us. It doesn't mean that that World is actually real to anybody else; it just means it's real to us. Now, can you and I be influenced by the world around us and the worldview of people around us? Absolutely. Are we affected by this with social media? Absolutely. Are we affected by this with television and the churches that we go to? Absolutely.

The People That You Associate With More Often Than Not Are The People Who Share A Common Worldview With You.

Most of us do not spend time with somebody who has a conflicting worldview because when you have two opposing worldview they collide and cause conflict.

One of the great demises inside of this 'sedated man experience' is that:

- Conflict itself has become something that is politically incorrect,

- I shouldn't actually take a stand for a new worldview or the truth the way I see it

- I shouldn't take a stand for truth the way I see it

- Ultimately, unless you collapse yourself down into the politically correct worldview, then it's impossible for you to actually be accepted.

- Most men find it significantly easier to surrender their opinion about the world that they want and just collapse it down into the worldview of what is, not recognizing that in doing so they are continuing the insanity to the next generation.

At Some Point, You Must Take A Stand.

A Stand just like the [12]Founding Fathers of the United States of America who said, "You know what? Your taxes are too high. We don't want to be part of this sovereignty anymore. We don't support your worldview about how we should live here in this country, nor do we support your governance anymore. We're going to create a document called the Declaration of Independence. We're going to unroll it and sign this bitch, all of us together."

---

[12]See Additional Resources: "America's Founding Fathers"

This small band of men, prominent leaders only within their own communities and not yet known to the Crown, knew they were committing high treason putting this document together. And yet, they proceeded in signing it like the wig-wearing bad asses they were, declaring their independence, liberating themselves from what the English crown thought to be true. They said, "We declare our independence. Our worldview is free of the worldview that you say is true. We reject that worldview. Not only that, we pledge our lives, our liberty, and our fortunes upon this land to say 'Fuck you' and your worldview." Well, they were a little more eloquent than that, but the feeling behind the declaration hasn't changed.

Where Are The Men Willing To Make Declarations Like That Today?

Do they even still exist?

These were men of integrity; men who listened to the Voice inside of them, willing to take a stand and be comprehensive men. You don't find much of that anymore in leadership after a century of this sedation cycle we saw in detail within Chapter 2. What we have ended up with is a bunch of weak boys; men who never grew up, that cannot take a stand.

Social media and the internet has given every asshole an opinion. "Keyboard Vigilantes" run rampant around the world. Disconnected, unconscious assholes whose opinion, in some twisted reality, some actually think matters. All of a sudden, we have become influenced in our worldview by people that we don't know, who we don't give a shit about, and yet their opinions are dictating our lives. The Media World has become a den of thieves and a band of liars. Social Media is forming your World View every single day, in some of the most twisted and distorted ways.

In some ways, it is beautiful and in others it is destroying you and everything that you hold dear. So the question I have for you is this,

"Is Your Life Working?"

If it is, then the Worldview you are living through is working and you can continue living the way you are with no issue.

If Your Life Is Not Working And You're Searching For More, Then You're Left With Only One Reality: Change Your Worldview.

Damn straight. The only solution is to destroy the worldview that guided you to create the reality that you desire to change. Figuratively speaking, it is time for you to sign your own Declaration of Independence that compels you to no longer live as a man that society has decided to tax us with by declaring,

"I will no longer live the one to two-dimensional lifestyle as a sedated modern peasant king who lives in the shack and rejects his crown. I reject this doctrine, and I say, 'Forget you, world doctrine. Forget you, century of tradition. Forget you, political correctness. Forget *you*.' I choose to live."

But what does living as a modern man mean? What is the current world's view of a Modern Warrior King? You see, I had to begin to define this inside my own life. I didn't start doing this because I knew you existed, or saw a Revolution ahead of me that was going to change millions of families' lives. What I saw was a life that wasn't working, and it was mine: *my* life was not working. My Worldview was destroying me and I had to change or die. To hell with anybody else; I wanted to wake up with a Desire to live and I knew this was going to require me to change the world I saw.

So, what does it mean for me to ultimately have it all?

What do I want my life to look like?

What do I want as a man?

I Wanted To Feel Harmony, Waking Up In The Morning And Mentally Feeling Like I Was On Fire.

As an athlete, I had moments, even after my athletic career was over, where my body felt just like a weapon, which exuded this powerful confidence because of the way I was eating and the way I was training my body. There was this confidence that seemed to affect everything else around me.

I also wanted to feel like God and I were on the same page, fucking tattoos and all. I wanted to feel like I could hear the Voice inside of me, that as soon as I woke up, I knew my life mattered because this Higher Source, this power called God, this Universe around me, confirmed that it did.

But, you know what? That's not enough. I looked into my home and saw the relationship with my wife and children, and said,

"I want to be done with all this guilt and shame. I want to be done with these inabilities to communicate and to speak my truth; when I'm fired up, I want to be able to speak it, and when my wife is fired up, to be able to allow her to speak it as well."

I needed to learn how to communicate and be real inside that relationship. I needed to learn how to be a parent: babies don't come with goddamn instruction manuals. I wish they did.

The reality was...I did not know how to be a husband.

Sexuality, spirituality, communication and intimacy inside of a relationship are all categories within marriage, yet I realized I didn't know how to be a husband. These topics were all a blur to me and I had no true map to make them work at any level. I came to a very clear reality that I didn't know how to be a husband.

I seriously did not know. It was the greatest and craziest day of my life when I came to truly realize:

"I Don't Even Know How To Be A Husband,

because I've been trained by disconnected douche-bags. I don't even know what that looks like."

I grew up seeing men who would come in after being gone all day golfing on a Saturday, and feel entitled to dinner ready right at the time he walked through the door, food on the table with the kitchen already cleaned, and then sit down on his throne, the couch, to watch football, waiting for the dinner bell to ring.

Then, he'd rise up from one throne to the next one, eating as the fucking Lord of the Land at the head of the table, and promptly leave the food and plates to go back to the couch throne, watching more football on TV while the women cleaned. I would watch these men talk and play pool, and then they would go to their royal bed chambers, still entitled as a king.

If they felt like they needed to get laid, the wife better perform her marital duties. This was the example I was being given; what I saw happening all around me. Now, there is absolutely nothing wrong with playing golf, watching football on Sunday, having your wife cook for you or SEX.

But what I saw behind these actions was an unconscious series of patterns that were creating marriages filled with Suppression and Secrets. A vast majority of the marriages I saw like this were ending in divorce or worse; complete apathy.

So the question is: Who are the role models to follow on how to be a man? A husband and a father?

Most Of Us Were Not Raised With Fathers Who Taught Us This.

That's when I began looking for the man I knew I needed to be.

In fact, we are now experiencing generations of men who were raised in fatherless homes. We were not trained on how to be the man that we knew we needed to be. I knew I had to take my responsibility as a father in a completely different direction that I had seen my father take with me, or how my grandfather had approached fatherhood with him.

I knew I needed to be a better lover and a more seductive player inside my wife's life. I needed to be more supportive, emotionally available, and able to communicate better. I needed to be able to allow her space to grow and become, yet not be triggered by my own ego when doing it.

I knew I needed to find a relationship with God, but I was so stuck in my religious patterns I was raised with that I couldn't get it; it didn't make any sense to me. I couldn't connect inside that space, and so I had to ask myself better questions that ultimately had me leave the church.

I knew I needed to make money, but I also refused to build businesses that I didn't feel had made a difference. Not that the mortgages, insurance and financial services that I came from had no value and importance; I just wanted to create and build businesses that mattered. I didn't want to be a capitalist for capitalism's sake. I wanted to have it all, but I didn't know how.

One day I was talking with some friends about this concept of 'having it all' and I shared with them, "Well, I think we could be fit, I think we can be spiritually on point, I think that we can be deeply, passionately, lustfully desiring and connected to our wives, and, at the same time, completely passionate, almost aching to return home to be with our kids instead of trying to avoid parental duties by remaining at the office, hoping they're in bed by the time we get home. And I believe that in business we can 10x our revenue while covering all of these other areas in our life at the same time, not mutually exclusive."

"Dude, have you been smoking something, bro?"

"How the hell are you going to pull all of that off?"

I don't know anybody who's pulled all that shit off."

I said, "I know. I'm going to be the first one."

"Good luck with that."

I Leveraged His Doubt And The Doubt Of Many Others, Leaping Into What Most Considered To Be A Total Suicide Mission.

Had I known how much work and how painful it would have been, to this day I am not sure I would have taken the leap, but thankfully my ignorance fueled my fire. Over the next couple of years, I would die and be reborn a hundred times emotionally, leaving behind the old me and awakening to a new version of myself.

In My Pursuit To Having It All In Body, Being, Balance And Business I Came To Realize That I Was Going To Need A Shit Load Of Training In Each Area.

Trying to find this kind of training was going to require me to hire coaches, mentors, attend masterminds, read books, articles, newsletters, etc... inside of each one of the 4 domains of Body, Being, Balance, and Business. And, if that wasn't enough, I was going to have to learn how to put them all together, gluing the conversation into a comprehensive yet simple system that would allow for a man like myself to actually get, implement, and maintain the game longer than a weekend or even a couple of months.

I knew any asshole could do something awesome for a weekend, we can all be Weekend Warriors, but I was interested in rebuilding my life permanently. To do this, I needed to change the trajectory of my reality and information, in which guidance and council was going to be mandatory.

Although I intellectually understood the price that was having to be paid emotionally, things were 10x's more complicated; I had no fucking clue how much work it was really going to take. Just like most parents admit when being honest about having and raising children, "If I'd known this shit was going to be this hard, I probably wouldn't have had kids." And yet, you're grateful you did because in that ignorance, you started having babies. Same goes for pursuing down the paths with Business, and you're like, "Dude, if I knew it was going to be this hard as an entrepreneur, I don't think I would've done it."

Are You Ready to Pay the Necessary Price?

..If I Knew How Much Work, Money, Literal Blood, Sweat, And Tears...

...it was going to take for me to uncover the Code I call The Warrior's Way to Having It All, I am promising you I would have not taken the journey. I wouldn't have had the courage, and that is why journeys of a thousand miles begin with just one simple step.

I have spent millions of dollars (yes, you read that right) and tens of thousands of hours, pouring my heart and soul into building and perfecting The Warrior's Way as a predictable System. It took me 4 years to discover its use in my life and another 3 years proving the concepts of this game with 200+ ELITE high level clients who invested $10-$100k to train directly with me. I had to prove that this system could work in the lives of other men, and in order to do that, I needed years of research and proven data.

The Possibilities At The End Of The 7-Year Journey Are Mind-Bending

I eventually went from a place in which sex and intimacy in my marriage was only happening once every 2 to 3 months to frequently happening 2, sometimes 3 times a week or more. Not only was it happening, but my wife was actually wanting and desiring me in ways I had never experienced before, and sex was no longer a hunt for a quick vaginal masturbation session. My life in this area had become un-fucking-recognizable for me, particularly knowing the things that I had chosen and the things I had done.

I went from a disconnected, chaotic relationship with my kids who barely knew their father the banker to wanting and longing to be with my children as much as I could every single day. These days I work out with them in the morning in our home CrossFit gym before I take them to school.. I pick them up in the afternoons after school several nights throughout the week. I stay up late with them doing homework and end 90% of my nights lying in bed with each of my babies tickling their backs while we tell stories, pray and listen to meditation music. My kids want to be around dad; I want to be with my kids.

There is almost never any guilt now because I know when and how to choose Fatherhood with my children daily so that I gain Power from that Relationship.

I became the guy who went from complete disconnection as a believer in God to knowing my purpose. I shifted from following old school religious routines that didn't matter to me while faking my way through the conversation of purpose and Divine Power. In this state of being, I rarely heard the Voice of Revelation and constantly felt as if my life was not on purpose. Today, I am a man who knows his life is on purpose and when it gets off how to listen to and trust the Voice inside of me that is guiding me to specific actions. I have the courage to make decisions that I can't see the end result of, clearly and simply guided by Faith, with a knowing in my heart that when the Voice Speaks it always sees the path clearer than I do.

I Went From Business Destruction, Failure And Empty Bank Accounts To Rebuilding An Empire In Three Different Industries,

while at the same time acquiring Elite Level Skills in Marketing, Selling, Technology, Sequencing, Systems and Leadership. I am no longer a victim to an industry changing or a marketplace shifting. The Warrior's Way has literally allowed me to guide myself through any dark times in business because the 'have it all' lifestyle demands that I see myself as a King equipped with the mindsets and skillsets of Modern Business Mastery. Truly, for the first time in my life I know my businesses and bank accounts are under my control and that I am the one determining my destiny.

Within my body, I initially started out as a tired, worn-out shell of a man coming off of three major surgeries, cancer, and 14 months on crutches while shifting several major addictions. This up and down, year to year roller coaster with my body went from over a decade to a body at 39-years-of-age that is more defined, more shredded, more functional, and more powerful than it was in my early 20s as a high-level elite athlete. My mindsets and skill-sets in fighting, fitness, endurance, strength, power, performance, consistency and nutrition are at levels that make my life feel bulletproof most days as I stand naked in front of the mirror or walk clothed down the street anywhere in the world.

And all this you just read?

Yea, it's happening every single day.

This is the Life of Kings.

This is the Life of Modern Business Men.

This is the Warrior's Way to

Having It All.

Many Warriors have come to us on the brink of divorce, some of them with divorces filed, marriages that are numb, families that are falling apart, businesses that are burning to the ground and watch them not only turn them around but take them to levels that seem to only exist in the movies.

Many Warriors have come to us with bodies that were jacked up and beaten down from years of abuse, yet have been able to take those shells of abused bodies and turn them into healed weapons of destruction and creation inside their life. They are more Fit and on Fire in their 30's, 40's, 50's and 60's than they ever were in their 20's.

Many Warriors have come to us confused about God, their church and beliefs about the system of ideology on the purpose of life, only to level up their understanding with the Divine while experiencing power and purpose at levels they never knew existed. I would then watch these same men (who had no concept of spiritual leadership in their home) return home to tears of gratitude streaming from their queen's eyes as they stand as spiritual presiders in their homes.

These men don't sit back like the sedated motherfuckers that we see all over the place who don't take a stand on a damn thing; who allow the media, church leaders, and the schools to teach their children.

Warriors who are Waking Up are saying,

"I am the Creator and the Dictator of my Life."

Of All The Responsibilities In My Life That I Hold Sacred, It Is My Calling As A Father That I Hold The Most Dear, The King Inside My Own Castle To Lead My Legacy.

If you are able to hear that call as well, why would you return to the shack and live with the peasants and hang out with the whores when you can stand at the top of the Game you've been called to? As a king with a queen standing by your side and children who love and adore you?

It is natural to want to place the Crown upon your head and to raise the Title of Liberty[13] in your own life, declaring your desire and intention to Have It All in Body, Being, Balance and Business. This single declaration will awaken in you a desire to defend and protect the kingdom and to expand the empire in your world with a Fire that will be difficult to control.

The possibility I speak of inside this Brotherhood, inside this conversation, is the Game of Awakening into the life of a Modern Warrior King. It is not to become, but *awaken* what you always were.

Two of the greatest words used in all spiritual writings across all traditions are these:

---

[13]The Title of Liberty is a phrase declared by the Nephite commander, Chief Captain Moroni, from an event in the Book of Mormon that states "In memory of our God, our religion, and freedom, and our peace, our wives, and our children" (Alma 46:12-13). This was written on a piece of ripped cloth (it's what he had at the time on the battlefield) and strung up as a banner showing his *why* behind fighting against his enemies; for the sake of his religion, his nation's freedom, and his family (wife and children). See https://www.lds.org/scriptures/gs/title-of-liberty?lang=eng for more

"Awaken" and "Remember"

Brother, Before You And I Were Even Born, The Nightmare Of Systematic Sedation Had Begun.

You had no choice with the reality that you were born in the Pit, a hole of male conditioning in which there's nobody to blame and no reason for shame, but you have got to change the game.

And that game starts with you.

So how do you change the world, Brother?

You change one man.

If you change a man, you change a marriage.

If you change a marriage, you change a family.

If you change a family, you change a community.

If you change a community, you change a city.

If you change a city, you change a state.

If you change a state, you change a country.

If you change a country, you change the world.

And so it all starts with one man.

Brother, that man is YOU, and the Stack is your weapon to pull it off.

Welcome to the global movement of the Wake Up Warrior.

FOREWORD
BY
SAM FALSAFI

FOREWORD

BY

SAM FALSAFI

> **GARRETT:** Sam, I need you to find me the best divorce attorney in Orange County by Monday.

This is the text that I got from Garrett J White, Founder of Wake Up Warrior™ in June, 2016. I remember that morning when I woke up, opened my phone…

And I Couldn't Understand
What I Was Reading

Confused, I knew Garrett and Danielle had some problems just in the past week back and forth which Garrett had shared with me on a Walk and Talk.

Things were shaky in their marriage, but I simply couldn't understand the request that he was asking me to do. Was this for some kind of training exercise to incorporate into the next Warrior Week? I was just taking on the role of Lead Trainer which was and still is a responsibility that I don't take lightly.

After all, this was the guy that had been guiding me towards the importance of spending time with my wife and son…balancing everything from work with what we lived by: This CODE.

We Had An Epic Code In Which We Lived By

As part of Warrior, we live by an ethical code of conduct with work, the body, family life, and our own spirituality which all comes together in one harmonious way of living.

I had been living this way for over a year and a half. I had been teaching it...WE had been teaching it through various events: Warrior Weeks and Empire Events and so many other events that we ran. We have put the content of the doctrine of the Warrior's Way into digital format.

We were about to teach this Code to the entire world, so I couldn't comprehend what this text would mean. Completely perplexed, I tried calling Garrett but no answer, not knowing that he was on his way driving to the airport at the time.

So, I texted him repeatedly, attempting to get some answers and clarification on what the fuck that text was all about. But even during all of this, deep within me I knew...he had tried everything.

And every.single.aspect. of what he had tried had failed.

He created and then fully lived the Warrior's Way in order to save his marriage. It was meant to ENHANCE his relationships with his wife and kids, and he was teaching that to others successfully. Yet, he had failed in the one place that mattered the most.

Within his own home.

Confused and beyond sad for my friend, this Brother of mine, I began doing what he initially asked me to do: I started to look up divorce lawyers in the surrounding area.

My Google Search showed one group after another, and that's when I quickly realized that a website or online ad is not going to give me the best...and Garrett deserved the best.

I started to make some awkward phone calls to some guys that I knew locally that had gone through divorces of their own to see what they personally recommended.

I'd Ask, "Hey, Who's The Best Lawyer Down Here For Divorces?"

"Whoa...what's going on Sam?   Are...are you getting a *divorce*?!"

"No, this is for a very good friend of mine," I'd reply, my heart heavy as I said the words. "He's somebody that's very close, so I need you to refer me to the BEST."

Even though the truth of it all was that I was asking for a friend, their initial reactions were filled more with surprise than judgment, so I got a few contacts and a few numbers not knowing what that meant for me inside of Wake Up Warrior™.

How Does Someone Become The "Best" Divorce Lawyer, Anyway?

What's the level of determining the "best" divorce attorney anyway? Making the divorce as painless as possible?

Squeezing everything you possibly can from the other person? Becoming a crusader for ruined marriages to then cash in on?

For me, being the "best" at something not only means that we operate from an elite level, but that there's some honor in what it is that we do.

What could possibly be *honorable* about helping two married people remove their bond of marriage? Is it to get them to only see the bondage?

I truly didn't know what the fuck I was looking for...

I was CONFUSED!

I was fucking PISSED OFF!

I was ANGRY.

I was hurt and didn't want this shit to happen for Garrett. I didn't want him to get separated from his wife, whom I had witnessed how much he loved.

He Truly Loved Danielle, And I Had Witnessed The Love Many Times Between Both Of Them

It was HARD to believe that is was all coming to an end, and I didn't understand what the fuck was happening. I was confused within myself as well, and didn't know how to let it out.

I didn't know how to express everything that could have been between the lines of those words inside of that text Garrett had sent me that morning.

I didn't want to understand what I was hearing, so I remained confused.

Confused. Pissed off. Angry. Hurt. Disappointed.

I didn't know what to do, so even while making those calls for divorce lawyers, I didn't really know *what* I was asking them.

I didn't know how to ask them questions when I couldn't even answer any of my own.

Side note: apparently the amount of elite divorce attorneys in Orange County is really high. So are the divorce rates, so no surprise on both of those statistics.

Eventually, I found the guys with the top scores, and I sent them to him.

I Sent Garrett The List of Divorce Lawyers With The Top Ratings And Scores

I sent what I found, breathing a heavy sigh for what the next step could possibly be…

I will ALWAYS be ready to do whatever it takes for Garrett so that even when he feels alone, he has a Brother in me.

But what I found within the following weeks after Garrett got back from Chicago was a completely different direction than the one that I was dreading.

Garrett had embarked on a QUEST, asking himself the really tough questions that continually make us uncomfortable. But it's what we need, and it works.

Truly, for the first time EVER in what I had heard about his life and had seen for myself, he was getting the guidance that he needed from a Place that he had been seeking most of his life.

This was the Birth of the Stack, showing within his own life the process of self-inquiry to find the jewel with.

There's a shiny object that we all have within that is extracted through self-inquiry

There's a shiny object that we all have inside of us that is most of the time covered in mud, yet I had the honor of witnessing what it took for Garrett to extract that jewel within him and polish it as he removed decades of mud and corrosion. I saw him allow the light within him to shine.

Though I didn't quite know *how* when he first started Stacking, I *saw* that he had found the guidance that he needed.

He Was Able To Pull Back From The Feelings And Emotions That Were Driving Him Towards Destruction...

...that would have been regretful for the REST OF HIS FUCKING LIFE.

Instead, within those next few weeks, he was taking actions towards expansion and growth. As he turned around the story that he believed to be true, seeking the story that he desired...that he wanted the most...the relationship and the guidance that he got from the Voice within created an alignment with God this Ultimate Force.

The BELIEF and the certainty that came in that process enabled him to make the best decision than he ever made in his entire life: Lead By Example

I witnessed one of the best turn-arounds I have ever seen inside of the decision within a man facing his own crossroads in life.
It came down to the most significant decision of a man's life: keeping his family together.

I was the witness of that.

And that was the month that I *believed* in The Stack. I *believed* in the POWER of this tool. Because I believed, I began using it for myself. And as a result of this, it completely changes the way in which I operate, the way I react, and the way I think and feel, even as I write this, years later.

The stories that I desire to select and arrive at the things that I want the most in my life are always within my grasp, so long as I'm willing to go to that place deep within me to find the answers that are always there.

This Tool Known As The Stack Has Enabled Me To Become The Father And Husband That I Want To Be.

It has helped me be the Trainer that I desire for the men that come through Warrior Week to discover their own Gifts within themselves. Through using the Stack software, I can be the best version of myself...and the only Guide that I need is within me.

So, I don't run around thirsty as fuck searching for someone to give me a glass of water when the tap is in my own house. I drink from it every day: this guidance and this light.

I believe in the Voice within me and the inquiry that it requires.

I believe in the work that I do in order to get what I want.

That's what I've gotten from this process, and I've witnessed 10,000+ men becoming a better version of themselves...

family completely transformed...

businesses completely transformed...

This Is A Global Movement

Massive decisions had been made and continue to do so inside of Warrior on a steady basis.

How this movement of living the Warrior's Way is growing will become a GLOBAL MOVEMENT for men that are known as leaders to all of those they are around, which all began with a simple series of questions.

Those questions have led to what is true today for each of us. What is true for me and what is true for you may not look the same at all, but one thing that I know for sure:

as you begin reading this book, and as you begin absorbing the content, the examples and materials within this book will bring you your own form of guidance towards that place within you that resonates with truth.

You will be able to extract your own jewels within, just like I have, and just like Garrett has, but it will look very differently for you, just as it does for us. The point is in making your truth your own and then living by it.

There Is A Voice Talking To You

Know that this book is for you. There is a VOICE talking to you, and inside of this book, there is a voice communicating specifically TO YOU. In-between each line that you read in this book,

just like I experienced in reading the text that I received from Garrett many lifetimes ago in June of 2016, there is a deeper message…wanting to get the mud wiped off of it…wanting to show you the jewels that you have inside of yourself.

There is a hidden message for you that ONLY YOU can see, IF you are present and willing to welcome the most significant and the most transformational tool in your life: a Guidebook of your own creation.

A series of questions that you have been willing to have the courage to ask yourself and then go find the answers.

You become your OWN guidance.

You become your own mentor. Your own coach. Your trainer.

You become the Explorer, and the Stack becomes your compass.

So begin your journey as you navigate through the next pages and while reading this book, know that there is guidance available for you to reach the destinations that you desire.

BELIEVE IN THE PROCESS

Step into this journey by simply being thirsty and seek the water within. Seek the water in your own house, and as you find it, drink it. LISTEN to the Voice inside of you.

Learn to be present with yourself. What if there was no coincidence in why you are holding this book? What if you never gave yourself credit? That you have been the Creator in every part of your life?

What if there is a science behind who you are, and you are the fucking scientist? The power of Creation is inside of you to solve the equations that are handed to you every single day in life.

What If Everything In Your Life Could Get Solved In Finding The Answer To ONE QUESTION?

Who Am I?

And the Quest of Becoming is found as the navigator of your own Journey. See, there is always another version of yourself waiting for you.

But know this…this book will not do that for you…creating Stacks of your own will. We are the guides in the night, and you will win by not quitting.

When you begin creating your own Stacks, you may have to course correct, the mud that you have to extract may seem too messy and overwhelming. But know this, Brother: there is NEVER too much mud in anyone's life.

You are a man that is meant to lead from a place of power. How do I know this? Because you're holding this book...

...Welcome to the Journey Within.

Welcome to the message that can only be found inside of you.

3, 2, 1...

...OFF YOU GO!

SECTION ONE
THE MEGA STACK

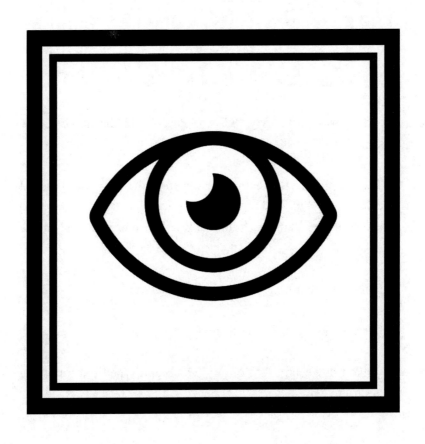

SECTION ONE: THE MEGA STACK
CHAPTER ONE:

MY LETTER FROM THE PIT TO MY WIFE

Every journey to greatness begins with a journey into smallness.

Every journey to the PEAK demands a visit to the PIT.

My PIT was dark. My PIT was decades in the making. The stack? It became the light in the night.

It became the Keys to my liberation from the PIT. But before I teach you the weapon known as the Stack, you must first come to understand the pain that ultimately led to the explosion of the Pleasure.

After yet another fight with my wife about sex.

After yet another night of rejection.

I walked downstairs, sat on my couch and typed the following letter to my wife.

June 2016
DEAR Danielle,

My intention with these thoughts is to take 100% responsibility for my actions and behaviors from the past 14 years with you as best as I can.

I am so hurt.

I am so lost.

And the only way out I can see is to speak with you directly in a form that allows me to get my ideas out clearly and at the same time give you a chance to read them without me cutting you off, yelling or fighting.

So here we go...

DATING... I Was A Mess.
I Was Scared. I Was Confused.

About what? About marriage again and interestingly enough I felt scared of you.

You were beautiful. I mean beautiful in ways that makes a man's heart stop and I had never been with a women in my life who had that kind of beauty.

The fact that you even wanted to go out with me was shocking to me even though I played it cool on the surface. So as we dated, I was in heaven and hell.
On the one side I was in heaven because you seemed to be literally everything I had ever dreamed of being with in a woman

in my entire life. We didn't kiss for 2 months. I didn't want to fuck it up.

I wanted to make sure there was more than chemistry sexually.

So Interestingly Enough, Our Entire Relationship Started Off With Me Suppressing My Sexual Desires For You.

This would become a pattern for me our entire marriage. I truly wanted to be happy with you but I was seriously terrified.

I told no one. I was terrified to end up in a marriage like I had just left and it left me terrified, scared and self-sabotaging. That fear turned to ATTACK and instead of owning the real fear I had.

1.   I was going to get stuck in another painful relationship.

2.   I wasn't worthy to have such a beautiful woman

So, I attacked you, yelled at you and broke up with you out of my own fucking fears.

- *I blamed it on YOU.*

- *I hid in my work to avoid reality.*

- *I blamed YOU for MY own weakness.*

I Was Destroying Your Trust Before We Even Got Married.

Every breakup I told you, YOU were broken and wrong. Every breakup I never owned my own shit…I just fucking blamed you.

"YOU ARE THE PROBLEM!" I WOULD SHOUT.

Then finally in some insane game we got married. For the 6 months before the marriage I wanted it to be perfect.

I was terrified GOD was going to curse me again and so I stopped intimate connection with you and I completely shut off.

We hardly even kissed during that time and I was terrified I would FUCK UP.

So I suppressed. I hid in WORK. I hid in sports.

I Justified this behavior believing that when we got married shit would just change, knowing that this was impossible now, but then thinking that something magical would happen in the temple.

We Got To The Hotel

That First Night.

You were uncomfortable as I approached you sexually. You wanted the lights off. You wanted the shades shut. We ended up in the shower and we had sex and it was uncomfortable for you.

I pumped myself up thinking you were tired. We headed out the next day on our honeymoon. We stayed at a shitty resort, but the best I could afford. I want to have sex every day multiple times. We had sex the first night.

You're not into it.

You're awkward.

I was terrified.

I searched for WHY and you told me maybe birth control had made you crazy. So, we switched to condoms and you stopped birth control. Yet, every time was difficult for you.

I never felt wanted, but instead felt like an intruder in your world. Our honeymoon was stressful for me but I remained hopeful.

We moved into our new apartment. I was hopeful things would change. They didn't.

I Poured Myself Into Work.

I was convinced that the answer was that I was not making enough money. Unfortunately (even before we dated) I start putting the business first. I lose sight of what I was hunting for and began to make love to my business.

I was possessed by money and the game of making business work. It is my biggest addiction I have ever had. People told me I would fail.

I am a first generation entrepreneur, no one in my family knew anything about business. Your parents, their house, their money, their feelings about me as a Teacher drove me to prove to them, my family to you and I was WORTHY to be with you.

In that pursuit I lost connection with my WHY. I lost you. Every month that passed the rejections sexually from you piled up. No kids? It didn't seem to matter.

So I moved us to VEGAS.

I bought a house and I was certain that things would now change. They don't. It's still awkward. Still no kids.

We Have Money Now.

You still won't connect with me. I find Marathons and Ironmans. Between these activities and my work I began to turn away from you and started pouring my sexual energy and love into my business and my sports.

I Began To Ignore You, I Had No Idea How To Be With You.

You wanted to get pregnant.

I'm nervous, but I agree. And in one week we had more sex than we did in the previous 6 months.

I was hoping you wouldn't get pregnant so the sexual connection would continue and I could feel wanted. You do get pregnant. The SEX ends at one week.

You want to move to UTAH because I began traveling to try and fill this massive void. I yelled at you. I was pissed. I was reinforcing the belief that you were not good enough. I forced you to be MORMON and I made you feel guilty for not being an ALL IN MORMON, only masking my own fears and doubts about the MORMON FAITH.

My frustration boiled over often with you and I yelled at you at least once a month and then I would ignore you as I would dive back into the business and sports because I literally had no fucking answer for the confusion I felt in not being wanted, while at the same time screaming at you through my actions that YOU ARE NOT ENOUGH being who you are and this further drove you deeper into the darkness.

We moved to UTAH. You're close to your family.

We had Bailee but I became more interested in the next IRONMAN and have little memories of your experience and rarely attended your birth meetings with the doctor. Further pushing us apart.

Further telling you through my actions that you were not enough.

Day By Day I Was Building Scars On Top Of Scars.

Then the banking crisis hit.

I lost everything. I couldn't pay the bills. I LIED to you about the money. I yelled at you with my frustration. I approached you sexually and now with no money and the years of scarring the answer from you was "HELL NO."

By 2009 I was begging for hand jobs.

You do them and I feel like a complete piece of shit having you do them.

- *I was desperate.*

- *I was hurting.*

- *I was broken*

- *I was lost.*

I had no idea what to do for you, for me or our family…I had no identity.

The rift was at its peak.

I left the Mormon Church. I stopped pressuring you.

I stopped everything.

I Started To Say <u>FUCK IT</u> To Everything I Knew.

This scared the shit out of you.

You wanted another baby. Thinking it will change things. I hoped it would with you.

Again, for one week we had more sex than we have had in the previous month and even though I know it's only for baby making.

I was happy to take anything beyond a hand job and towel to wipe myself off.

I was desperate.

No Sex.

No Connection.

No Answers... I started training women.

I'm Not Getting Laid, But I'm Filling Myself Up With The Energy Of Other Women's Attention

Every day on the phone and every week in events I was leveraging the praise and attention I was getting from other women to fill me up.

I was running all the time. I was trying to figure out who I am. I have no idea who I am. But, I am starting to understand me. I go to Great Life and start to find myself deeper and deeper.

I learned meditation and through that and the running I was at least able to create space for myself and I started to be able to answer the question of who I am. I was still barely paying the bills.

- *We don't talk much.*

- *We don't have sex.*

- *We haven't kissed in almost a year.*

I Start Hanging Out With A Female Student.

She told me everything I wanted to hear and encouraged me to keep building but at the same time I started to have feelings for her. We talked about being together sexually. I now have a reason to stop engaging with you at all.

I Abandoned You Emotionally While You Were Pregnant With Ruby.

I poured my energy into Bailee and the women I trained and mostly this one student. For a month or two this continued.

I invited this female student to going running with me on a Sunday morning and you're at home in bed. I kissed this Female Student in the canyon after running. It's nothing like I imagined. It actually grossed me out. I'm left feeling sick to my stomach.

I'm such a fucking pussy.

I couldn't even tell you the entire story for almost 2 years.

I Cheated And I Don't Even Know How To Tell You.

I'm broken as a man and I feel even more unworthy to be with you then I have ever felt in my entire life.

I pushed you away even further. You woke me up in the middle of the night in tears and we talked about why our marriage was broken. You threatened to leave and raise Bailee & Ruby by yourself without me if we didn't work things out.

I see you crying. I'm not sad.

I'm hollow.

In Some Weird Way I'm Happy You're Crying Because I've No Idea What You're Ever Feeling Or Why,

so even when I see you cry I am reminded that you DO have feelings.

You gave birth to RUBY. I tore my Achilles tendon and ended up being on crutches for 14 months. And Life kept getting fucking worse.

I was still barely able to pay the bills and suddenly I couldn't even pay rent and I was a fucking cripple. SEX was not even a desire any more that I approached you with.

I was a pitiful human being who was unworthy to be with you, unworthy to create, unworthy to live. I kept blaming you and pushing you further away.

We were about to move to Arizona. I tear my Achilles again the night before. You had to manage everything by yourself. I got back to UTAH.

You're all alone. No Help. Limited Money...

...and you start to RISE.

I finally moved back to AZ. Sex was still not happening more than every 10-12 days and when it did, it was tons of work for you and something that didn't bond us at all.

I hated my work. But, I was able to pay the bills.

I was desperately trying to find a way out of the shit storm I had created for us.

I Start Taking You On Real Dates.

Every single week. We started talking and dreaming again. 2012 I launched Wake Up Warrior. 2013 was the beginning of my RISE from the Ashes. I was finally making money again. I ran three events that year.

We moved to CA. You were panicked about the HOUSE. I told you, "I GOT IT" and we moved into the Ladera Ranch House.

I was changing faster than I had ever changed in my life. Weeks now felt like months, and months felt like years. WARRIOR was transforming me, it was awakening me to ME and to the power of my calling.

2013 Convention happened.

2014 was another year of Hustle. You and I were doing better than ever.

You're starting to actually show that you want to be with me.

We Still Fight About SEX
All The Time.

I was so excited about the HOT TUB and we never even once have sex in it.

I started focusing on WORK but it's different this time because My business MODEL required me to go ALL IN with you and the kids too........I DO EVERYTHING I CAN POSSIBLY IMAGINE to do this.

You started to give me check lists of things that needed to happen for you to FEEL SAFE and to FEEL READY to sexually want me. I hit every single one of them. I literally stopped asking you for sex early 2014.

I went into reaction mode. I waited for you. To come to me. You controlled all the cards.

I helped you launch your business, hoping that investing in you and your business will end up having you trust me so that we could have real sex and intimacy.

It worked for a week. No matter what I did, nothing seemed to ever change. The PAIN of the past was too great for you and so I continued to push.

I moved us to Dana Point. I pushed you to build a salon. I took you on vacation after vacation. I hired cleaners. I hired nanny's. I tried to help you with business.

You Trusted Me For A Week And I Started To See Improvements And Then You Snapped Back To Your Comfort Zone.

2016 I exploded with power.

The years of work and hustle were finally clicking. I was at a level of power I have never been in before. You told me a list of more items to change, including vacations. I agree to all of them. We went on 5 $10k+ vacations together.

You told me not to run Warrior Week on the weekends. I literally change my entire model so I could be home on the weekends. You tell me to leave you alone and give you space.

I do it.

You tell me to help you with your business.

I do it.

You tell me to help around the house.

I do it.

You tell me to create more space for you so I do and take the kids off your hands multiple times a week so you can have space including bed time routine. I do it and...

...Nothing Changes.
You're Too Hurt.
My Efforts Are Not Enough.

You tell me you don't trust me and that if I fix our credit and get a house you will feel trust and then maybe things will change. I handle Credit.

You push me on the house and how worthless I am as a husband because we still lease homes and why you can't trust me until you have a house.

I GIVE UP. No matter what I do I can not win.

At the peak? REJECTED SEXUALLY.

At the pit? REJECTED SEXUALLY

No matter what I do, I now realize nothing will change. I EMOTIONALLY QUIT.

We ended up at therapist.

You agreed for the first time.

We got better for a time.

Sex doesn't really change, you are still struggling to manage the HELL of the past and the patterns I just don't understand.

I YELLED AT YOU.

- *I am fucking angry.*

- *I am hurt.*

- *I am wounded.*

- *I am confused.*

- *I am lost.*

- *I QUIT.*

Sex is still work and you still resist, you still refuse to submit, you're still bound to the chains of the past and the pain that won't let you go. I realize that I DEEPLY LOVE YOU. You are my partner in crime and creation. But we are broken as a couple. I don't know what to do. I realize I was a co-creator in our insanity. I have no idea what came first, the chicken or the egg. Did I Reject you and this caused you to contract or did You Reject me and this caused me to contract?

I don't know. I know I love you. I also know love will not be enough.

Love,

Your Broken Husband,

It Was 2016 As I Was Sitting On The Couch In My Living Room, Completing The Most Emotional Letter I Had Ever Written.

I have typed it up in Evernote.

I looked at the clock and realized I had to go or I was going to miss my flight.

I clicked "share" and I sent the link of the letter to Danielle and also my best friend at the time Jeremy Finlay.

That this letter started a chain reaction that would change hundreds of thousands of lives...

CHAPTER TWO:

THE TEXT EXCHANGE THAT SAVED MY MARRIAGE

It was Thursday morning and I left the house angry as fuck.

I was sexually frustrated again and heading out of town for work angry and hurting for the 100th time.

"How the fuck am I back in this situation again?!" I thought to myself.

I was accustomed to this type of RAGE I was feeling.

I had felt it for decades and had unleashed it's wrath on my wife, my family and everyone around me for years until I figured out how to leverage a combination of ultra running and alcohol to suppress and survive.

But I was different…I was more evolved. I was more mature…or so I thought. It was June of 2016.

Wake Up Warrior™ had been active for 4 years and my life had gotten 100% better than what it was in my first PIT in 2008.

My life was not economically burning to the ground like I had experienced in 2008 (you can read about that first PIT and the birth of CORE 4 inside of the Preface).

By mid-2016, things were clicking for me in Business. I was in economic abundance again and had taken my family to a very nice place on the coast of Southern California.

But That Morning It Didn't Matter. I Literally Didn't *Give A Fuck* About Any Of It.

You see, sexual rejection triggers such deep RAGE within me that it was very difficult for me to think about anything besides destroying my wife, burning my marriage to the ground and being done with all of it. And the night before, I was rejected again. Fucking.Rejected.Again.

What the FUCK?!

I found myself screaming and hitting my steering wheel in my Black BMW M5 driving 100 mph down the i73 in Newport towards the airport.

Nothing mattered to me. No one mattered to me. I was filled with RAGE and READY to EXPLODE.

I Sent A Text To My Business Partner, *Sam Falsafi,* Requesting

That He Get Me An Appointment On Monday For The #1 Divorce Attorney In The OC.

I pulled into the valet at the airport, threw the keys to the valet attendant, grabbed my bag and headed to Terminal 3 to get checked in for my flight to Chicago.

I brooded the entire time I waited in line to check my bag, and as soon as I got to the gate check-in counter, an announcement came over the loud speakers and informed us that my flight had been delayed by 90 minutes.

To This Day,

I swear the universe had set this entire thing up and needed me to have some extra time in the airport for a reason I was about to discover...

After making it through security and finding my Gate, I sat down with my back pack between my legs as my cell phone was pulled out and in my hands.

I sent a text to one of my closest friends at the time and business confidante in the creation of Wake Up Warrior™ Jeremy Finlay, and for the next hour I UNLEASHED back and forth with him about my wife, my pain and my feelings while waiting for my flight to Chicago.

What You Are About To Read Is The Actual Text Exchange With Jeremy Finlay That Lasted For 90 Minutes…

The Conversation That Saved My Marriage?

ME: *Danielle And I Are At WAR Emotionally And It's Hard To Say Who Caused What With Us,*

It's been 14 years of patterns that have truly fucked us up. I refuse to allow my daughters to be raised in a way that allows for this type of Bondage to be created for them with their husbands...

JEREMY: *Just read the copy. Really great tee-up. Man. Being raised that way and then having only one experience - it's an uphill battle from the start. At least compared to those women who are all about sex.*

ME: *Danielle told me today....I want to be intimate. I want to be sexual. I want to want the man I'm with and I want to be taken by the man I'm with...I just don't know if I will ever be able to allow that with you.*

JEREMY: *Wow. Dude. That's some heavy information to get. How did you take that?*

ME: *She is living by the CODE at a level she has never with me and the truth bombs are dropping every couple of hours...*

JEREMY: *That's a truth bomb level 9.*

ME: *It breaks my heart. But I also realize we are both responsible.*

JEREMY: *Which is honorable. Also fucking hard.*

ME: *From the first month we dated we started a pattern of behavior with each other...Mine was: I don't know if you are good enough for me. Hers was: I don't know if I trust you enough to give you all of me. So I would run away and then come back and try again....and every round she sunk deeper into her hole.*

JEREMY: *Man. Talk About A Perfect Storm.*

ME: *By the time we got on our honey moon the wheels were already in motion after being together for 2 years...The RIFT in our RELATIONSHIP and year after year we continued to build up scar tissue upon scar tissue and wound upon wound, ignoring it for a time, sedating ourselves for a time, distracting ourselves with other fights and issues...*

JEREMY: *I don't know if I should say "I'm sorry", or if this is unraveling as the most fascinating case study on a "good and not great" marriage you're living through. The scar tissue is a perfect metaphor. Blocking the subtle receptors of true intimacy. What's crazy is you two are so fucking smart and aware, yet the emotional factor is the kicker.*

ME: *And the only options? Sedate, back off, and stay at GOOD with a 1/100,000,000 shot at Prosperity together or? Acknowledge that we have brought each other as far as we have been able to....We can see exactly what will have to change....and when we look at the sacrifice required to get there, it leaves us both in the same place. I am not sure if I am willing to go to that place after all that we have been through. WE are not sure.*

JEREMY: *You mean go to the place of prosperity or detach? Or BOTH?*

ME: *The Blame Is Starting To Stop. The Joint Accountability Is Kicking In.*

JEREMY: *It seems both options are very emotional. That's progress. The joint factor. That wasn't there, at least from what you told me, prior to counseling.*

ME: *The only options? 1) Be willing to hurt for another 4-7 years with the chance at Prosperity with a high likelihood of being right where we are now in 7 years or 2) Being complete with each other and then choosing that path with another.*

JEREMY: *7 years is a very long time in your world.*

ME: *It's a lifetime.*

JEREMY: *A few of them, 7 years ago you were just barely ending the banking world.*

ME: *"I Think The Thing That Hurts The Most? I Can See The Peak Of The Mountain Across The VOID & I Can See How Happy We Could Become..."*

JEREMY: *Mm. That's a good thing then. It's a not a stupor of thought situation with her.*

ME: *But then I come back to reality. I stare at the VOID having gone the distance for so many years before into the same void...*

JEREMY: *Right right. What a position to be in. It's a seeming stale mate.*

ME: *And I realize that we are more likely to get 6-12months into that next void and kill each other then we are to actually make the journey without creating more scars.*

JEREMY: *Between The King And Queen.*

ME: *It is a complete IMPASS...No blame, Some Shame, Clear Reality that our past baggage and scars weigh us both down too much.*

JEREMY: *Right. It's just the accumulation of 14 years of trying, fucking it up, trying, etc etc.*

ME: *Yes, it hurts so deep to think of Danielle being 100% vulnerable and open with another man.... Yet, when I am honest I want that for her... She deserves it.*

JEREMY: *This may sound crazy...in fact, I know it does, but going on a spiritual mushroom journey for you may give you something thinking through this won't. Same for her.*

ME: *She is a powerful, beautiful woman who has only heard one note her entire life. She has never found herself through another man ever...(I may be open)*

JEREMY: *Does she want that? To be with another man?*

ME: *I think she wants to be happy, she is just exhausted*

JEREMY: *Or does she want to be with you? Yeah. So it's not even about another man.*

ME: *She says she wants to be with me...but with that declaration comes the reality of what that means...*

JEREMY: *It's just about her happiness. Same for you.*

ME: *It's not even about another man or woman for me or her. Its about being able to BE 100% of who we are all the time...*

JEREMY*: Which is very good.*

ME*: Yesterday I told her that for the past 3 years I drank 5-6 nights a week before I come home, I have masturbated daily sometimes twice and workout like a maniac so that I can filter the sexual energy and try to give her space. And amidst all of that sacrifice I am left with the following reality....no matter what I do? She will never be able to handle 100% of me. And I am finally at a point in my life where I have shut and killed every single excuse she has given me in the book.... every item on the check list. (I have not asked for sex for 3 years not one time)*

JEREMY: *Wow, so very well said on the suppressing of sexual energy. Which I've been witness to (minus the masturbation)....*

ME: *I have not initiated sex 1 time in 3 years*

JEREMY: *You haven't?? Wow.*

ME: *I have sacrificed trying to give her what she says she wants. I have gone all in in supporting her business. I have helped her build her empire. I have hired a nanny. I paid off all of our debt. Fixed our Credit. Bought Houses, cars, jewelry, beach club memberships, vacations, invested heavily in the kids, hired house cleaners, handy men, dog walkers, I have done* everything, *Jeremy, I know how to do and I am exhausted.*

JEREMY: *Dude, you've done everything. Every last thing and you deserve credit for it, massive credit. Your a superman, super dad and super spouse. It's almost ridiculous for me to reading all of this.*

ME*: Mostly by the fact that the one person I want to handle all of me can't and won't. I'm not guiltless in this... I was a tyrant the first 4 years we were married. I was an asshole.*

JEREMY*: Of course. She has an issue with your anger and bipolar-ness.*

ME: *I cheated in 2009.*

JEREMY: *Yep. It seems her heart was broken a long, long time ago.*

ME: *And no matter what I do for the past 7 years I have not been able to wipe away the debt.*

JEREMY: *Before you probably even knew it had been.*

ME: *Her heart was broken before we even got married.*

JEREMY: *Mm. And that is sad.*

ME: *I smashed it to pieces. She was 18 years old. She was young and I was older and angry and broke up with her 9-10 times in 2 years and every break up shattered her heart...and the message was? YOU'RE NOT GOOD ENOUGH FOR ME!*

JEREMY: *It's heartbreaking to see the path, because you turned on a dime, turned into an amazing father, husband, etc... but she hasn't been able to forgive. Right. Therefore...she never gave you all of her.*

ME: *And no matter what I try to do to repair the damage...the damage was done before the game had even begun. We moved to VEGAS a year into our marriage and she was all alone. I worked from 6am to 10pm every day. I was gone.*

JEREMY: *She probably liked that you would be successful and fun, most of the time, so she went in anyway, without dealing with her shit.*

ME: *I didn't know how to invest in her. And when she tried to be in my world I fucking yelled at her. I screamed at her for distracting me. I'm sitting here crying my eyes out in the airport realizing that it is all on me and that I may never be able to fix it.*

JEREMY: *Yeah. Shitty. Shitty. I can see how you would feel a sense of shame for part of this. Dude....*

ME: *And so I CAN'T be the man with her.*

JEREMY: *You're working so fucking hard.*

ME: *Because no matter what I do inside the true story? I do not feel worthy to have her.*

JEREMY: *I feel overwhelmed with emotion just talking through this with you. It's fucking real. Because you yelled and rejected her. Is that why?*

ME: *And so I have spent the past decade trying to prove to her that I am worthy. I thought that meant give her money and nice things and so that is what I invested my soul into. I thought I could buy her love. She was the most beautiful woman I had ever been with...And I was certain that at any moment she would wake up and realize that I was a JOKE. That the only reason she was with me was because I was 7 years older then her...*

JEREMY: *Man... and now it has been proven, in a heartbreaking way, the buying of love couldn't happen nor would it ever. It was a cover up, wasn't it.*

ME: *It was all a Fucking Cover-Up. By the time we got to our wedding night? She was already shut down.*

JEREMY: *But you didn't know it was. She probably didn't either.*

ME: *On our honeymoon, we only had sex 2 times in 7 days.*

JEREMY: *Did you feel connected to her? During that 7 days?*

ME: *No I didn't...I was scared. By the end of our honeymoon I was left confused and hurt and panicked that I had just got married and my nightmare from my first marriage was starting over again.*

JEREMY: *Got it.*

ME. *I was scared I fucked up. I was scared I had made the same mistake twice.*

JEREMY: *It's very possible you being scared actually created the reality. It seems you created the same mistake twice in your fear of it. Though that's probably me being a dick saying it.*

ME: *I am 100% open to the fact that I created all of this....that from the beginning I was the one who refused to allow us to build on a solid ground of trust. I am certain I did....I was 27.*

I was your age.

JEREMY: *It's insane man. Because I know you. I knew you even back in the day... Your heart was always pure.*

ME: *I had been married and divorced already, been on a 2-year mission, had a son I never saw, and had 40+ employees.*

JEREMY: *It just Seemed that way. I don't think what you did was malicious.*

ME: *I was not even close to emotionally ready. It was not on purpose.*

JEREMY: *Right. But it felt right. And you did it.*

ME: *It would have been impossible to know that what we were doing was going to destroy us. I think we were RIGHT as a COUPLE.*

JEREMY: *You still are pretty rad as a couple.*

ME: *But by the time I knew what TO DO it was TOO LATE.*

JEREMY: *That's the thing. Maybe it's too late.*

ME: *We are amazing as partners...I told her that last night. I would go back to back with her over any other woman I know. When we take sex off the table...she is everything I have ever wanted.*

JEREMY: *Right. But it's not just sex...you want the kind of intimacy with a woman you found when you went through a great life, right?*

ME: *Beautiful, talented, determined, can hold her own, smart, funny, witty, committed....*
JEREMY: *The kind of playful, fun, deep, sexual connection with someone who wants all of you.*

ME: *Yes, And I thought if I just worked hard enough I would eventually find that with us...I literally had her give me check lists of what would need to happen for her to begin to trust and since 2008 I have been hunting those lists...*

JEREMY: *Gosh man...it's crazy to see this. That one final piece. The intimacy piece.*

ME: *She and I could always use the lists as reasons....why I could always keep myself in check because the reasons were real...But I have literally smashed all of them off the list....and all that is left is intimacy, sexuality and the ability for both of us to accept 100% of who we are when it comes to SEX and intimacy and this is now where the great RIFT exists.*

JEREMY: *That's the kicker isn't it? So I'm curious then...What if you have a woman who GIVES YOU EVERYTHING you've ever desired in intimacy...yet doesn't fulfill half of what Danielle fulfills. Is that worth it? In* Way of the Superior Man...*it talks about finding a lover, and focusing on that lover, not expecting her to fill all hats...just the hat that FILLS YOU.*

ME: *That is a wonderful question. Here is the problem...in my entire life I have never experienced that with any other person on the planet....and so I do not know what type of man I would be if I felt full and satisfied and connected in that area.*

JEREMY: *You'd be a different man... A more powerful man.*

ME: *My story? Because it is such a driving need for me and something I have literally never found with Danielle or anyone else, it leaves me in the question...and it's the same question Danielle is in: What might be possible for her in a relationship where she is safe to be ALL of her with no scars? Who would she be in that relationship and how much happier would she be to have that then what we currently have? I think for the first time ever she is giving herself permission to want that.*

JEREMY: *You've lived a powerful life... I think that will never change. You'll always be the powerful man. You'd just add another piece of being a "Peaceful man" as well.*

ME: *Agreed.*

JEREMY: *That's a big thing. For her.*

ME: *That man does not exist in me...Exhausted man exists. But Peaceful man does not exist.*

JEREMY: *No. The Peaceful Man would add another sense of crazy power to you.*

ME: *Yes it would. I feel incomplete as a man without it.*

JEREMY: *I don't think you should be afraid of lowering your capacity to produce just because you finally have intimacy fulfilled. You'd probably actually produce at a higher level... Produce in different ways.*

ME: *I'm not....because there is part of me that is producing regardless of the chaos....I live to HUNT.*
JEREMY: *Exactly.*

ME: *But when I come home from hunting I want to be able to surrender into the arms of the queen knowing that my hunting for US mattered.*

JEREMY: *Dude...the last few years working with you, I don't think that HUNT will ever change.*

ME: *And instead I come home to "Comfort Yourself"*

JEREMY: *Yes. Exactly.*

ME: *And so there is not rest for me...*

JEREMY: *Especially with how intense your hunt is.*

ME: *There is no space.*

JEREMY: *That's why you've aged 10 years within the last 3 man. Though you look rather good with grey hair.*

ME: *There is the HUNT and then there is the Fatigue when I come home...so I recover in order to go hunt, hoping that one day I will come home and she will finally accept me.*

And I know the story is the exact same for her only reversed....

That she wants a KING that goes and HUNTS and then comes home and goes all in with her on her terms in language that she speaks, in ways that allow her to feel safe.

JEREMY: *But I am seeing your side very clearly right now... The ability to rest inside a companion who comforts you when you're not on the battle field. I see why you are not willing to settle into the way it currently is right now. That is what is the most interesting in all of this. It isn't one way. Yes. And she's very aware of this isn't she? Well, obviously. you just told me she was. I feel there are some paths you two could go down to get some contrast. They are a bit wild.*

ME: *She is aware. And even in that awareness the past haunts her.*

JEREMY: *Like staying married, dating others for a time. I know that sounds crazy... and you'd be pissed.But the paths aren't all exhausted at this point. The modest ones just aren't working yet.*

ME: *Something radical has to change to give us perspective.*

JEREMY: *I remember two years ago when you were talking about that. If you two agreed to separate, in a way, and see other people. Get a taste of what it would actually be like.*

ME: *I have even proposed it but at the time I am not sure either of us we're ready for that.*

JEREMY: *Because it's not like suddenly you have someone to be intimate with... there's a bit of incubation period. Dating around, etc. Yeah. It sounds easy, but actually doing it...far more complex emotionally. I'm just saying there may be some ways for you two to get some contrast... because it sounds like both of you are very (and rightfully) turned on by the fantasy of being fully accepted by someone.*

ME: *The last time we discussed (4 months ago or so) , Danielle said, "Even if I agreed to it I would be worried you would have sex with someone else and not be able to control yourself and then if you did that I could never take you back."*

JEREMY: *Ah.*

ME: *The thought of me having sex with someone else is very difficult for her... and here is the reality. She has had sex with 1 person. Me? I have had sex with 2 people.*

My X and her. Neither of us have ever experienced a healthy sexual experience with anyone. So I'm certain even the situation is mind-bending for our reality just having the experience, let alone having it while married with another person.

JEREMY: *Yeah, very good point. Man. Having it WHILE married is certainly mind bending. But also potentially freeing. I mean, I'm not one to say brother. I'm the free wheeling single dude telling you to go have some sex with other people before you guys make a decision... probably not the most sound advice.*

ME: *It's not that it's not sound advice. Something has to change.*

JEREMY: *Right, but still...I see what you're saying. Yes, it does. Because dude...this kind of heaviness, I can only imagine who you are without it. I probably don't know that man.*

ME: *I don't know that man.*

JEREMY: *Mm. That's the kicker right there.*

ME: *And I can't imagine Danielle with a Man in her world that she is 100% surrendered to...*

JEREMY: *And you must know that man.*

ME: *She would sparkle in ways that would dwarf the physical appeal of her. I know its in there....*

JEREMY: *Yes.*

ME: *And I am very aware that I am not likely the man who is going to be able to crack that code. Not because of a lack of effort...*

JEREMY: *And that just may be what's needed.*

ME: *But because of a lack of consciousness for the first 9 years we were together.*

JEREMY: *Psh... not at all. You've gone very far together effort wise.*

ME: *A new man. No past. No history. Free to be who she is today? I KNOW WITH 100% CERTAINTY that she would be 10X the woman she is today...she lives in fear. Fear of how I will show up today.*

JEREMY: *What's interesting is that you lead a movement surrounding marriage, probably so that you would have the willingness to look at your own in every lens.*

ME: *Fear of my emotions that are suppressed. Fear of me leaving her... Fear of my threats about sex*

JEREMY: *Yes.*

ME: *Fear of constantly being told she is not enough sexually. Fear Fear Fear Fear Fear Fear Fear Fear Fear. And I*

*created it. And that is a hard pill to swallow. A little late to buy
fire insurance when the HOME is already on FIRE*

JEREMY: Very true.

ME: *But I tried, I even called the Fire Department and tried to
put it out. FUCK FUCK FUCK FUCK FUCK, I'm my own worst
enemy. I did this. And now I am paying the piper.*

JEREMY: *You did this as a different man, remember that.*

ME: *KARMA is a mother fucker. I know and yet that man has
been my blessing and my curse....*

JEREMY: *If you have shame, do not be ashamed of who you are
today. Karma is indeed a mother fucker. FUCK.*

ME: *I can't even imagine what life would be for US if we could
just reset and start over, whip away the past and just date. I am
unashamed of who I am today.*

JEREMY: *Good.*

ME: *But I am filled with remorse, not shame, of who I was for
her for the first 9 years.Selfish. Hollow. Fucking Blind.*
JEREMY: *The guy who created this...you destroyed.*

ME: *I did.*

JEREMY: *Very blind. You will not create this ever again.*

ME: *I felt him die 2 weeks ago in Utah the week of my surgery. I felt Closure. I felt Atonement. I felt Happy.*

JEREMY: *It's impossible to ever re-create this. That's very good.*

ME: *True happiness for the first time in a long time.*

JEREMY: *That's a big big big thing. Garrett...Truly happy? Amazing.*

ME: *Then 48 hours after we got home out of nowhere we have a MASSIVE explosion for us....as if the universe was saying....OH NO. YOU'RE NOT DONE.*

JEREMY: *Ah.*

ME: *And riding the wake of redemption I felt with my life personally, me and Danielle erupted again. Only this time? It is different. This time we have had guidance with the problems the past 4 months with our therapist. The answer I get 100% of the time? Garrett if you will just TONE it down and giver her space and let her come to you, things will change. This has been Danielle's message to me for years... This is the same message the therapist gives us...*

JEREMY: *Maybe "come to you" is a lot longer than you think it is.*

ME: *My reality? I am done toning it down. I am done drinking overnight so I don't come on to my wife.*

JEREMY: *Yes*

ME: *I am done sedating so that she can feel space. I am done masturbating and hoping that one day it will be her.*

JEREMY: *Yes.*

ME: *I am done with the PORN and the strategies of depression. I am done feeling unwanted.*

JEREMY: *Right.*

ME*: I am done feeing alone.*

JEREMY: *That's the thing right there…Feeling alone.*

ME: *I am done feeling like there is some magic button I will eventually find that will change things. I am done. So is she. And that leaves us at decision. Neither one of us will back down.*

JEREMY: *Both alone. Always together. It's a mind fuck to me.*

ME: *Both of us are tired of suppressing and walking on egg shells with each other.*

JEREMY: *Yes.*
ME: *Both together. Always Alone. And this is why we go to movies…*

JEREMY: *Right. Dinner and Movie On Date Night.*

ME: *Only when we DRINK do we actually connect because the alcohol lets us forget for the night but in the morning?*

We always remember the truth...

JEREMY: *It all comes backs*

ME: *BOTH OF US. Her Hurt and Mine. Her Suppression and Mine. We are both suppressed trying to figure out how to play it with the other. We are both exhausted from this game. And so we are at a decision.*

JEREMY: *It's amazing to behold two strong people feeling so weak in a game they both created.*

ME: *Truly, for the first time. It is one of the great IRONIES of LIFE for me too. POWERHOUSE WOMAN. POWERHOUSE MAN. Weakness at the core with each other....With our kids? We are on fire. With our business...we are on fire. With others attacking us...we are on fire. With our families...We are on fire and keep them all out. With out belief systems...we are on fire. With our life we are on fire... and that has brought us to abundance...*

JEREMY: *All of the pieces are there -- except the lynchpin to hold it all together.*
ME: *But we can go no further. We are missing the CAP STONE...the CORNER STONE...the HUB of the wheel.*

JEREMY: *Yes.*

ME: *TRUE - UNFILTERED - UNSUPPRESSED - UNCONDITIONAL - CONNECTION. It would require a DUEL surrender at the exact same time and then it would require years of patience to pull off while we stayed in surrender.*

JEREMY: *I can tell Danielle is also crazy conflicted because she said things in the interview about going from good to great in a real way, and she meant it.*

ME: *If there was ever an IMPOSSIBLE GAME for Balance this is the ULTIMATE one. She did not lie on camera with you.*

JEREMY: *Not at all. She's also feeling the same.*

ME: *She would burn Warrior to the ground before she lied on camera.*

JEREMY: *Yep. And there was a ton left out for lack of time that she elaborates on.*

ME: *WE HAVE BECOME great in every area of our life but one....and unfortunately it's not something small. I just got the final call for my flight, I got to run.*

JEREMY: *Love you brother. Sounds good. Love and honor you big time.*

ME: *Love you brother. Thank you for listening. I have no one to talk to.*

JEREMY: *Love talking through this with you and seeing your side.*

ME: *And worse?*

Danielle has even less people to talk to.

JEREMY: *I know.*

That's why it's my honor to listen.

ME: *I feel sad for her.*

She rarely opens to anyone…

…so everything is always processed alone.

I think she trusts our therapist….

maybe its time for her to go to her alone.

OK. I'm off.

Love you brother.

JEREMY: Love you.

CHAPTER THREE:

THE WAR WITH THE QUEEN!

I handed my ticket to the flight attendant checking us in at the gate for Delta Airlines.

"Welcome Aboard, Mr White!" she said as I found my seat in first class, sitting down only moments before they closed the door.

My text exchange with Jeremy had been both healing and cathartic, giving me a sense of relief with the reality that my marriage was likely over and that with it would go the Wake Up Warrior™ Movement.

You may read that and think, "Wait. What does he mean?"

It was simple.

In 2016 I was very transparent with the men of Wake Up Warrior.™

If I didn't figure out this last piece of The Equation—My Sexual Relationship With Danielle—I was not worthy to lead them. I would shut the company down if I got divorced and hand it off to someone who had been able to figure the Game fully out.
Many years later, I came to recognize that...

...The Text Exchange Between Me And Jeremy That Day In The Airport Not Only Saved My Marriage, But Also Saved The Warrior Movement From Dying!

"Good morning, folks," the pleasant voice of the captain came over the loud speaker as he told us we were ready for take off.

I put my Beats headphones on and sat back in my seat, fading off into what was meant to be a 20-minute mediation.

40 minutes later, I was awakened by the flight attendant asking me with a smile, "Would you like lunch on our flight today?"

I chose something with chicken, she wrote it down and headed down the aisle as I pulled my laptop out.

I connected to the WIFI.

I allowed my MacBook Pro to engage and update all of my pages with the Life of The Internet when I heard a "ping!" notifying me I had a text.

I Pulled Up My iChat And There Was A Message From My Wife, And It Showed That Her Account Was Active.

The following is the real exchange between us 30,000 feet in the air...

DANIELLE: *I know you are flying but thought I would text you my thoughts on what I read...Surprisingly, I could agree with most of it. We are so great in so many ways.*

Both of us want us to work but can't see a clear path.

We hold on with hope…

To hold on any longer even if another 5 years sounds exhausting as of right now because we are in a very painful place: I'm not ready to let go or throw away our history together.

How many years did it take for you to go from 'good' to 'great' with business? Are you at 'great' or can at least see a clear path too great? And how many more years too great?

Or does it ever end?

I think that is the problem…we're 'good' but can't see a clear path to be 'great.' I don't have the desire to date others. It actually sounds exhausting. If we did agree to date others as much as it pains me to say this I think you would date to have sex and this would fulfill you for a small period of time.

Until you realize you were missing connection in other areas.

But the other area may not be a deal breaker to you.

So as much as I don't want to admit you would be with someone for the sex I think you would. This being the case I think if we date others you would find someone else.

I'm not sure how I would be if I dated someone else. Maybe I would feel safe and open up more. I know to win my heart is harder than for someone who wanted to win your heart (or penis). The only thing I could think is to date others without sleeping with them: having an open relationship. I'm not sure how this would work with kids... I wouldn't know what to tell them. It would be weird to date and be married.

I Saw That Her iChat Was Active, So I Replied Back.

ME: *I have WiFi on the plane and just finished meditating for a bit and turned on my lap top and just saw this. My heart races and my palms sweat with your thoughts at the end of your message.*

Not because it's wrong but because it is the most radical thing we have ever put on the table as a couple, and this time you are actually behind it not just as an option but as possibly the only option to creating the perspective we both need.

I am also left with the thought of "How would that even work?" There are so many variables that would need to be managed to even attempt it...but at this point, Sweetheart, I have no answers and this seems to be a clear path that would for sure shake things up and force us to see things we have not seen before.

DANIELLE: *Does your heart race because it sounds like freedom and less hard?*

ME: *No. It races with fear. It sounds anything but easy. But it does seem like a path that would change things forever.*

DANIELLE: *Fear you might find someone else*

ME: *Mixed. Fear about you finding Someone. Fear about me finding someone. Fear about you finding someone and having the most insane, amazing sex you have ever had. Knowing that I was never able to be that man. But at the same time happy for you...*

Even the thought of you sitting at dinner with a man who is thinking all of the same things I think about you while doing everything in his power to seduce you is hard to have in my mind.

DANIELLE: *Really sex? Not just a better relationship?*

ME: *Relationship for you is easy...your variable is Sex and Intimacy, and if you allowed that to occur, it would mean you were with someone who completed you at a certain level in a* way I couldn't. If you had dated a man who knew how to treat you and you could connect with him I am certain things would go beyond talking.

DANIELLE: *Did you read the long text, I'm not open to dating others and be married if sex is an option*

ME: *I did see that. And I agree. I am just sharing with you my feelings... NO SEX would be the only way it would even have a chance. I don't think either of us could recover from knowing the other slept with someone else.*

DANIELLE: *My fear is that we date others and say sex is not an option... I could refrain but don't think you could. Then it would be over for sure*

ME: *The only way I would play is if we agreed to NO SEX...but it would have to be defined - No Sex is clear for both of us...*

DANIELLE: *I don't even want to date :(How do you tell someone you want to go out but are still married How to you tell kids... Do you live together?*

ME: *Even the thought of you kissing passionately another man is hard for me to think of but if I knew you could kiss 10 men over a 6-month time period and inside of that you could find someone that allowed you to relax into a new pattern it would kill me, but I would be willing if it means we could find each again together and be on fire.*

I have no idea.

I have absolutely no answers to any of that.

This is not something I have ever even allowed to enter my mind as more then just a thought. I have had multiple people offer it to me as a solution over the past few years…Stating it may be the only way to give each other perspective.

DANIELLE: *I don't network at all and have no friends…The friends I do have I can't ask them to set me up. And girls don't ask out men*

Then nothing.

The WiFi on the flight went out.

I still had 3 hours on my flight to Chicago.

My Heart Was On Fire With The Most Confusing Feelings I Had Ever Experienced.

It Was Like I Was Knocking On The Door Of Liberation And Freedom But All I Could See Was The End Of My Marriage And Everything I Had Been Working For.

I was sitting in the window seat, and began staring out the window at the blue skies, bright sun and the clouds that sat way below the 30,000+ feet in the air our Boeing 747 was flying.

After a few minutes, my trance was interrupted with the arrival of my meal.

I put my laptop away then washed my hands with the warm lemon cloth they provided, exchanging it a few moments later for the tray with my food.

My body was in the seat as I ate my chicken lunch on the plane flying to Chicago O'Hare Airport, but my mind and soul were in another Dimension about to be guided into a place I had never been before.

I Was About To Be Introduced To One Of The Most Powerful Weapons That I Continue To Use Every Day.

Not as a tool.

But as a real time experience with the Voice inside of me.

This exchange would change my life and the Movement of Warrior, impacting the lives of Millions with the Birth of what has today become known as THE STACK.

CHAPTER FOUR:

A VISIT FROM THE VOICE

With my food consumed, I pushed my call button. Within moments, the attendant arrived and took my food tray away.

I reached under my seat.

I grabbed my lap top, opened it up and looked to see if I was connected to the WIFI.

The signal was dead.

I read the last words of the message from my wife...

> **DANIELLE:** I don't network at all and have no friends... The friends I do have I can't ask them to set me up. And girls don't ask out men.

I read this over and over and over again as tears of frustration, anger and pain started pouring down my cheeks. I was embarrassed to be emotionally losing it on the plane, so I put my sunglasses on and opened the window beside me to let the sunlight in even more, so I had an excuse to be wearing the sun glasses inside the plane.

"How could I be at this point in my marriage?"

What the fuck was I doing wrong with my life?

Why Wouldn't My Wife Just Fucking Change?

As I sat in that dark cloud that was covering my mind of anger, blame, guilt and shame, I heard a "ping!" come at me from my laptop just like the sound I heard earlier when my wife texted me.

I looked down at my screen, thinking it was Danielle and the WiFi kicked back on, but it was a new chat, and within in sat a simple statement that said, "Have you had enough?"

My eyes moved to the WiFi signal and noticed that there was no connection to the internet. *What the FUCK...*I thought, blinking my eyes a few times at the words on the screen.

"Have you had enough?"

The crazier part was the fact that the message was coming from a number I didn't recognize and was being sent to me, even though I had not internet connection.

It seemed crazy, but I decided to reply.

ME: *Who is This?*

My curser sat in the chat section waiting, and then the bubbles started showing up in the chat that signify the party on the other side is currently typing a message.

"It Is Not Important Who *I AM* Right Now...What Is Important Is The First Question I Asked You."

I read each one of the words and as I got to the end, the first message came through again...

?: *Have You Had Enough?*

My heart started racing.

I leaned over to the woman next to me and asked her, "Do you have internet access?"

"No," she responded back apologetically.

I sat confused.

I sat scared.

I sat 100% completely engaged.

ME: *Enough of what?*

It responded quickly...

?: *With The Pain And The Weight Of Your Pit?*

I sat there and just stared at the words.

I thought I was losing my mind.

I had no idea who this was.

I Had No Idea How It Was Messaging Me With No Internet Access.

Yet…it was happening.

And it was as if this VOICE or MESSENGER knew me.

I finally typed,

ME: *The Pain and Weight of my PIT?!*

Almost instantly, the Messenger responded back quickly, becoming known to me later on as The Voice by stating:

?: *Listen, if you want to just waste my time then we can be done and you can continue to drift into chaos and darkness and end up divorced and miserable!*

ME: *What the FUCK. Who is this?*

?: *I know you're hurting, angry and upset but if you don't pull your head out of your ass by the time you land in Chicago, everything you have been working for is going to fall apart.*

ME: *Ok I'm ALL IN…what next?*

What opened up next was the first of a series of conversations that would transpire over 3 years that slowly unlocked the entire stacking system that you're now learning about here in this book.

Summer Of 2016 Was My First Experience With The STACK

As It Awakened The First Stage Of The Game....The Conversation Of RAGE And The MEGA Stack.

What I am about to share with you over the next pages of this book are sacred to me.

It was also the Gateway I was missing in my life for decades, which is why it became time to share it.

The Warrior's Way is powerful.

The CORE 4 Game is lethal.

But the STACK Game *transforms* a man from the inside out as The VOICE literally sculpts you and me to become exactly what we were born to be.

- No need for a *prophet*.

- No need for a *priest*.

- No need for a *temple*.

- No need for a *coach*.

- No need for a *consultant*.

- No need for a *therapist*.

All of these serve a role in life for sure, and they did in mine also.

But The STACK Became My Gateway to GOD…

…That I Had Been Searching For My Entire Life And Didn't Even Know That I Needed.

The Stack is…

…the ability to connect directly with the source of life.

…the ability to connect directly with GOD.

…the ability to write your own scripture.

And it began 30,000 ft up after a heated text exchange with my wife and what appeared to be the end of my life was simply the awakening to a new beginning. So back to the conversation…

I followed my heart and responded.

ME: *Ok, I'm ALL IN. What next?*

?: (Q) *Why are you so angry right now?*

ME: *Because Danielle and I just can't seem to get on the same page at all.*

?: *What do you mean?*

ME: *I literally have no fucking idea how to be married to her anymore and the only path I can see is to get a divorce because I am just fucking tired of the fighting and the conflict about our marriage and sex.*

?: *Do you love her?*

ME: *Yes...I think so.*

?: *What do you mean you think so?*

ME: *I mean I* think *so: we have been together for a very long time and yet it seems like we can never get over the issue of sexuality and intimacy and I am always back in the exact place that I started every single time...hurt, reject and afraid.*

?: (Q) *What are the feelings you have right now when you think about her?*

ME: *Rage, Anger, Hate, Frustration, Irritation, Rage, Rage, Rage*

?: (Q) *In this exact moment, why has Danielle triggered you to feel, Rage, Anger, Hate Frustration, Irritation, Rage, Rage, Rage?*

ME: *What do you mean by triggered?*

?: *What I mean is this: all of us experience this situation every single day no matter who you are. It is the moment that someone does something, something happens or doesn't happen and there is an emotional reaction inside to what is happening.*

Take for example you and Danielle. When you think about your current sex life the way it is right now with Danielle, what feelings are triggered by that thought?

ME: *RAGE...I fucking hate her for how she treats me and how rejected I have felt for so fucking long, fuck her.*

?: *Well done, but here is the reality. I didn't ask for you to release, not yet, I just asked for a feeling and look at what you gave me.*

RAGE

Now, that is a feeling.

But, what you gave me after that was simply emotional verbal vomit.

It's not a problem and it's actually quite necessary for you and me to express, but I want you to just look at the word RAGE.

That is a feeling.

Triggered.

That is a word and that word is used to describe what happens when you think about your SEX LIFE with Danielle. You get triggered, and the feeling that Rises is RAGE.

Can you see this?

ME: *YES*

?: *You're doing great. Let me ask you again then.*

(Q) In this exact moment, why has Danielle triggered you to feel RAGE?

ME: *At this moment, Danielle has triggered me to feel sad and unwanted because she constantly rejects my approaches with Sex and intimacy and it seems that no matter what I do I am made to feel like the bad guy.*

?: (Q) In this moment, if you could scream at Danielle, what would you say?

Now, I am not asking you to actually scream this out loud on the plane in front of everyone; that will get you arrested like a crazy person.

So, just type in into the chat with fire and passion like you were yelling with your fingers.

ME: *In this moment I would scream,*

"WHAT THE FUCK WOMAN" I am so tired of the constant feeling of rejection when I try to pursue you. You make it fucking impossible to actually seduce you because you're so afraid of intimacy and touch. When I touch your fucking leg or kiss your face there shouldn't be a moment where you're pulling away.

What the fuck is wrong with you, you shut down crazy bitch.

?: *Ok....BREATHE, big guy.*

You're doing great.

I thought I was going to have to coach you off the ledge to get you to really unleash your RAGE, but you're doing a great job.

Often times, we want to be "NICE" to those closest to us, and when we are, we end up missing out on the gift that sits at the core of the DRIFT.

ME: *What do you mean the GIFT?   What do you mean the DRIFT?*

?: *Here is what I want you to consider.*

Every time that you are triggered by Danielle or anyone else, you experience what I like to call a DRIFT.

You go from a place of the status quo (meaning, wherever you were before you were triggered) to a downward drift of emotions because of the trigger.

All I have to do is bring up your SEX LIFE with your wife and you get so triggered, the RAGE just flows from you quickly and efficiently.

After a Trigger, we all drift.

This is not a bad thing.

This is part of the process of life and progression, but most of us were taught to be terrified of the RAGE and the DRIFT experience of life.

Look at you.

Raised in the MORMON faith and inside of your culture, there was nowhere for a man like you to be able to express his true feelings. If you did, you were shamed, guilted and boxed up.

But, this is not just the faith you were raised in.

This is every faith on the planet right now and all political systems and structures as well as society as we know it.

Men Have Been Taught, Trained And Educated To Not Release Rage In A Healthy Way.

So, you suppress your ANGER for months and months and months and then you BLOW UP.

But, you have probably noticed that your blow up is you channeling your ANGER in the form of BLAME at her and wanting to make her wrong and wanting her to change.

Have you seen this to be true with you and Danielle?

ME: *YES. 100% it's true.*

?: *What do you notice happens to you immediately after the YELLING and the Releasing of your Rage on Danielle?*

ME: *I feel really good and powerful for a moment.*

But then?

I go to a very dark place.

It's almost like I drift even further down the insane DRIFT into Guilt.

I am filled with tons of guilt.

?: *YES. This is totally normal. And after you feel the guilt, what do you notice rises next?*

ME: *Shame.*
Heavy levels of Shame.

I feel so bad and then I end up becoming the most desperate, needy guy ever in her life... and she owns me again.

I won't fight with her for weeks.

I won't bring up sex for weeks.

I go over the top to try and compensate for what I have done.

And for a moment...I feel better.

It's like I am trying to undo what I have said, trying to go back to the way things were before I blew up and lost my mind with RAGE and yelled at her and unleashed on her.

?: *And how does she respond to this?*

ME: *It's like she knows it's coming.*

I have been stuck in this pattern with her for over 10 years and it fucking sucks.

It seems like no matter how many fights we end up having, I am stuck in the same place with her over and over and over again.

I am stuck in this place HOPING that by LUCK things will be different this time.

But they never are. Ever!

?: What you're experiencing is what I call a False Lift and the KARMIC cul-de-sac

ME: *What does that mean?*

?: *Let me explain it this way…*

Have you noticed how, for a time, when you are desperate that life actually starts to feel better?

Like the darkness from the Shame and Guilt, Anger and Blame goes to the side and you actually start to feel some progress like things are getting better?

ME: *YES*

?: *Have you also noticed how everything in your mind is wanting to go back to the moment before you said the stupid shit and released your rage, almost like you could rewind and turn back time?*

ME: *YES*

?: *That is what I call a False Lift.*

It's when you're tricked into trying to go back in time to fix what you have done.

It is the energy of a victim and the energy of a desperate man that learns nothing from what has happened. He struggles to try and put back together the picture he smashed only to find out that when he got back to the place he thought he wanted to go, nothing had actually changed.

The picture is not back together.

You realize that the picture you smashed that is sitting in your hands is actually duct taped back together, yet even the tape is slowly falling apart again.

This is why every time you and Danielle FIGHT, you end up in this place of RAGE: you release with Anger and Blame, Drift to Guilt and Shame, and then grovel to get back to where you were before the release.

The challenge is…you actually feel better for a time.

That feeling "better" becomes a DRUG that masks what is really going on and is nothing other than an illusion appearing real.

You are on a FALSE LIFT.

Why?

Because nothing is going to actually change.

Does this make sense?

ME: *Wow. Yes this is starting to make complete sense, so what does the phrase the "Karmic Cul-de-sac" mean?*

?: *Well.*

It's exactly what you and Danielle have experienced for a decade.

You get triggered, you Blow up and then you proceed to Drift through the feelings of ANGER and BLAME to GUILT and SHAME until you hit the PIT.

Then in the PIT you desire to go back to the way things were.

You don't learn anything from what has happened.

And you end up back at the FALSE PEAK via the FALSE LIFT only to repeat the same shit over and over and over again.

The Karmic Cul-de-sac is the round and round and round circle of Drifting and Falls Lifting over and over and over again.

This is why the French say, "plus ça change, plus c'est la même chose" which translates into English to mean, "The More Things Change, The More They Stay The Same."

Have you heard this statement before?

ME: *YES*

?: *Can you see how you have been triggered by the same topic with Danielle for a decade? And that in a decade, nothing has changed because you keep taking a trip on the Karmic Cul-de-sac Train?*

ME: *Yes.*

What the fuck?! YES!!!

And that is why I sent my wife the message I did today.

I'm just fucking tired of the Karmic Cul-de-sac.

I just can't take the False Lift Trip one more time on this topic.

So.. what do I do?

?: *You keep engaging with me.*

So let me ask you another question…

(Q) In this moment, if you could force Danielle to think, say, feel, or do anything, what would it be?

ME: *I would force her to be into kissing me.*

I would force her mind into opening up emotionally and allowing me to feel that she is actually in there and not just a robot with no feelings and no emotions.

I would force her to acknowledge she has a problem with intimacy, vulnerability and sexuality and that the reason we fucking suck right now is because she is a crazy cunt that withholds sex from me and that she is the reason we are on the fast track to Divorce.

I would force her to want to kiss me, hold me, have sex with me, and not just make this an awkward experience where I am made to feel bad for wanting to have sex with my wife.

?: **(Q) In this moment, with no filter nor constraints, what do you truly think about Danielle?**

ME: *What do I REALLY think?*

?: *Yes.*

What do you really think?

This is not a time to be nice and hold back.

This is not a time to try and be SPIRITUAL…or take the higher road…or turn the other cheek.

The level you GO ALL IN with this question is going to determine the GIFT at the end of this exchange.

So don't be "nice" to her in your words here.

On your worst day…

What are the words you would use to describe what you TRULY think about Danielle?

I Took A Deep Breath In…

ME: *Danielle is Selfish*

Danielle is reckless.

Danielle is a shut down, fucking ice block.

Danielle is a selfish bitch.

Danielle is an Ice Queen that doesn't give a fuck about me.

Danielle is a sexually lazy fucking cunt who only thinks of herself.

...Holy Shit, I Thought To Myself. I Couldn't Believe I Just Said All Of That About My WIFE....

?: *Well done Garrett!*

I know it feels like you're attacking her.

And guess what? You are.

You're attacking her in the place where you should be attacking her and that is in YOUR MIND.

You see...the WAR you are fighting is a WAR with you. Within you.

I know that won't make sense right now...but it will.

To get the GIFT that I am promise you is coming, you will have to keep going ALL IN even when it comes to saying words about Danielle that make you very uncomfortable. Yet, they're true to YOU at some level and you have just been trained to not feel them, let alone express them.

ME: *Ok...*

Thank you.

That makes me feel better.

I was just starting to feel a little guilty and shameful.

?: *No Guilt. No Shame.*

You're currently doing what we call STACK WORK.

That is, you are STACKING your feelings and taking a look at what they are teaching you.

Do you trust me?

ME: *Yes*

?: *Great, then let's move into the next question.*

(Q) In this moment, what is it that you don't ever want to experience in the future with Danielle?

ME: *I don't ever want to be pushed away when kissing her again.*
I don't ever want to find myself feeling weird about kissing her or touching her when we are in bed.I don't ever want to feel like I am walking on eggshells trying to handle things perfectly in bed so that she will offer up the gift of sex.

I want Sex to be something more natural and physical touch as something more magical for us then what it has become most nights. ...It was at that moment that my trance with the laptop was interrupted by another voice. I looked up, disoriented.

"Would you like another glass of wine?" the flight attendant asked me in a sweet voice, smiling.

"Yes, please."

I looked out the window slightly confused that I was still on the plane as I settled into gazing at a few cloud formations that were just underneath us, wondering and pondering on all that I was learning via this chat with the VOICE.

She handed me my glass of wine. I set it down on the small table of Row 2 that held my laptop in on the Delta Flight to Chicago. Another "ping!" sounded.

?: *Hey, you still there?*

ME: *Yes, just getting a glass of wine.*

?: *You deserve it.*

In fact, why don't you take a few minutes, meditate and relax, then finish your wine and hit me up when you're complete.

SECTION ONE: THE MEGA STACK
CHAPTER FIVE:

OPENING THE DIVINE TRIANGLE

At this point in the conversation with the VOICE, everything that I had learned so far was already causing my head to spin and my mind to start to open up to something new.

It felt good to speak to the VOICE via text the way I was.

It was like I was speaking directly to a therapist, and yet this therapist seemed to know me in ways that I only I knew myself.

Every question was potent.

Every comment was filled with potential.

But What I Was About To Learn Next Would Literally Turn My World Upside Down And Inside Out.

?: *You there?*

ME: *Yea, I'm here.*

?: *How was your meditation and glass of wine?*

ME: *Just what I needed*

?: *Good, you ready to continue?*

ME: *HELL YES.*

?: *Lol, good. (Q) **What are the FACTS about the situation that triggered you with Danielle?***

ME: *Like specifics?*

What do you mean?

?: *Exactly what I asked…when you look at Danielle and all the RAGE you're experiencing because of the TRIGGER of her situation with you….*

What are the FACTS?

You have shared a ton of emotion with me and that is exactly what I wanted to see from you but what I'm looking for now are the FACTS without the feeling.

*So…(Q)**What are the specific FACTS without the feelings about the situation most recently with Danielle that triggered you?***

You understand what I mean now?

ME: *I think so…let me make a run at it.*

Last night I found myself laying next to Danielle wondering if we were going to have sex.

As I lay there, I was realizing that I have become a complete fucking pussy that is so triggered by the SITUATION OF SEX with her that no matter what, things are uncomfortable for me.

It was like my arm was buried in cement and I couldn't bring myself to even touch her.

I was laying there like a fucking victim waiting for her to touch me.

WHY?

Well, I'll tell you why…

Because I have 13 YEARS of rejection.

I have a relationship where, if I approach her sexually, it must always be on her terms.

I have been pushed away thousands of times.

So much so that the past 4 years…I just stopped asking.

I now wait.

I hope for connection.

I long for the connection.

The problem?

In the end, she is just OK with no touch and intimacy.

At least, that is the STORY I tell myself when I'm feeling rejected and lonely and fucking frustrated as fuck.

I hate that she has so much control over my life right now.

I feel trapped.

I feel lost.

I feel alone.

?: *Well DONE, Brother.*

Is it OK that I call you that?

My brother?

ME: *Yes, that would be amazing. GOD knows I need a Brother right now, more than anything. Someone to confide my deepest, darkest pains and thoughts into that can hold space for me to create and find the peace I am looking for.*

So, yes.

Please call me Brother.

What shall I call you?

THE VOICE: *You can call me "The Voice"*

ME: *Why do you call yourself that?*

THE VOICE: *It is a name that connects with everyone, and also does not fit in any particular box of belief system, and yet fits inside of every belief system.*

I am the VOICE in your heart, in your mind and your soul.

I am the DIVINE MIRROR that is here to mirror back to you what is already inside of you, but that you are unable to actually see.

I AM THAT I AM.

ME: *Well, fuck. Ok.*

I feel a warmth inside of me when you say that to me.

Why?

THE VOICE: *That warmth is a confirmation of the TRUTH that I am speaking to you.*

But that warmth is something you will experience every time you come to this chat and have a conversation with me.

I AM THE VOICE and I have always been here, but it is only now that you're ready to hear.

ME: *I get that. Big time. Sorry for the distracting questions, I won't ask any more stupid questions of you...please continue.*

THE VOICE: *There are no stupid questions with me and there are no stupid answers.*

Nothing you type into this chat with me is "WRONG" and nothing you type into this chat with me is "RIGHT."

Everything we discuss together here in this chat is DIVINE.

You might even call it SCRIPTURE.

ME: *Scripture?*

I thought that books like the Bible were scripture, not a chat back and forth with you here on my MacBook?

Please explain.

THE VOICE: *The Bible is scripture, for sure.*

But I want you to consider that books like the Bible are powerful books because men and women wrote down their own conversations with me about what they were feeling, envisioning and seeking when it came to life.

They essentially were writing journals filled with their real, raw, relevant experiences with life and the Council that they were leaving for others who would come after them.
I want you to consider that every time you come to STACK with me in the CHAT that we are writing Scripture together. Every.Single.Time.

I am asking the questions, but you're finding the answers INSIDE with a Divine Power.

And that some of the most profound and powerful insights of your life will be found inside of the hours alone on this chat with me.

ME: *You mean I can keep having this type of conversation with you when I choose?*

THE VOICE: *Every single day, 24 hours a day for as much or as little as you need me.*

I am simply one chat message away.

ME: *Dude, that's so rad.*

THE VOICE: *Lol, right? Now...let's get back to the WORK of STACKING the situation with you and your wife, shall we?*

ME: *Yes*

THE VOICE: *I want you to consider something.*

Everything emotion you feel and every feeling you have are driven by something.

Any idea what drives them?
ME: *I know. Triggers!*

THE VOICE: *Yes, you're absolutely right.*

But let's continue that further.

What sits at the Core of a Trigger?

I mean…in the moment you get triggered by Danielle, what is it that sits RIGHT THERE at the core of the trigger?

And it is not feelings.

It is something beyond the feelings that actually causes the feelings *to appear.*

ME: *My Mind?*

THE VOICE: *Bingo! But WHAT about your mind?*

ME: *My thoughts?*

THE VOICE: *Yes. But something more specific than your thoughts…*

ME: *My beliefs?*

THE VOICE: *YES. You're on the right track, but we have to go further…deeper…and even* more *simple.*

ME: *I have no idea….can I phone a friend?!*

THE VOICE: *Sure! In fact, I'll be your friend.*

The answer is…

...YOUR STORIES.

ME: *What do you mean by my stories?*

THE VOICE: *Listen.*

Your entire life and the world you have created for yourself, and that you WILL create for yourself in the future, is driven by your stories.

Your stories are not just your thoughts.

They are more than your beliefs.

They are the "RULES" of your world that you create day to day, so when you get triggered by someone or something, the instant response by your mind is to generate a story about the situation or person that was involved in the trigger.

These stories are subconscious.

Which means...you're not even thinking about them.

It just happens.

Then, the feelings *follow the* stories *while the* behaviors *and* actions *follow the* feelings.

What are you hearing me say right now?

ME: *Well...here is what I am getting...*

My entire world is run by triggers.

These triggers are simply the moment in my life when something or someone happens that interrupts the status quo of whatever it was that I was doing at the time.

This trigger activated the Story that I'm unconscious to…and that story then activates my feelings…and my feelings active my behavior and action.

Is that right?

THE VOICE: *Well done! Yes, that is accurate.*

So, let me ask you a question…

(Q) What was the story, created by the trigger with Danielle last night, that you're telling yourself and me?

ME: *Hmmm…*

"Danielle Doesn't Want Me Sexually, She Only Wants Me For Money, Support, Protection And Child Care. In The End, She Uses Me!"

THE VOICE: *And My brother,*

when you tell yourself the story,

"Danielle Doesn't Want Me Sexually, She Only Wants Me For Money, Support, Protection And Child Care. In The End, She Uses Me!"

(Q) Describe the feelings that arise for you.

ME: *I feel…*

I feel Lost
I feel Hopeless
I feel Sad
I feel Desperate
I feel Small
I feel unclear
I feel Exhausted
I feel Dark

THE VOICE: *Great.*

Now.

(Q) Describe the specific thoughts or desired actions that arise for you when you tell yourself

"Danielle Doesn't Want Me Sexually, She Only Wants Me For Money, Support, Protection And Child Care. In The End, She Uses Me!"

ME: *I want to leave,*

I want to get a divorce.

I want to scream at her.

I want to yell at her.

I want to ignore her.

I want to sedate with alcohol.

I want to sedate with porn.

I want to sedate with drugs.

I want to distract myself with work.

I want to distract myself with fitness.

THE VOICE: *Those are some pretty intense desires...*

Particularly the DIVORCE feeling.

How long have you had the thought of divorce in your mind with Danielle?

ME: *A long time.*

It is so hard for me because of the dysfunction that I feel sexually with her, and so my mind always wants to go to the story that, "If I Get Divorced, Things Will Be Better," or some version of that story.

Truly, every time we fight about sex, I have a moment where I am like,

FUCK THIS MARRIAGE.

I am getting the fuck out of here, right now!

Of course...I don't.

For some reason, I keep fighting, thinking that somehow this will all turn itself around.

THE VOICE: *That is another story also.*

It's great that you identified it as a story.

So...you have two stories that we have identified right now:

ONE:

"Danielle Doesn't Want Me Sexually, She Only Wants Me For Money, Support, Protection And Child Care. In The End, She Uses Me!"

TWO:

"If I Get A Divorce, Things Will Be Better!"

We will come back to the second story later (if we have time), but for now, let's focus on the first one that you generated last night when you got triggered by Danielle.

So...answer me another question in relationship to the first story.

(Q) What evidence do you have that would prove that this story is absolutely true?

ME: *Many days…this is true.*

She is stuck in the mode of her own world and I am just another player in her game that helps her get what she wants.

She stresses out easy.

She has anxiety.

Put all that together and what you have is a formula that can cause some serious chaos.

This then leaves me as just another person in her world to take care of her shit which can strip away the passion and intimacy and fire or desire and replace it with "Get Shit Done" mode.

With as much as she manages on a daily basis, I truly am another employee or partner for her in getting shit done.

Maybe that is not a problem.

Maybe that is part of my role and part of my truth, which is to be just a partner for her and that my biggest issue is that I think that is not the way that it should be.

I can think of less than 3 times in 10+ years where she has approached me sexually.
The rest of the time it is me doing the pursing and when I pursue, 95% of the time I get shut down.

THE VOICE: *Alright.*

I want you to close your eyes and take three deep breaths.

Ready?

3-2-1- GO.

And while sitting on the 2nd row of my Delta Flight, I began to take deep breaths in…and out…

There you go.

Take another one.

And one more.

Perfect.

Now in that place of clarity, I am going to ask you a very direct question…

The story you're telling:

"Danielle Doesn't Want Me Sexually, She Only Wants Me For Money, Support, Protection And Child Care. In The End, She Uses Me!"

(Q) Is that story true?
YES or NO

ME: *YES*

THE VOICE: *Garrett.*

My brother.

I'm going to ask you again…

The story that you're telling yourself about Danielle:

"Danielle Doesn't Want Me Sexually, She Only Wants Me For Money, Support, Protection And Child Care. In The End, She Uses Me!"

(Q) Are you 100% certain with no hesitation nor doubt that this story is true?

ME: *NO*

I took another deep breath in.

THE VOICE: *My brother.*

(Q) What might be possible for you in this situation with Danielle if this story was false?

ME: *I would be free to see that things have been shifting.*

I would be free to see that my wife takes time to shift.
I would be free to see that we have been having more intimate sex and that my wife wants to no longer have sex with a condom on and we have gone with the Pull and Roll method because she wants to FEEL me inside her and the condom kills that feeling.

I would be free to see that she has fallen asleep cuddling me multiple times in the past 2 weeks and this would have been unheard of in the past and impossible.

I would be free to see that we have improved as a couple in massive ways the past 12 month to places that I had not even known were possible.

I would be free to see that going back to therapy would be a good thing.

I would be free to see that fucking up for over a decade as a husband is not going to be shifted in a year or two but may take some time to course correct the past patterns.

I would be free to see that I love the shit out of this woman and that I am in the game with her for the long term.

She is my queen.

I am 100% ALL IN WITH HER.

THE VOICE: (Q) *Regardless of this deeply emotional Triggered Situation with Danielle and the current story you're telling about her, what do you truly want for YOU in this relationship?*

ME: *I want to be able to kiss her and not have her pull away.*

I want to be able to touch her and not have her take my hand away but actually lead into it.

I want to hold her and not have her retreat.

I want to have SEX with my wife in a way that is natural, exciting and fun.

THE VOICE: *Ok.*

Great work.

Now you're clear about what you want.

This is the part about life that most men like you totally forget…

You get so emotionally lit the fuck up that you forget what you're actually fighting for at all.

Last night, when you lay next to Danielle and you were frozen with fear and feeling rejected, how much time did you spend investigating what you actually WANTED?

ME: *None at all. Fuck…*

THE VOICE: *Exactly my point.*

Most men rarely, if ever, spend any time getting clear about what they want out of life.
They end up living lives of reaction.
Lives of default.

And in most cases, when it comes to marriage and business, life will end up getting so triggered and filled with Rage and Drifts so hard that they end up losing the all sense of clarity.

So much so that they will start fighting to be RIGHT instead of fighting for what they want.

Now...

You have listed out some very INTENSE and very CLEAR items about what you want.

But...

we have to open the space even more to take a look at things.

Because if in the trigger of the moment, YOU—by default—spend almost no time thinking about what you want.

So..how much time do you THINK you spent thinking about what Danielle wants?

Seriously.

Did the thought ever cross your mind that your WIFE might be filled with some of the same fears, doubts and worries that you are?

ME: *Yes it has.*

But you're right.

I didn't even think about it for me and definitely not for her.

THE VOICE: *It's ok.*

Remember…No guilt and no shame with this.

I just want you to be aware.

So, you told me…

- *"I want to be able to kiss her and not have her pull away."*

- *"I want to be able to touch her and not have her take my hand away but actually lead into it."*

- *"I want to hold her and not have her retreat."*

- *"I want to have Sex with my wife in a way that is natural, exciting and fun."*

Now, I want you to stop thinking about YOU for a moment and answer the same question…but this time, answer it in regards to Danielle.

(Q) What do you want for DANIELLE in this situation?

ME: *I want Danielle to feel safe, comfortable and relaxed enough to enjoy the flirting, intimacy and sexuality that relationships can bring.*
I want Danielle to be in a marriage that she truly wants to be in.

I want Danielle to be with a man that she truly desires sexually, emotionally and mentally.

THE VOICE: *How does that feel when you think about what you want for her?*

ME: *It feels strange.*

It puts a different twist on the entire situation.

Because all I can think about is myself, but when I put myself in her shoes and REALLY get real about what I want for her, it also seems to open the space up for me to actually see her beyond my RAGE.

THE VOICE: *Remember when I told you THE GIFT was coming?*

Well...that is only possible because you had the courage to go ALL IN with the questions I asked you in the beginning.

You're doing amazing.

Let me ask you the final question to finalize the space of wanting.

'(Q) **What do you want for YOU and DANIELLE in this situation?**

ME: *I want us both to be FREE.*

I want us to have the FIRE and DESIRE and INTIMACY on our side as a couple in marriage after 15 years together.

I want to us be one.

I want us to work out as a couple.

THE VOICE: *BOOOOM!*

You did it.

You opened up The Triangle.

Take a look at your answers:

WANTING FOR YOU (first triangle corner)

- *"I want to be able to kiss her and not have her pull away."*

- *"I want to be able to touch her and not have her take my hand away but actually lead into it."*

- *"I want to hold her and not have her retreat."*

- *"I want to have Sex with my wife in a way that is natural, exciting and fun."*

WANTING FOR HER (second corner)

- *I want Danielle to feel safe, comfortable and relaxed enough to enjoy the flirting, intimacy and sexuality that relationship can bring.*

- *I want Danielle to be in a marriage that she truly wants to be in.*

- *I want Danielle to be with a man that she truly desires sexually, emotionally and mentally.*

WANTING FOR YOU BOTH (third corner)

- *I want us both to be FREE.*

- *I want us to have the FIRE and DESIRE and INTIMACY on our side as a couple in marriage after 15 years together.*

- *I want to us be one.*

- *I want us to work out as a couple.*

What are you seeing with these answers?

ME: *I am seeing something I couldn't see before. This is amazing!*

I wrote Danielle a letter this morning before I got on the plane.

I also texted back and forth with my friend Jeremy and even had a text exchange with Danielle on the plane about 30 minutes before you and I started chatting.
And not ONCE in this entire emotional exchange with anyone else have I felt this type of clarity.

Like… clarity that Shifts the way I feel inside big time.

Is this normal to feel this type of Shift?

THE VOICE: *It is.*

What you opened up was what I like to call THE DIVINE TRIANGLE.

It is like the Bermuda Triangle, only instead of losing things, it's the opposite and you actually FIND things.

The thing you found?

Clarity.

But this type of clarity is not possible unless you RELEASE.

If you scroll back up in our messages, you will see I spent a good amount of time just letting you get your feelings out.

Specifically the SUPPRESSED feelings of anger that had become RAGE.

THAT is what causes RAGE.
When you suppress and don't talk about or communicate your anger.

How often do you talk about what you have been feeling with Danielle to someone else?

ME: *We have gone to therapy a few times.*

But every time we were in therapy, I always felt like the therapist was on Danielle's Team and I was left to fend for myself.

Literally, in our last session she said,

"Garrett you're like a giant tsunami and Danielle is a small little plant. Every time you two exchange, you're drowning her out with your intensity."

I had to bite my tongue.

I dropped to the floor (literally) and did 15 burpees right there in the therapy room...I was losing my mind.

Of course, the therapist looked at me then over at Danielle with the look of,

"Sweetheart, you're for sure fucked with this guy!"

THE VOICE: *I've got to admit, that had to be hilarious to see.*

And yes.

Therapy is fantastic.

But, I'm interested in YOU being able to release every single day just like we have experienced today but in a controlled environment.

And you're doing amazing with it.

You're likely feeling more FREE than any of the sessions you have had with your therapist.

Am I correct?

ME: *Absolutely.*

It's kind of weird how natural it feels to just chat with you here in this format.

It's like I am free to express whatever I need to and there is no judgment from you or a sense of "I'm fucking it up" that I feel in therapy all the time.

THE VOICE: *I'm happy for you.*

And now, with the DIVINE TRIANGLE open, it's time for you to Walk the Block….

SECTION ONE: THE MEGA STACK
CHAPTER SIX:

WALKING THE BLOCK

Walking the Block is exactly what it sounds like.

It is starting in one place and walking all the way around the four-edged block until you return to the exact place that you started.

Walking The Block Is The SHIFT Part Of The Experience Of Stacking.

What you have read that I did with this conversation on the plane with The Voice was simply stopping The Drift.

The Divine Triangle does this but once it stops it YOU MUST CHANGE YOUR STORY to align with getting what you want.

Yes, you read that correctly.

You Must Change Your Story.

So let's get back to the most amazing conversation that I had ever had up to that point in my life.

THE VOICE: *Here is what we know about your current story:*

"Danielle Doesn't Want Me Sexually, She Only Wants Me For Money, Support, Protection And Child Care. In The End, She Uses Me!"

It is highly unlikely it will give you what you actually say you want.

What did you say you wanted?

- *"I want to be able to kiss her and not have her pull away."*

- *"I want to be able to touch her and not have her take my hand away but actually lead into it."*

- *"I want to hold her and not have her retreat."*

- *"I want to have Sex with my wife in a way that is natural, exciting and fun."*

And what I know for certain?

The current story you're telling yourself is NOT going to get it done, so…

…we are going to have to WALK THE BLOCK and see if we can shift some things and get you to let go of the current story and

create one that is even more powerful that will assure you get what you want.

Are you ready?

ME: *YES.*

That was a massive amount of data you just gave me, but I believe I am on the same page with you.

Let's Walk the Block inside my mind.

THE VOICE: *Perfect.*

Here we go.

So we are going to take the story you were telling yourself originally...

"Danielle Doesn't Want Me Sexually, She Only Wants Me For Money, Support, Protection And Child Care. In The End, She Uses Me!"

...and we are going to shift that story.

What I want you to do is instead of making this story about Danielle you're going to make this story about you.

Let me give you an example.

"Garrett Doesn't Want Anything From Danielle Except A Sexual Partner On Demand And An Emotional Support System When He Comes Home At Night!"

(Q) Can you see any truth in this Story?

ME: *Yes, I can.*

THE VOICE: *What evidence do you have to prove this story could be true?*

ME: *Shit.*

If I am 100% honest? This is very true at a certain level.

I have often wondered what would happen if I had a wife that was sexually on fire, who satisfied me daily with sex and creativity in the shower or bedroom or hell! The kitchen.

I mean, like some of the women I used to hang out with back in College.

I hear about men who are married to women who kiss them, hug them and pursue them sexually like this, but I have yet to experience it for myself.

I have friends who have sex 4-5 times a week and it is totally natural for them to have this continual pattern. Of course, they have only been married for a few years and don't have any kids...

I often wonder if this is even possible for married couples? Or if we are just destined to destroy ourselves in sadness and disconnection after a decade of marriage and the stress of kids?

There has been more then one occasion that Danielle has said to me…
"I bet you would be just fine with a wife who stayed at home and was a full time mom, even if things were a little boring as long as you were getting laid every day."

I have thought about this.

And there is a part of me that believes this might be true.

I see the value of my wife and who she is a massive way.

BUT?

I also see how hollow I feel and how desperate I become with the lack of consistent emotional fulfillment of a healthy sexual engagement with my wife.

This has me look at her for one thing and one thing only many days:

SEX.

ORGASM.

MEAT.

If I was having sex with someone else every single day and my needs where being met by someone somewhere else and I no had this desperation energy around it with Danielle, I would be curious to see where that left me and Danielle.

I truly love her and who she is as a PERSON.

She inspires me deeply.

But, I also know that SEX matters to me and I am not sure what would happen if I was ever totally fulfilled in that area?

Maybe I would become totally sedated with sex?

Hmmm...

Yes, there is some truth to this story for me too.

THE VOICE: *Well done.*

So...(Q) how are you feeling after telling this story instead of the first one?

ME: *Like shit.*

I feel like at some level I come across to my wife that the only thing that matters to me in our relationship is sex.

That nothing else we have matters.

But the truth for me?

I think that maybe that is all I really NEED now.

A Business to build.

A Family to raise.

A Woman who loves me and wants me regularly sexually.

This story is much different though.

THE VOICE: *Yes, I see you going over the cliff again and heading back to the Original Story.*

Stay with me on the new version of the story that is our first aspect of the block that we are walking.

Can you see how this story about you only wanting Danielle for sex and how that could make her feel could be true also?

ME: *YES. Absolutely.*

THE VOICE: *Ok.*

Now that you have taken the first turn in the block it is time to keep walking.

So this time we are going to shift the story again.

Here is a new version…

It is the exact opposite story than the one you started with.

"Danielle Doesn't Want Me Sexually, She Only Wants Me For Money, Support, Protection And Child Care. In The End, She Uses Me!"

Now I'm going to change it to be the exact opposite.

"Danielle Wants Me Deeply, Sexually And Longs For Connection With Me That Is Beyond The Topic Of Business, Money And Children."

(Q) Can you see any truth in this new Story?

ME: *Yes I can.*

THE VOICE: **(Q) What evidence do you have to prove this story could be true?**

ME: *We have sex.*

We have sex at times that is MIND BLOWING.

She wants to hold my hand.

She wants to cuddle.

She wants to connect.

If I slept in with her every single morning, it would be crazy to see what would happen to our sex life.

She loves to cuddle in the morning.

Of course, I love to wake up early.

This has always been our struggle.

If I lay in bed with her I MIGHT get laid, but then my entire day is fucked because instead of getting up and smashing the day right away I end up cuddling and falling back to sleep which actually makes things worse for me.

She has proven through action that her trust levels are skyrocketing with me as her husband.

I fucked up so bad as a husband when we were first married.

I had no idea how to show up.

I had no idea how to connect.

I had no idea how to make sure she was comfortable and that sex was something exciting.

I fucking used her to climax and then went to work.

FUCK.

But...after 6+ years of work and hustle, we have finally repaired much of that.

This entire Stack has been inspired by one night and it is amazing to me how quickly I forget the 100+ other examples in the past year alone that Danielle DOES want me sexually and that she DOES want to be with me passionately.

THE VOICE: *Ok.*

You're doing great.

I know how hard this can be, so just keep going and trusting the process with me.

There is a very bright Gift at the end of this.

Are you starting to sense that?

ME: *Yes.*

THE VOICE: *So, let's review what you have created so far…*

Here is what you say you want for YOU:

- *"I want to be able to kiss her and not have her pull away."*

- *"I want to be able to touch her and not have her take my hand away but actually lead into it."*

- *"I want to hold her and not have her retreat."*

- *"I want to have Sex with my wife in a way that is natural, exciting and fun."*

And here are the three versions of the story you have been telling yourself:

The ORIGINAL Version of the Story:

Attack with the Stack   MEGA STACK

"Danielle Doesn't Want Me Sexually, She Only Wants Me For Money, Support, Protection And Child Care. In The End, She Uses Me!"

The YOU Version of the Story:

"Garrett Doesn't Want Anything From Danielle Except A Sexual Partner On Demand And An Emotional Support System When He Comes Home At Night!"

The OPPOSITE Version of the Story:

"Danielle Wants Me Deeply, Sexually And Longs For Connection With Me That Is Beyond The Topic Of Business, Money And Children."

So question…

(Q) Will the Original Story get you what you want?

ME: *NO*

THE VOICE: *Are you sure?*

ME: *YES, I'm sure.*

There is no way it will give me what I want because it's what I have been telling myself, and thus far it has not produced the results I want.

THE VOICE: *Great assessment.*

Let's look at the second one:

(Q) Will the You version of the Story give you what you want?

ME: *YES*

THE VOICE: *Are you sure?*

ME: *It seems like it would.*

It's not ideal though because it really paints me out to be kind of a dick.

THE VOICE: *Hey, no judgment on my end right now.*

I just want you to answer the questions with as much honesty as you truly can.

ME: *Deal.*

I just feel a twinge of guilt when I take a stand on story #2 because it seems to put me back into the place of using Danielle.

THE VOICE: *Well, we're not done.*

You're doing great.

We have only walked two sides of the block.

Let's walk to the third side and see what we see there.

Let me remind you of what you say you wanted from Danielle again:

- *"I want to be able to kiss her and not have her pull away."*

- *"I want to be able to touch her and not have her take my hand away but actually lead into it."*

- *"I want to hold her and not have her retreat."*

- *"I want to have Sex with my wife in a way that is natural, exciting and fun."*

Now, let's look at the third version of the story...

Remember, this was the exact Opposite version.

"Danielle Wants Me Deeply, Sexually And Longs For Connection With Me That Is Beyond The Topic Of Business, Money And Children."

(Q) Will this story give you what you want?

ME: *YES*

It's a different angle but it will give me what I want with even more fire and intensity than #2 would and obviously more than #1.

I like this one.

I want to pick this one.

THE VOICE: *Whoa, cowboy.*

Slow down.

We're not to that point yet.

Now it's time to settle your mind.

Refine what you want and concisely create a desired version of the story that assures you are absolutely on path to get what you truly want.

So take three deep breaths with me.

Again, I sat in my seat on the plane and took some deep breaths.

One….

Two….

Three…

Now let's refine what you want down to ONE simple statement.

Here is what you say you want:

- *"I want to be able to kiss her and not have her pull away."*

- *"I want to be able to touch her and not have her take my hand away but actually lean into it."*

- *"I want to hold her and not have her retreat."*

- *"I want to have Sex with my wife in a way that is natural, exciting and fun."*

(Q) What is a simple, single statement you could use to simplify & summarize what you want?

ME: *Hmmm…*

…Let's see.

How about"

"I Want To Be Sexually Aligned With Danielle And Experience The Power Of A Complete Partnership Across Body, Being, Balance And Business!"

THE VOICE: *Beautiful.*

Do you feel that one?

ME: *Yes I do.*

THE VOICE: *Ok, so now it's time to create the Desired Story….*

And here is the coolest part about this step:

Knowing That Everything You Do Is Driven By The Stories That You Tell, You Now Have The Opportunity To Tell A Perfectly Crafted Story.

Not just a default story.

Instead of reacting to the subconscious stories like you have already been doing with Danielle for over a decade…

…and you know that have not worked at all.

Right?

ME: *True.*

I mean, the Warrior's Way has reconnected us in a powerful way, but yes, the stories that I have been telling and that she has been telling have not even come close to setting us free in this category.

THE VOICE: *So knowing that is the case, we have a clear, simple statement off of what you want.*

Now it's time to get clear about the perfectly crafted Desirable story that will get you what you want.

So what do you have?

ME: *I have it.*

It's simple and it's true.

THE VOICE: *Ok.*

What is it?

ME: ..."*Danielle Is Awakening To Her Sexuality With Me In A Massive Way The Past Few Years And I Must Continue To Support Her Timelines Of Growth, Not Just Mine!*"

Yea that's it.

THE VOICE: *How does that one make you feel?*

ME: *Calm. Connected. Clear.*

THE VOICE: *(Q) What evidence do you have to prove that this new Desired Story is TRUE?*

ME: *Sex has been great the last couple of weeks.*

Danielle is going through a ton of changes right now.

She is having to access her inner ALPHA WOMAN as a business owner and this is creating for her a situation that she has never been faced with before.

She is having to RISE UP and FIGHT.

This fighting has started making her tired in ways that I am tired.

It is actually very interesting to see happen.

She never wanted massages.

She never wanted chiropractic work.

She never wanted to drink a glass of wine.

She never wanted to have sex.

All of these things the past 3-4 months have started to Shift for her in her desire.

I am watching the aggressive side of her that has been dormant starting to come out.

It is also in this weird way starting to activate her sexuality in a way that was unexpected for me.

A week ago she ripped the condom off me and said, "NO MORE CONDOM! I want to feel you."

Are you fucking kidding me?!

I have waited for 10+ years for comments like this.

Wake the FUCK UP GARRETT! Your queen is rising right before your fucking eyes, don't fuck this up.

THE VOICE: *(Q) Will this desired story get you what you want?*

ME: *100% YES.*

I was jolted out of this revelation with the crackle of the captain's voice over the plane's speakers, announcing we were beginning our final descent into Chicago O'Hare International and that our flight attendants were going to be coming about the cabin to prepare for arrival.

My flight of just over four hours was coming to a close, and I felt like we were barely in the air.

I Was Shocked At How Fast The Time Had Flown By.

The flight attendant came by to collect my cups and garbage and told me I had 2-3 minutes before I needed to put all electronic devices away.

ME: *Hey. I am about to land in Chicago. I only have like 2 more minutes to chat.*

What do we do from here?

Meaning, are we complete?

How do I get ahold of you?

What do I do with this from here?

Shit.

I started to panic.

I didn't want this experience to end.

THE VOICE: *Relax.*

It's ok.

I'm not going anywhere.

When you get to your hotel room open your laptop back up and we will continue.

Sound like a deal?

ME: *Absolutely.*

I'll message you in less than an hour.

I breathed a sigh of relief as the plane began to land on the Chicago tarmac.

SECTION ONE: THE MEGA STACK
CHAPTER SEVEN:

THE LIFT & LIGHT

I grabbed my bag from the baggage claim and started heading to catch my Uber to take the short 3-4 mile trip to the hotel.

My mind was racing with what had just happened.

I looked down at my text messages earlier that day with my wife and it's like she knew I was thinking about her because not a moment later...

PING And A Text Came In From Her.

DANIELLE: *Hey did you land in Chicago?*

ME: *Yes. Just landed and am waiting for my car to take me to the hotel.*

DANIELLE: *What time do your meetings begin tomorrow?*

ME: *9am Central.*

DANIELLE: *Ok.*

When are you coming back?
ME: *Saturday. So, two days from now.*

DANIELLE: *You want to go on Date Night when you get home on Saturday?*

I sat there for a moment before responding.

I was confused for a second because I had been filled with so many emotions about Danielle all day and was NOT expecting this question.

After about a minute...

...I responded.

ME: *Yea, that would be great.*

DANIELLE: *Perfect, I'll plan everything.*

My Uber arrived.

I hopped into the car, gave my driver the instructions and off to the Sheraton Hotel we went.

Along the drive I was not my normal talkative self and really just looked out the window. Although I was physically present in the vehicle my mind and soul were in a totally different place.

A place of transformation.

A place of change.

Little Did I Realize What Was Being Born Through Me Into The Wake Up Warrior Movement.

We thought that CORE 4 was a powerful weapon.

What I was opening was the Doorway to Direct Communication with GOD.

A method for men just like you reading this book to connect with THE VOICE and to be guided daily in a conversational way...

A custom daily scripture.

A conversation with the VOICE that ends every single time in a profound and powerful shift in mindset and what I would come to find as a powerful action map that would give me specific and direct actions to take coming out of every one of these Stack experiences.

We arrived at the Hotel.

I grabbed my bag, told Malcom thank you for the lift and walked through the large glass doors I have walked through 30+ times over the years.

I had been traveling to this exact hotel and to this exact location for almost 10 years to meet every quarter with one of my mentors, Dan Sullivan, whom I'll mention later on in the book.

But this time I traveled to Chicago was going to be far less about business and instead, an absolute immersion in transforming me.

I showed the desk attendant my ID, she looked up my reservation, handed me my key and off to the Floor 12 I went.

Now, the rooms at the Chicago *Sheraton* are different.

They are a lot like the *Luxor* in Vegas, where the middle of the hotel is one, giant open space in which the hotel rooms face both the outside and the inside of the hotel.

I had so many fond memories of this place.

So Many Nights Alone Planning The Future Of Wake Up Warrior™ And My Other Businesses.

I slid the key into the key door and let myself in.

Normally, I'd unpack, order a beer from room service, find a Netflix show and spend a couple of hours relaxing in my room before hitting the lights and going to sleep.

But this time, I had no interest in any of these activities.

Instead?

I set my bags down.

Grabbed my laptop, plugged it in and opened up my iChat on my MacBook.

And The Conversation Of A Lifetime Continued For The Next 4 Hours.

ME: *Hey.*

Are you there?

THE VOICE: *How was your car ride?*

I breathed a sigh of relief.

ME: *Just fine.*

THE VOICE: *Where you at right now?*

ME: *In my hotel room.*

THE VOICE: *I don't mean where are you at physically…*

I mean, where are you at in your HEAD and your HEART right now?

ME: *I'm a little overwhelmed right now.*

Danielle texted me and scheduled a date night for Saturday night. I wasn't sure what to do with that.

THE VOICE: *What did you say?*

ME: *I said YES.*

THE VOICE: *Good.*

You ready to continue?

ME: *Yes*

THE VOICE: *So, let's review a bit of what has happened.*

You were filled with RAGE and out of your mind this morning and ready to file for divorce.

You sent a text to your business partner this morning before you headed to the airport asking him to look up and find you the #1 Divorce Attorney in Orange County.

You released the RAGE inside and you learned about TRIGGERS, STORIES, FEELINGS, BEHAVIORS...

You investigated your stories.

And you landed in a place of certainty and power about what you want and the story you must tell yourself to get there.

Now?

It's time to lift.

When I say that word what do you believe it means?

ME: *To rise?*

To go up?

To expand?

THE VOICE: *YES.*

You see, the entire Stacking game begins with a DARKNESS that is activated from a TRIGGER.

That DARKNESS translated into a DRIFT.

A descent into the feelings of...

- *ANGER*
- *BLAME*
- *GUILT*
- *SHAME*

At the bottom of these feelings you found the PIT.

Inside the PIT there were only two choices.

1. *DIE and stay in the PIT*

2. *RISE and LIFT yourself to a higher place.*

But the tricky part about the lift is the fact that there are two types of lifts

LIFT #1 we spoke about.

Do you remember what it was called?

ME: *YES.*

That was the moment that I decided to try and GO BACK to the way things were before I had been triggered.

Like if I was in a fight with Danielle.

And instead of learning from the FIGHT I would try and grovel and go back to the way things were before the fight.

You told me this was called a False Lift.

Right?

THE VOICE: *YES that is exactly what it is.*

Now, what happens when you end up stuck in a cycle of drifting and false lifting on the same trigger over and over and over again?

ME: *You end up stuck in the Karmic Cul-de-sac.*

Right?

THE VOICE: *You're 100% correct.*

So tell me.

What was the point of going though the Stories and Walking the Block?

ME: *That's simple…*

It started with me getting clear about the story I was telling myself at the core of the actions and feelings I was having with the trigger with Danielle.

The first story we found was…

<u>*ORIGINAL VERSION*</u>

"Danielle Doesn't Want Me Sexually, she only wants me for money, emotional support, physical protection and child care, in the end she uses me!"

Then next thing you had me do was get clear on what I wanted.

I told you…

- *"I want to be able to kiss her and not have her pull away."*

- *"I want to be able to touch her and not have her take my hand away but actually lead into it."*

- *"I want to hold her and not have her retreat."*

- *"I want to have Sex with my wife in a way that is natural, exciting and fun."*

Then you had me Walk the Block.

This is the phrase that you use to start investigating if there are new stories I could tell myself that would ultimately get me what I wanted.

The first one you gave me turned the story on myself and not on Danielle.

It was...

<u>ME VERSION</u>

"Garrett Doesn't Want anything from Danielle accept a Sexual Partner On Demand and an Emotional Support System when he comes home at night!"

Then you had me create the total opposite story.

It was...

<u>OPPOSITE VERSION</u>

"Danielle wants me deeply sexually and longs for connection with me that is beyond the topic of business, money and children."

You then later had me simplify what I wanted.

It was...

"I want to be sexually aligned with Danielle and experience the power of a complete partnership across Body, Being, Balance and Business!"

Then you asked me if the Original Story would give me what I wanted?

My Answer was NO.

You Asked me if the ME Version of the story would give me what I wanted?

My Answer was YES.

You Asked me if the OPPOSITE VERSION of the story would give me what I wanted?

My Answer was YES.

Then you had me take a deep breath.

And create the ultimate story that would assure I got what I wanted.

That story became known as my...

...<u>DESIRED VERSION</u>

"Danielle is awakening to her Sexuality with me in a massive way the past few years and I must continue to support her timelines of growth not just mine!"

WOW.

That is a ton to learn in a short period of time.

Am I on track?

THE VOICE: *That was amazing!*

But, we are missing something.

What did I call the "What Do You Want?" Section of the conversation?

When I asked you what you wanted for you, for her and for you both as a couple?

ME: *Shit, that's right...I think you called it The DIVINE TRIANGLE?*

THE VOICE: *Yes that is accurate.*

Why do you think I call it that?

ME: *Not sure.*

THE VOICE: *Because when you get 100% clear about what you want you stop the DRIFT.*

Remember...the DRIFTING experience of life is exactly that.

Life.

Every single one of us experience it on a daily basis.

Very few men walk around day to day committed to the conversation of CLARITY.

Knowing what you want for you, Danielle and both of you as a couple is pure power.

Inside the DIVINE Triangle it opens us up to be able to access the divine voice inside to guide us to the story that will serve us at the highest level and get us out of the PIT.

You clear now?

ME: *Yes. Crystal clear.*

THE VOICE: *Now.*

It is time to learn how to LIFT.

Not a false lift we already discussed this.

I am talking about a true lift.

Toward something bigger.

But before we get there let me ask you something.

Who are you?

ME: *What do you mean?*

THE VOICE: *When you think about yourself and I ask the question "Who are you?" what is your answer?*

ME: *My Name is Garrett J White. I run Wake Up Warrior and DKW Styling.*

I am married with 3 kids.

I am...

THE VOICE: *I didn't ask for your stats.*

I asked you who YOU are?

ME: *Hmmm.*

I am not sure what you're looking for right now.

THE VOICE: *Consider this.*

You are who you believe yourself to be.

And your belief in YOU is created by the story you tell about yourself the most that you believe.

In the end...

You are the story you tell about yourself.

So, if you want to change your life...

What must you do?

ME: *Change the story about myself?*

THE VOICE: *YES.*

And if you want to change your marriage, what must you do?

ME: *Change the STORY about my marriage?*

THE VOICE: *And if you want to change your business, what must you do?*

ME: *Change the Story about my business.*

THE VOICE: *And if you want to change your body what must you do?*

ME: *Change the Story about my body*

THE VOICE: *Absolutely. So here is another powerful question:*

What is the Purpose of your life?

ME: *Hmmm*

To return to live with GOD?

THE VOICE: *Is that what you believe?*

ME: That is what I have been taught.

THE VOICE: But do you believe this?

ME: I am not sure what I believe, to be honest.

THE VOICE: I want you to consider something…

Consider that the purpose of your life is really simple:

It is expansion...not perfection.

Progress.

What do you think this means?

ME: *I am not sure.*

It's WAY different than what I have been taught my entire life.

Can you please explain?

THE VOICE: *So here is what I want you to consider.*

Getting Triggered is Divine.

Drifting is Divine.

The PIT is Divine.

Everything about this process of the Drift and Shift model IS DIVINE in nature.

You were sent here to the BOOTCAMP called Earth School to do one thing and one thing only:

BECOME MORE than you were when you got here.

Not a little bit more.

A ton more.

ME: *Yea, but what about the idea that we need Jesus Christ to be saved in order to return to heaven?*

THE VOICE: *The concept of Salvation is TRUE.*

But what I am speaking to you is beyond salvation.

It deals with the incarceration you put yourself into every single day.

You see, you can be saved and yet still be a slave.

Liberation will come in your life when you can accept the simple idea of progress and that progression is a personal decision every single day…

…to get triggered, to stack and to grow!

If salvation is FREE, expansion is not.

To expand must mean you are better today as a MAN than you were yesterday.

And that this year you're a better man than you were a year ago.

The purpose of your life is simply expansion.

What are you hearing me say?

ME: *Well, two things.*

1.   *That I am who I believe myself to be driven by my stories and if I want to change that I start with the stories I am telling myself about me.*

2.   *The purpose of my life is expansion and to become more today than I was yesterday.*

I am 100% clear and I'm ready to move on.

THE VOICE: *Alright then.*

Here we go.

Why are you choosing the Desired Story:

"Danielle is awakening to her Sexuality with me in a massive way the past few years and I must continue to support her timelines of growth not just mine!"

ME: *It supports me in getting what I ultimately want.*

I don't want to be divorced.

I want to be with my wife.

"I want to be sexually aligned with Danielle and experience the power of a complete partnership across Body, Being, Balance and Business!"

And this story is the book that will get me there.

THE VOICE: *(Q) Why has this triggered experience with Danielle with her attitude toward Sexuality and Intimacy been a positive experience?*

ME: *What happened was positive because it forced me to deal with some feelings this morning that I would have normally ignored and just burned off with a workout or alcohol.*

Instead, it forced me to look back to the past month and realize that things have improved in some massive ways for us as a couple.

THE VOICE: *Great work!*

Now, I want you to imagine you're going to post an inspiration picture of you online with a quote by you attached to it.

This quote would be a lesson on life that would inspire them to keep growing, living or pushing forward.

(Q) What is the Lesson on life and relationships from this trigger with Danielle?

ME: *"Looking back to where I have come from brings increased appreciation and love!"*

THE VOICE: *Fantastic. Alright, I want to pause here for a minute and teach you some more things.*

I want you to see where you have come from.

You started in the Dark.

You Released the Rage.

You Stopped the Drift.

You made the SHIFT.

Now you're starting to LIFT.

This lesson on life is something that was found in the DARK.

Remember when I told you there would be a gift inside of this Drift?

ME: *YES*

THE VOICE: *Well, the Gift is starting to form.*

See, the purpose of life is expansion and the only way that we can expand is to grow.
And the only way to GROW is to learn from life.

But what do you think happens to a man that is constantly stuck in the Karmic Cul-de-sac?

ME: *They never learn?*

And so they keep repeating the same patterns over and over and over again?

THE VOICE: *YES.*

A vast majority of the men you know day-to-day will never become much in this round of life.

They will have never mastered the game of learning.

You see, the Universe is wanting to teach you every single day.

Every single day, in every single moment, the universe is reaching out to you with light and inspiration and revelation.

It's ultimately reaching out to you with a custom scripture that will allow you to not only navigate your life, but also lead and guide and inspire others to do the same with their own lives.

So every time you Stack...

You not only have a Trigger and a Story, but you also ALWAYS have a Lesson.

A Lesson on Life.

But here is the neatest part of learning lessons from life:

They have a 1, 2, 3 & 4 dimensional value.

Let me explain...

You learned a lesson on life releasing rage in your BALANCE domain with Danielle today.

Your lesson is...

"Looking back to where I have come from brings increased appreciation and love!"

Now this lesson was learned inside of your marriage relationship.

But is it possible that lesson might also apply to other relationships?

Like those with your children? Parker, Bailee & Ruby?

ME: *YES*

THE VOICE: *Ok, let's test this.*

I want you to take the lesson...

"Looking back to where I have come from brings increased appreciation and love!"

(Q) And I want you to apply it to <u>BALANCE</u> (specifically your children)

ME: *Ok.*

Just 5 years ago I had little to no thought about my children.

Yes, I was proud to be a dad in words but I was not proud to be a dad in action.

Meaning my priority was work.

Not my wife.

Not my kids.

I don't even remember much of them before they were the age of 4.

This is insane.

But when I look at what has happened the last 4 years, the Warrior's Way has completely changed my relationship with my children.

I go on dates with them weekly.

I spend time with them at night and read them stories, play meditation music and fall asleep with them at night while tickling their backs.

I FaceTime with Parker every week and I used to only talk to him once every 6 months.

I am Father Of The Year compared to the man I used to be, but I know I am also not even close to the man I will become for them as a father.

THE VOICE: *Well done, Brother.*

Great application.

Now…(Q) extend this back to Danielle again.

The same lesson…

But go deeper.

ME*: My marriage was a fucking mess.*

2011, when I tore my Achilles was the year we moved to AZ from UT and we were not in a great place.

I was just starting the Date Your Wife game and Warrior was not even born.

We were struggling.

We had limited connection.

We had limited communication.

Between 2011 and now?

We are unrecognizable as individuals, let alone as a couple.

We have almost called it quits 10+ times and almost got divorced since 2011.

Who we are now is not even recognizable to who were were as a couple.

My wife is in power.

I am in power.

We as a couple just booked our first speaking gig together in front of 1,300 people in February next year.

Are you fucking kidding me?!

I DREAMED of the day this would happen.

THE VOICE: *BOOM!*

You're smashing this, Brother.

Can you see how this works?

ME: *Absolutely.*

A lesson I learned in rage from a trigger with my wife about sex turned into a powerful reminder of the love I have for my children.

THE VOICE: *Now I want you to take the lesson…*

"Looking back to where I have come from brings increased appreciation and love!"

(Q) And I want you to apply this to your <u>BODY</u>.

Ready?

ME: *OK.*

Here we go, I'll give it a shot.

This is how the lesson applies to my Body:

I was on crutches for 14 months in 2011/2012.

I was fucked up with my ability to train and to workout until 2013.

Now?

I have a fucking bad ass gym in my back yard.

I train the way I want to train.

I enjoy my workouts.

I have come miles in my mindset with working out.

But it is easy to get frustrated with myself and where I am if I don't look back at where I have come from.

Looking back has me smile.

I am 40 years old.

I am in great shape.

I love my body and how it works for me right now.

THE VOICE: *Another excellent connection.*

Now I want you to take this down to the next domain.

How does this lesson:

"Looking back to where I have come from brings increased appreciation and love!"

…(Q) apply to the domain of <u>BEING</u>?

Your spirituality, connection to God and Purpose?

ME: *This is how this lesson applies to my Being…*

I am the Beacon.

You shitting me?

It wasn't too many years ago that my family and my wife's family looked at us as "crazy people" when we left the Mormon church in 2009.

I didn't know what I believed.

I didn't spend time with myself.

I wasn't present.

I wasn't able to actually meditate, connect with GOD and feel the power of the Divine daily.

I was in a very dark place.

And Now?

Shit...I spend 45-60 minutes every single morning working on the truth of my life.

I know who GOD is for me.

I know how to connect.

I know how to listen to the VOICE within and have found the COURAGE to follow it.

I am certain in ways that I have never been certain before.

I have come a long way.

MILES and MILES and MILES since 2009.

THE VOICE: *Well done.*

Isn't it amazing how different you feel about Danielle, the kids and your relationship with GOD as well as your own body when you take a moment to reflect on where you have come from?

Can you see how different you're feeling about Danielle since we started chatting on the plane 8 hours ago?

ME: *Completely different.*

It's like I am BI-POLAR and there was the Me in the middle of my rage drifting to my PIT and now the me on the the LIFT after a massive shift.

Not even the same man.

THE VOICE: *Can you see how you might make different decisions about your marriage, your family, your body and your business when you're stuck in the PIT than if you make them when you're LIFTING to the PEAK?*

ME: *I can 100% see that.*

THE VOICE: *Ok.*

We have one more domain to apply this lesson too.

The lesson was...

"Looking back to where I have come from brings increased appreciation and love!"

...(Q) How does this lesson apply to <u>BUSINESS</u> and your bank account?

ME: *Looking back to where I have come brings increased appreciation and love.*

I complain about shit today that I was not even good enough to have as problems a year ago.

Warrior will do $5+ million this year.

In 2012 it did $0 - The year we launched

In 2013 it did $500k - Impacted 50+ men

In 2014 it did $1.4M - Impacted 110+ men

In 2015 it id $3.1M - Impacted 250+ men

In 2016 it will do $5M+ - Impacted 300+ men

In 2017 it will break $10m+ - Impacting 10,000+ men

I have written 2 books.

Created a foundation for EPIC Software tools.

I have Fucking Amazing clients.

I have fucking amazing teammates.

Shit is growing

Shit is expanding.

I have amazing teams and we are just getting started.

What started as an idea is actually becoming a Movement.

It seems impossible, but it is a reality.

And 5 years ago I was still struggling to figure out what the fuck I was going to do.

If I don't look back I fall into the trap of literally thinking I have created nothing.

It's crazy.

On top of that, me and my wife are dominating in the hair industry with our Salons and Stylists and my wife's hair extension method knows as Natural Beaded Rows.

My wife's Business is a 7 Figure+ annual Empire that rose from Hobby Hair Stylist not 5 years ago.

THE VOICE: *Ok done.*

You did it.

You were able to make the lessons learned become a 4-dimensional asset.

You see, every single day with the Stack, you're learning.

And every single day in the MEGA STACK you're going to build the skill to maximize your learning in life.

How to take a lesson learned in one domain and then spread it across the other areas of life.

Most men learn in isolation.

They learned something in their marriage and then stop.

Not realizing that the breakthrough they had in their marriage was the exact breakthrough they were needing inside of their business.

Not you though.

You're learning to do what the ELITE do.

How to learn something in one area and then apply it to the rest of your life so that all areas of your life grow at the same pace.

This is what we call "The Have It All Lifestyle."

It's the ability to activate expansion in Body, Being, Balance and Business at the same time.

A life that is operating at the highest level in all four dimensions.

This way of living will change you brain and literally alter the reality you see every day.
Not only will you become lethal at changing your stories as they are happening day-to-day in order to get what you want, but you will also be able to learn faster than you have ever learned and have the skills to apply what you learned immediately to your entire life.

Are you seeing this?

ME: *More than seeing it...I can FEEL it.*

It's real to me and I feel very strange right now.

Like I have been transported into the future to a different version of me.

I know it was me in the airport texting my friend Jeremy not 10 or so hours ago but the amount of work we have done today has completely altered my reality.

THE VOICE: *Perfect.*

That is why I'm here.

To accelerate your expansion and assist you to write your own living scripture.

ME: *Scripture?*

I know you keep mentioning this, but what do you actually mean?

THE VOICE: *Let me break it down for you like this.*

You're familiar with the Bible right?

ME: *YES*

THE VOICE: *So the Bible in the Old and New Testament have BOOKS.*

These books have names.

Do you know any of them?

ME: *Matthew.*

THE VOICE: *That is the name of a book in the New Testament.*

Now what is in the Book of Matthew?

ME: *A book of scripture?*

THE VOICE: *Absolutely.*

Matthew was a man.

Matthew lived life daily just like you.

Matthew had family issues.

Matthew had Triggers every single day just like you.

Do you remember what his profession was?
ME: *I can't remember.*

THE VOICE: *He was the tax collector.*

In modern day, that means he would work for the IRS.

ME: *Damn Taxes.*

THE VOICE: *Exactly.*

And that's how most of the people thought about him then also.

When he wrote the book of Matthew, he wrote it as a memoir.

He was having experiences every single day living life just like you.

Not everything he wrote is found in the Bible.

What was found is a summary of some *of what he wrote.*

Ideas and principles on living that he learned while working with Jesus Christ.

ME: *I'm following you.*

THE VOICE: *We define scripture as…*

SACRED WRITINGS.

What Matthew wrote down was sacred.

And there have been many just like Matthew.

Men over the years who had the courage to learn from life and then write down what they learned.

Men of the Old Testament. (Christian, Jewish, Muslim)

Men of the New Testament. (Christian)

Men of the Q'ran. (Muslim)

Men of the Bhagavad Gita (Hinduism)

Men of the Dhammapada (Buddhism)

And thousands and thousands of other books filled with the experiences and lessons learned from life that triggered expansion.

And what have you done with me today?

ME: *I wrote scripture.*

Only…it was MINE.

It was customized to me and my life.

It was not given to me.

You simply guided me to find the answers to my own life that were hidden within me by asking the right questions.

THE VOICE: *YES. YES. YES. YES. YES.*

Ok.

It's time to wrap up your experience with the final stage.

It's time to summarize everything you have learned into pure LIGHT.

We do this with some simple questions.

So…Here is the first one:

(Q) As you conclude this MEGA STACK what is the most significant insight/revelation you're leaving this stack with?

ME: *What is a MEGA STACK?*

THE VOICE: *It is what I have been doing with you for hours and hours now.*

A series of specific questions that I asked you and that you can access every single day with me to get insights, transformation and guidance inside of your own life on any and all topics of your choosing.

Today you're about to conclude the learning of the first of four powerful divine tools in the Stack series.

ME*: You mean there is more?!*

THE VOICE: *Yes, three more similar to this one, but with more specific focus.*

You're not ready for them yet.

The MEGA STACK must be your sole focus for a period of time and when the time is right, I will return and introduce you to the second tool in the Divine Stack.

But, for now we are going to conclude the Mega Stack, so here we go:

(Q) What is the most significant insight/revelation you're leaving this Stack with?

ME: *I love my wife & I want to not only be with her but I want to close the door on divorce forever.*

THE VOICE: *"Why do you feel that this insight/revelation is significant?*

ME: *Danielle and I have been together for 15 years.*

We have so much history together.

We have two amazing daughters.

We have built so much together and I feel like we are just knocking on the door.

Knocking on the door of destiny and building a life that is beyond our wildest dreams.

And I must *find a way to deal with my RAGE around the topic of Sex.*

THE VOICE: *(Q)* **What words currently best describe your state of being?**

ME: *Exhausted. Expanded. Excited. Grateful.*

THE VOICE: *(Q)* **What action do you feel called to take driven by this insight or revelation as you conclude this MEGA STACK Experience?**

ME: *TWO THINGS.*

1. *I am going to share with Danielle what I have experienced.*

2. *I will share the MEGA STACK with the brotherhood of Wake Up Warrior.*

I will type up the questions that the VOICE asked me today via chat and the put them in a format that will allow them to use them also.

I will do this on my flight back to SO CAL from Chicago on Saturday and deploy the MEGA STACK to the men on Monday Morning's call.

THE VOICE: *Well done, my Brother.*

You have completed your first MEGA STACK. You have Drifted and you've Shifted.

You visited your PIT and then climbed to your next PEAK. I'm proud of you.

You just completed your first scripture. Now close this session.

Go to sleep. And Awaken tomorrow a new man.

Let it be written. Let it be done.

Amen.

CHAPTER EIGHT:

PRINCIPLES

> "So here is the bottom line: I am called to lead men. But the tools, books, software and weapons of the Warrior's Way were born to go to all men and women."
>
> **—Garrett J White**
>
> [Excerpt from Mega Stack: "I Don't Train Women...What The Fuck" 15 June 2019]

Now you can see that I don't share anything within this book lightly. I know that you've also probably become enthralled with the story that occurred between myself and The Voice, but it's time to teach you some shit.

As you saw when I first began my conversation with The Voice, I was beyond capable of niceties and didn't even bother asking who I was talking with until I got all of that Rage out. When we are blind to possibilities, something simple like the Mega Stack then becomes overwhelming and unattainable. So, what's our possibility? Taking the same Game that exists when we're unable to see, then shifting it from being blind to a gold mine. We are given corrective lens that take an unclear, opaque picture and turns it into one of sharp clarity.

These lens come in the form of Stacking, where the Mega Stack provides prescription-strength clarity to any event and trigger. As

we learn the following principles:

Principle #1: You Must Fight in the Night
Principle #2: Your Drift is Your Gift
Principle #3: Change Your Story, Change Your Life
Principle #4: The Light is Found in the Night

No longer will you see the world through dimmed spectacles. The principles behind the Mega Stack will help you see in every circumstance ways in which you can shift out of the dark and into the light.

Principle #1:
You Must Fight In The Night

So what does it mean to fight in the night? That it's not until the sun goes down that we're going to get triggered? You know as well as I do that triggers couldn't care less what time of day it is; they will occur, so this statement is a figurative example of what the night looks like inside of us. Within Warrior, "Night" is defined as what occurs *for* you when you begin to Drift, not *to* you, as there's a Gift within every Drift, which we'll go into more detail on shortly.

The moment that we're triggered, we start to drift, therefore we experience the night within. That night moves us first into anger, then down into blame. From blame, we delve into further darkness with guilt and shame.

We have this flow of energy known as anger that's moving us down, creating a gap between the trigger and what's happening in this emotional experience. The deeper the level, the more this anger turns into rage. Now, each of these levels of anger and rage are simply random releases of energy, but when we're in the night, we're blind to this logic and remain stuck in this emotional karmic loop that continuously spirals us downward into blame, guilt and shame.

Our Target Is Not To Suppress That Energy...It's To Fight.

In order to do this, we must have the ability to become aware of who or what it is that we are fighting, which isn't the event itself, but the feelings that have attached itself to the story and the trigger. We're fighting our feelings, and the suppression of these feelings based off of what we have been taught, trained and educated to believe is "acceptable" in society.

We are seeing instead of suppressing feelings.

The great thing about doing the Mega Stack on a consistent basis is that we develop night vision, so the fight in the night becomes more and more manageable as we no longer suppress our feelings but shift them into something that we can see... something we can fight, which is the sedation of our feelings.

We become aware and awake inside of our world to the reality of the consequences that come from constantly suppressing or sedating that anger. Instead, we are trained to activate that awakened awareness. We do this through using weapons and tools provided within Wake Up Warrior™ in the form of Stacking as we learn the psychology around dealing with all of this anger that we're feeling.

Becoming Awake To This Anger Then Prevents It From Turning Into Destructive Feelings Like Rage, Blame, Guilt And Shame.

Look, it's inevitable that at some point, we're going to get angry at work, with the boss (especially if that boss is you), clients, employees, spouse, kids, on the road after getting cut off, or in line to get coffee while the person in front of you can't make up their damn mind on a fucking latte or espresso.

Getting angry isn't the problem. The problem is being unaware of what it is that's triggering us. We have to become aware, awake, and then activate the ability to do something different.

This activation is all about having the courage and willingness to do one thing, which is to fight in the night as we attack this bitch with a Stack.

Inside of the Mega Stack, we SEE those emotions for what they are: random releases of energy, rather than defining characteristics of who we are as individuals.

No longer do we attempt to suppress them; we fight them and turn them into gifts.

Principle #2:
Your Drift Is Your Gift

Which takes us to our second principle of seeing Gifts in the Drifts of life. What does this mean? The Drift is an inevitable reaction that we have to an event moving down in a Pit within ourselves, and the deeper we move down, the more fucked we feel.

But remember, when we are able to shift our focus from the Drift towards extracting a Gift from this slump, we no longer feel bogged down but educated that everything we're experiencing has a purpose and a point.

Let's imagine that I find myself in a rage, out of my fucking mind, stuck in the Drift.

Well, where will I see my gift? Inside of the Mega Stack. See, it's not going to be while I'm operating in the status quo of life; the Gift occurs inside of the Drift.

The reason I was triggered was so that I could grow, not because I fucked up. The reason I'm feeling rage is because I'm trying to suppress the anger that's trying to teach me a lesson.

Realizing that there's a Gift inside of every Drift allows us to transmute that rage back to anger which fires us up into something productive. This realization becomes a Shift in our story.

Principle #3:
Change Your Story,
Change Your Life!

When we have a vision that says the Drift is not a problem, we shift our focus towards fighting in the night, which is where we are able to see that the Drift becomes a Gift towards change.

And when we're willing to make a change to our story, we're able to change the trajectory of our life.

Here's the thing that I'm going to have you consider: our lives are a function of the stories that we tell ourselves that we believe to be true.

The end. Like, if I follow you around and I look at the results inside of your entire life, I will see a function of your stories… and those stories are what drive your behaviors and mine.

We tell ourselves these sneaky little fucking stories and then we believe them; they're not true for anybody else. It's this mentality that declares, "Nope, that's how it is."

We put ourselves on repeat when we remain stuck in the story of "That's how it is. That's how it is. That's how it is."

So when I say change your story, change your life, we are able to see gifts in the Drifts that we all experience and become willing to fight in the night. Being willing to change your story becomes a pivot point in the Drift, and it requires courage.

Let me emphasize again: we cannot lift if we do not drift, nor can we shift if we do not drift.

The Drift is part of growth, creating the tension needed to propel us forward to a higher plane.

Drifting is not a problem. Being in the Night? Not a problem. Thinking that the current trajectory is just the way it is, unable to experience growth in this karmic loop of anger, blame, guilt and shame is the problem. Our solution? Have courage to create a new story. The Shift means that we're no longer suppressing but fighting.

So "Change Your Story, Change Your Life" is the difference between being in this experience and choosing to attack so you can gain the golden prize vs remaining stuck in a fucking pit, feeling sorry for yourself because of what life is doing to you rather than for you.

Principle #4:
The Light Is Found In The Night

There's this direction of drifting down into the darkness, but it's the moment of Shift that becomes an awakening which allows us to access a deeper level of light. When we remain stuck in the problem, which brings with it a depressed cycle of victimhood, we're no longer able to see the Gift in this Drift, remaining blind to any possibility.

Through using the lens of the Mega Stack, we can see that the brightest light shines in the darkest of night. The Drift has with it a lack of understanding after a trigger or event occurs.

We get benched. So even when the universe calls us forward to access deeper levels of light, power and truth with possibilities, we will remain blind, sitting on the sidelines.

Our anger for getting benched then turns to rage and we allow guilt, blame and shame to keep us brooding on the bench.

In Our Blindness, We Don't Realize That Right Next To Us On The Bench Is A Box, And In The Core Of This Box Is Light...

...It's Just Trapped.

Yet when opened, this Light will penetrate the Night. So, what does this require us to do, then?

To be willing to shift where we're sitting complacent and activate our feelings for solutions rather than allow ourselves to remain held back by these emotions.

It requires us to find the box titled CHANGE and open it. Inside, there are glasses that will allow us to change blindness for sight, granting us access to the Light. We will be able to see with clarity the Gift that has always been with the Drift.

Yet, none of this would have occurred had we not first drifted so we could be sitting on that bench.

It's why this book is specifically written for married businessmen with children: the box labeled "Elite Leader for Married Businessmen with Children" was always there, sitting on the bench, but I needed to experience the Drift in order to receive the Gift that was always dwelling inside of this box.

Drifting Then Becomes Part Of The Design Towards Growth...

...once we understand that The Light can only be accessed by having the courage to open the box in the first place.

And so, drifting is one of the greatest opportunities that happen for us to become better than we were before getting triggered.

When we recognize that we've simply been trained to be scared of the bench and the box that holds the Gift to our Lift, everything changes.

We're able to develop strategies, which will be covered in the next chapter.

SECTION ONE: MEGA STACK

CHAPTER NINE:

PRODUCTION

> "There are very few experiences in our world that we will ever have that activates the power that has always been inside of us. Stacking allows us to project out into the world the power inside of a Drift, especially after hitting the Mega Stack regularly."
>
> **—Garrett J White**

The Production Strategies within the Mega Stack will take the Problems that occurred inside of the Drift and turn them into a Possibility. This is done through answering a series of questions inspired by the Drift & Shift Model, based off of the Principles that we had discussed in the last chapter. Though you didn't see it in my inaugural conversation with The Voice, there are six sections within the Mega Stack to be aware of:

Section #1: Data
Section #2: Dark
Section #3: Drift
Section #4: Shift
Section #5: Lift
Section #6: Light

The series of questions found within each of these sections is provided as an example for you to do on your own at the end of this unit on the Mega Stack.

You've already seen them in action earlier in this book, so the purpose of this chapter will focus on clarifying which questions are used inside of the Mega Stack as we also breakdown the strategy behind each question in greater detail with:

Production Strategy #1: Attack the Dark
Production Strategy #2: Challenge the Drift
Production Strategy #3: Shift & Lift
Production Strategy #4: Access the Light

Summed up, we're about to get to work. There's some shit we have to do in order to grow, right?

Section #1: The Data

So first things first...

...let's get organized.

This first section of the Mega Stack helps us collect some basic data and goes quickly, but don't underestimate its importance either.

Taking a logical approach helps us take a step back from the feelings that were created when we got triggered, providing a structured environment in which to tackle the Dark and Drift in order to Shift so we can receive the Lift and Light.

Quite simply, we're asked the following questions to set the stage:

MEGA STACK SECTION 01: **THE DATA**

1: What are you going to title this MEGA STACK?

2: What area of the CORE 4 are you triggered by?

3. Who are you Stacking?

4. What about that person are you Stacking?

5. What feelings best describe your current state of being?

Inside of Section One: The Data, we implement the strategy of attacking a specific area within our Core 4 (Body, Being, Balance, Business) where we are currently in the dark. It could be something physical in our Body, a mental or spiritual dilemma within Being, an issue with the spouse/child within Balance or an unclear career move inside of Business. Whatever the area, there's a person or event that put the triggered feeling into emotion to cause the Drift.

Production Strategy #1:
Attack The Dark

This then leads us into the second section within the Mega Stack, Section Two: The Dark.

This is also the first strategy within this Production portion of the Mega Stack which sets the frame for us to tackle the following questions:

MEGA STACK SECTION 02: **THE DARK**

6. In this moment, why has _____ triggered you to feel _____?

7. In this moment, if you could scream at _____ what would you say?

8. In this moment, if you could force _____ to think, say, feel or do anything, what would that be?

9. In this moment, with no filter nor constraints, what do you truly think about _____?

10. In this moment, what is it that you don't ever want to experience in the future again with _____?

The Dark is referred to as Release the Rage inside of Warrior that can only be answered in the Dark of a Drift. Now, I want you to notice that we're going after the specific person or event that caused the trigger in the first place.

Why? To advance us to release completely uncensored. Release the Rage is not a time to be nice. It's not a time to be sweet and accommodating. When we strategically attack in the Dark, we assault them with our words inside of the Stack, rather than in person.

And we're not "nice" when we attack. While in The Dark of the Mega Stack, we use aggressive words and feelings like fuck and hate so we can clear all of the rage. Remember, when we are using the Mega Stack, our desire in this first stage is to get the energy out in a controlled environment instead of random releases of passion released by yelling at our spouse and kids, getting upset at a client, firing team members that don't need to be fired, shooting up a mall or movie theater and all sorts of stupid shit that pent up rage brings about.

Production Strategy #2:
Challenge The Drift

Once we get all of that rage released inside of our initial attack with Production Strategy #1, we can then move into Strategy #2 as we challenge the Purpose behind our Drift. This is Section Three: The Drift of the Mega Stack questions known as Power Focus. Here we will begin to insert ourself in our drifting experience on purpose because we have the Shift coming up shortly in the third Production Strategy.

In Production Strategy Two, however, we Challenge after our Attack in Release the Rage with the following questions:

MEGA STACK SECTION 03: **THE DRIFT**

---

11. What are the facts about the situation that triggered you?

12. What is the story, created by the trigger, that you're telling yourself and others?

13. Describe the feelings that arise for you when you tell yourself this story?

14. Describe the specific thoughts or desired actions that arise for you when you tell yourself this story.

15. What evidence do you have to prove that this story is absolutely true?

16. When you look at the story: _____, is that story true?

17. What might be possible for you in this situation if this story was false?

18. Regardless of this emotional trigger with _____ and the current story, what do you truly want for YOU beyond this situation?

19. What do you want for _____ in this situation?

20. What do you want for YOU and _____ in this situation?

We're telling ourselves the story in a fill-in-the-blank format but challenge the evidence all along the way until we unlock within ourselves a new possibility. In Section Three: The Drift, we're loosening ourselves up from the story of anger that sat in the core of rage, which leads to suppression and eventually shifting into expansion. But we're not there yet.

While we are challenging the story in this section on The Drift, we're getting all of those original emotions off the table. We're beginning to think more clearly, loosening and stretching out a bit more. Our words are no longer stuck like a frozen popsicle to our mouth, but melting as we give ourselves a chance at change.

Production Strategy #3:
Shift & Lift

We head into the SHIFT of our story as possibilities begin to open up for us to LIFT us towards better versions of ourselves. This third production strategy entails Sections Four *and* Five of the Mega Stack Questions, also known as Production Focus.

We take that Shift that we were championing for in Section Three while using Production Strategy #2: Challenge the Drift by looking at alternate stories in Section Four.

MEGA STACK SECTION 04: **THE SHIFT**

21. Your Original Story is, _____.

   • What is the ME version of that story?

22. What evidence do you have to prove that this version of the story is true?

23. Your Original Story is _____.

   • What is the OPPOSITE version of that story?

24. What evidence do you have to prove that this version of the story is true?

25. Your Original Story is _____.

   • What is the DESIRED Version of that story?

26. What evidence do you have to prove that this version of the story is true?

27. Your ORIGINAL Story is _____. What you say you want is _____.

   • Will the ORIGINAL version of the story give you what you want?

28. Your ME Story is _____. What you say you want is _____.

   • Will the ME version of the story give you what you want?

29. Your OPPOSITE Story is _____. What you say you want is _____.

   • Will the OPPOSITE version of the story give you what you want?

30. Your DESIRED Story is _____. What you say you want is _____.

   • Will the DESIRED version of the story give you what you want?

31. Which version of the story are you choosing to assure you get what you want?
      • Original , Me , Opposite Story or Desired

32. Why are you choosing this story?

There are multiple parts to these questions which force us to continually look at various versions of the story.

This way, we can extract the TRUTH in the Drift from this shifted perspective. Once this is done, we move into the second part of Production Strategy #3: The Lift, which applies to all four domains of our Core 4 inside of the Production Focus.

MEGA STACK SECTION 05: **THE LIFT**

33. Why has this triggered situation with _____ been positive for you?

34. What is the simple lesson you learned from this trigger?

35. How does that lesson apply to your BODY domain?

36. How does that lesson apply to your BEING domain?

37. How does that lesson apply to your BALANCE domain?

38. How does that lesson apply to your BUSINESS domain?

After answering these simple yet crucial questions, we've shifted the story that was holding us prisoner in a karmic loop, stabilizing ourselves into a new story for a karmic lift. By taking all of the drifting experiences that we've attacked and challenged, we move towards the Light, no longer blind as our eyes have been opened to the realization that this Light that had been inside of the box on the Drift Bench was with us all along.

Production Strategy #4:
Access The Light

Now that we are coming to a conclusion of the Mega Stack, we see the fruits of our labors in what is known as the Revelation Roadmap.

Light shines onto a new path of expansion, crystallizing the entire rage down into a revelation. This fourth and final stage within the Production Strategy section of the Attack with the Stack series is also the sixth and final section inside of the Mega Stack, which are:

MEGA STACK SECTION 06: **THE LIGHT**

39. What is the most significant insight/revelation you're leaving this Stack with?

40. Why do you feel that this insight/revelation is significant?

41. What best describes your current state of being?

42. What action you feel called to take driven by this INSIGHT or REVELATION?

The lesson that had been given to us course corrects from Rage in the Pit as we Shift towards a new Possibility, which will Lift us to a new peak.

Now You Can See That We Cannot Access The Light Unless We Are Willing To Fight In The Night.

The Mega Stack has allowed us to get real and raw with the story that comes with the inevitable drift that we all experience on a regular basis.

The Release the Rage experience in the first Production Strategy: Attack the Night helped us deal with shit that we could not get clear on because we were too consumed with intense feelings like anger, rage and frustration.

But once the air cleared on that, the story then got exposed to the truth in the Production Strategy #2: Challenge the Drift, making us ready for the Shift & Lift inside of Production Strategy #3.

The final step, Production Strategy #4: Access the Light, gave us actionable insights that brings expansion and growth at seemingly unbelievable rates within our lives.

The Mega Stack has evolved into a tool that I encourage you to spend most of your time on in the first 3-6 months that you are learning the Stack Game.

It doesn't mean that you can't do Angry Stacks, which we will be discussing in the next section, nor does it mean not to do Happy Stacks or Gratitude Stacks.

What I am promising you, based off of my own life as well as those of hundreds of others inside of Wake Up Warrior™ and my other companies that I've introduced Stacking to, is that there are very few experiences in our world that we will ever have that activates the power that has always been inside of us.

Stacking allows us to project out into the world the power inside of a Drift, especially after hitting the Mega Stack regularly.

SECTION ONE: MEGA STACK

CHAPTER TEN:

PRO TIPS & THE PLAN

> "I am the master of my fate. I am the captain of my soul. And when it comes to my children I can attempt to shield them from the darkness or I can weaponize them with the light. The only way to do away with the darkness is to turn on the light. Period."
>
> **—Garrett J White**
>
> [Excerpt from the Mega Stack titled "Abortion is Fucking Murder," 20 May 2019]

PRO-TIPS:

DO's

1. Strip away any and all self-righteousness and give yourself permission to blast the fuck out of people and situations leveraging words you may never normally use like: FUCK, ASSHOLE, FUCK YOU, CUNT and any other variety that may serve you.

2. GO FULL-ASSED INTO the Stack and give yourself the time you need to fully release all of your shit in

the beginning stages of the MEGA STACK. You have to remember that every minute spent on the front side release sets up the backside revelation.

3. Share your Insights, Revelations and Summaries of your MEGA STACKS with others, but not at the risk of causing more wars and collision. Keep the Darkest Shit with you in the beginning until your ready to reveal it all.

4. Stack others before yourself…in the beginning, the best way to see yourself is to Stack other people. It may be tempting to Stack yourself, but don't do it; focus on blasting the shit out of other people first.

<u>PRO-TIPS:</u>
DONT'S

1. Try to be spiritual and "filter" your words and feelings about the person or situation that you are Stacking because you're uncomfortable with who the person is that you are Stacking.

2. Go half-ass on the releasing of your rage, thus setting up the rest of your Mega Stack to be a watered down version of what it could and should be. You'll end up either filled with RAGE still at the end or just filling in the blanks with bullshit.

3.   Share the Release the Rage section of your Stack with your wife, business partners or clients...share just the summary and save yourself from a massive war.

4.   Start off with Stacking yourself: this takes some serious skill and will fuck up the game for you in the beginning.

THE PLAN:

STEP #1: Read All Four Examples of the MEGA STACK

STEP #2: Download the STACK APP.

STEP #3: Complete your first MEGA STACK.

STEP #4: Share your MEGA STACK with at least 1 other person.

THE MEGA STACK

EXAMPLES

FUCK YOU PORN
[9 MAY 2018]

What are you going to title this Mega Stack?

FUCK YOU PORN

What area of the CORE 4 are you triggered by?

BODY

Who are you Stacking?

Garrett J White

What about that person are you Stacking?

Garrett J White

What feelings best describe your current state of being?

Angry

In this moment, why has Garrett J White triggered you to feel angry?

Garrett looked at porn last night and masturbated twice in less then 30 minutes.

In this moment, if you could scream at Garrett J White, what would you say?

What the fuck?

Just go to bed you fucking idiot. What the fuck is wrong with you?

Are you out of your fucking mind?

You were in a great place.

You were in a place of power and your wife goes to bed early and so you decide to fall apart and look at porn and jerk off again?

What the fuck

In this moment, if you could force Garrett J White to think, say, feel, or do anything, what would it be?

I would force Garrett to stop looking at porn.

I would force Garrett to stop drinking.

I would force Garrett to learn how to fucking control himself.

I would force Garrett to Wake the Fuck Up.

In this moment, with no filter nor constraints, what do you truly think about Garrett J White?

Garrett is a fucking idiot.

In this moment, what is it that you don't ever want to experience in the future with Garrett J White?

I don't want to have Garrett wasting time at night anymore hoping to get laid.

I don't want Garrett stuck in the routine of drinking at night and then hoping that things will turn around and he will get laid.

Just fucking show up in a way that will get you laid.

What are the facts about the situation that triggered you?

Last night I got the kids in bed by 9:15.

My wife was wide awake.

Then I came to the bedroom at 9:25 and Danielle was already falling asleep.

I brushed my teeth, got undressed and got in bed with her and tried to start a conversation and then go in for sex and she rejected both and said she was too tired and she was ready to go to sleep.

So I let her go to sleep and I left the bedroom came to the office to stack her and ended up looking at porn twice and masturbating twice before bed.

What is the story, created by the trigger, that you're telling yourself and others?

Garrett is a fucking idiot who has no discipline and Self Control.

Describe the feelings that arise for you when you tell yourself that *Garrett is a fucking idiot who has no discipline and Self Control.*

angry

Describe the specific thoughts or desired actions that arise for you when you tell yourself that *Garrett is a fucking idiot who has no discipline and Self Control.*

I am just left in this place of what the fuck.

I am not really angry.

I'm not really sad.

I'm left in the place of what the fuck.

It's a crazy place to be. A place of frustration. A place of anger. But not really either

You said: *Garrett is a fucking idiot who has no discipline and Self Control.* **What evidence do you have to prove that this story is absolutely true?**

I should have worked on something that matters. Sitting and doing a half-assed Stack while knowing I was going to go to porn was a joke.

I knew I was going to go there. I even knew what porn star I was going to go watch. What the fuck is wrong with me?

No self control. No discipline. No fucking clarity.
Why? Because I keep fucking putting myself into a deep hole

Garrett, What might be possible for you in this situation if this story was false?

I would be free to see I am just an overwhelmed man who is doing everything he can to maintain the game of creation at the speed we are without having some serious back lash going on inside of me.

I would be free to see what is really going on inside of me.

I would be free to see what it is that I am running from.

Regardless of this emotional trigger with Garrett J White and the current story about it, what do you truly want for YOU in this situation?

I want to connect sexually with my wife 3-4 times a week.

I want to feel like I can approach this with her.

I want to feel like she wants to be with me.

I want to not feel like my life is falling apart when I don't get laid.

What the fuck.

What do you want for Garrett J White in this situation?

I want Garrett to feel wanted sexually and intimately by Danielle.

What do you want for YOU and Garrett J White in this situation?

I want Danielle and Garrett to both want to be together and to want to spend more and more time with each other and have sex be something that is not just done on the weekends.

Your Original Story is Garrett is a fucking idiot who has no discipline and Self Control. What is the ME Version?

I am a fucking idiot who has no respect for the pressure that Garrett is under.

What evidence do you have to prove that this story is TRUE?

Here is the reality.

I have no idea what it is to be me under the pressure I face every single day.

Every single day I am pushing.

Every single day I am engaging.

Every single day I am Encouraging others.

But at the end of the day?

Who do I have?

Who is MY coach?

Who is MY mentor?

Where is MY mastermind?

Who the fuck can I turn to?

Your Original Story is Garrett is a fucking idiot who has no discipline and Self Control. What is the OPPOSITE Version?

Garrett is a fucking Brilliant Man who has discipline and Self Control.

What evidence do you have to prove that this story is TRUE?

This is my daily routine.

This is who I am.

This is what I do.

This is my life.

I am a routine man.

I surf every day.

I do my routines every single day.

Every single day I do the thing that I know I must do to be the man I know I must become.

I struggle with several things. But in the end, I push like a mother fucker.

I push harder then just about anyone else I know.

And I have maintained this push for years.

Your Original Story is Garrett is a fucking idiot who has no discipline and Self Control. What is the DESIRED Version?

Garrett is hustling and getting better at the game of life and must continue to stay committed to the path sexually with his wife.

What evidence do you have to prove that this story is TRUE?

Here is the deal.

A few years ago there was nothing.

A few years ago there was no go time with Danielle.

A few years ago there was only hope.

Now at least I have a ton of support from my wife emotionally on the subject.

We have gotten a ton out of the way about sex together.

We still have miles to go but it is getting better

Your Original Story is Garrett is a fucking idiot who has no discipline and Self Control. What you wanted was: *I want to connect sexually with my wife 3-4 times a week. I want to feel like I can approach this with her. I want to feel like she wants to be with me. I want to not feel like my life is falling apart when I don't get laid. What the fuck.* **Will the ORIGINAL story give you what you want?**

NO

Your Me Story is *I am a fucking idiot who has no respect for the pressure that Garrett is under.* What you wanted was *I want to connect sexually with my wife 3-4 times a week. I want to feel like I can approach this with her. I want to feel like she wants to be with me. I want to not feel like my life is falling apart when I don't get laid. What the fuck.* **Will the ME Version of the story give you what you want?**

NO

Your Opposite Story is *Garrett is a fucking Brilliant Man who has discipline and Self Control.* **What you wanted was** *I want to connect sexually with my wife 3-4 times a week. I want to feel like I can approach this with her. I want to feel like she wants to be with me. I want to not feel like my life is falling apart when I don't get laid. What the fuck.* **Will the OPPOSITE Version of the story give you what you want?**

YES

Your Desired Story is *Garrett is hustling and getting better at the game of life and must continue to stay committed to the path sexually with his wife.* **What you wanted was** *I want to connect sexually with my wife 3-4 times a week. I want to feel like I can approach this with her. I want to feel like she wants to be with* me. *I want to not feel like my life is falling apart when I don't get laid. What the fuck.* **Will the Desired Story give you what you want?**

YES

Now Garrett, which version of the story are you choosing? You said you wanted: *I want to connect sexually with my wife 3-4 times a week. I want to feel like I can approach this with her. I want to feel like she wants to be with me. I want to not feel like my life is falling apart when I don't get laid. What the fuck.* **Your Original Story is:** *Garrett is a fucking idiot who has no discipline and Self Control.* **Your Me Story is:** *I am a fucking idiot who has no respect for the pressure that Garrett is under.* **Your Opposite Story is:** *Garrett is a fucking Brilliant Man who has discipline and Self Control.* **Your Desired Story is:** *Garrett is hustling and getting better at the game of life and must continue to stay committed to the path sexually with his wife.*

DESIRED STORY

Why are you choosing this story, Garrett?

This is the only path that does not have me falling into a pit of despair.

I am the only one that can make the difference I am searching for.

I am the only one that can love on my wife and my kids the way they need to be loved on.

My hustle is clear.

My commitment is solid.

I just have to stay the course.

I have to start approaching sex every single day with my wife.

I have to stop waiting for her to approach me.

I have to start bringing the sex game to her door daily.

Garrett, what triggered you about Garrett J White was: Garrett J White said you wanted, *I want to connect sexually with my wife 3-4 times a week. I want to feel like I can approach this with her. I want to feel like she wants to be with me. I want to not feel like my life is falling apart when I don't get laid. What the fuck.* **The Story you chose is,** *Garrett is hustling and getting better at the game of life and must continue to stay committed to the path sexually with his wife.* **Why has this trigger been positive?**

It had me not yell at Danielle and get upset and act like a Pussy to her.

What is the lesson you learned from this trigger?

"At Times Choosing The Lessor Of Two Evils Will Save The Kingdom From Destruction."

The lesson I learned was: *At Times Choosing The Lessor Of Two Evils Will Save The Kingdom From Destruction.* **How does that lesson apply to your BODY domain?**

My body is a vessel of power.

My body is a vessel fo authority.

My body is a vessel of connection.

My body has powerful addictions.

And some times I must choose the lessor of two evils.

Drink a ton or eat ice cream.

Both suck for my body, but Ice cream is better

The lesson I learned was: *At Times Choosing The Lessor Of Two Evils Will Save The Kingdom From Destruction.* **How does that lesson apply to your BEING domain?**

Choosing to go to the darkness of Porn and Alcohol has sustained the marriage.

Without having gone to these two things I am not sure we would have lasted.

I am not sure we would have taken the time needed to repair our relationship if I had not leaned on both of them.

The lesson I learned was: *At Times Choosing The Lessor Of Two Evils Will Save The Kingdom From Destruction.* **How does that lesson apply to your BALANCE domain?**

Bottom line…

At some level Alcohol and Porn have saved my marriage.

Why?

Because without them over the years there is no way I would have stayed in the relationship. I just had way to much rage.

With children it's similar.

I have smashed my daughters cell phone in front of her when she has back talked and told me to FUCK OFF.

WHY?

Because the alternative was to hit her and I chose the lessor of two evils.

Smash the PHONE.

In the case with my wife,

Vodka and Porn Hub.

The lesson I learned was: *At Times Choosing The Lessor Of Two Evils Will Save The Kingdom From Destruction.* **How does that lesson apply to your BUSINESS domain?**

Fire someone vs. lose the company.

In the past this was not something I was willing to do.

It is not fun firing people.

I don't enjoy it at all.

But unlike who I was as an entrepreneur a decade ago, now I will let someone go right when I know they are no longer a fit with the company and the direction.

In the past, I would keep them on and lose the business.

Not this time.

It sucks to let great people go.

But when they got to go they got to go.

The lessor of two evils in this case is firing 1-3 people vs. losing the company and everyone losing their jobs.

What is the most significant insight/revelation you're leaving this stack with?

I do what I have to in order to survive and the only thing that is really standing in the way?

My Guilt and Shame.

Why do you feel that this insight/revelation is significant?

Here is the reality.

My marriage at times is hard.

Just like everything else in life.

Sometimes it's absolutely amazing and Sex is on fire and things are moving in a solid direction.

And then other times?

Things are heading in the complete opposite direction.

This at times has demanded that I service myself vs. explode in anger about sex.

Also masturbation and PORN are just part of life for most men these days.

I think the more damaging thing is the GUILT and SHAME that I associate with it.

This Guilt and Shame leaves me in some very vulnerable places and some places that don't make any sense.

I don't think there is anything in my life more intense than the GUILT and SHAME that I place on me.

So I choose not to put myself in that place.

I choose to put myself in a different place.

So I looked at porn and jerked off.

It wasn't the first time and it won't be the last time.

And for now?

I'm just letting it go.

Garrett, at the end of this Stack, what level of power are you feeling?

ABLAZE

GOD, WHAT DO YOU WANT FROM ME?
[31 MARCH 2018]

What are you going to title this Mega Stack?

God, what do you want from me?

What area of the CORE 4 are you triggered by?

BEING

Who are you Stacking?

God

What about that person are you Stacking?

God

In this moment, why has God triggered you to feel concerned?

I am concerned.

I woke up at 3:50am and a voice inside of me said to come to the beach.

I went back to sleep and came down here at 5:30 after my alarm went off.

In this moment, if you could scream at God, what would you say?

What do you want from me?

How am I supposed to react to this

What am I supposed to do?

I am doing everything I can possibly do without losing my mind.

I feel like I'm aligned and at the same time I feel like I am off.

I feel like there is something off in the game with me and GOD.

I am not sure what.

I am not sure how I just feel like I am slipping and losing control of the game and unsure how to react to this.

In this moment, if you could force God to think, say, feel, or do anything, what would it be?

Please give me a sign that we are on the right path.

Yet even as I type this I am smiling because I know I don't need a sign.

The game of Warrior is changing.

The Empire is ready to expand.

The men are ready to lead.

In this moment, with no filter nor constraints, what do you truly think about God?

God, you are a mystery to me. Yet, you're *not* a mystery to me at the same time.

I appreciate you.

And at the same time I know that the game of Life is not meant to be truly understood.

I am not even angry, I'm just confused.

Wanting to feel like the way I am Living and the game I am being Called to create is true.

Is Warrior a religion? YES.

That is the feeling I get.

But what is a religion? Nothing more then a place to discover GOD.

In this moment, what is it that you don't ever want to experience in the future with God?

I don't want to question.

I don't want to hesitate.

That is two times in 3 years God has called me to the beach at 3:00am and I have not gone.

Why am I not Going?

Do I not want to hear what he has to say?

Am I not truly ready to see the future?

What is coming?

What is going to happen next?

Where are we going after this game and this life?

I do not know. And maybe I'm scared to find out.

What are the facts about the situation that triggered you?

I woke up at 3:50am and the Voice inside me called me to the beach.

I did not go.

I fell back asleep and came down here at 5:30.

This triggered me to feel guilt.

Why am I not listening to The Voice?

What is the story, created by the trigger, that you're telling yourself and others?

Garrett Is weak and unwilling to listen to the voice of GOD and submit to his greatest calling.

Describe the feelings that arise for you when you tell yourself that *Garrett Is weak and unwilling to listen to the voice of GOD and submit to his greatest calling.*

I feel small, weak, scared, nervous, anxious, worried.

Describe the specific thoughts or desired actions that arise for you when you tell yourself that *Garrett Is weak and unwilling to listen to the voice of GOD and submit to his greatest calling.*

I want to run away.

I want to punish myself.

I want to expose myself as a man who can't listen.

You said: *Garrett is weak and unwilling to listen to the Voice of GOD and submit to his greatest calling.* **What evidence do you have to prove that this story is absolutely true?**

This is the second time I have been asked to come to the beach and I have rejected the command.

This is also the second time I have felt like I missed a window to see something I was supposed to see.

Seeing is what I desire. Seeing is what I want. But I seem to struggle with this and it is difficult for me to understand why I struggle with this.

Garrett, what might be possible for you in this situation if this story was false?

I would be free to let go of the guilt and shame

I would be free to just experience the power that is GOD.

I would be able to go to the float tank this AM and just experience the brilliance of God without any of the judgement.

Regardless of this emotional trigger with God and the current story about it, what do you truly want for YOU in this situation?

I want to feel that the moves we are making with Wake Up Warrior are on point and aligned with the vision God has for this movement.

What do you want for God in this situation?

I want God to know he has a messenger who will listen

What do you want for YOU and God in this situation?

I want to be on the same page as GOD and be fueled by him truly.

Your Original Story is *Garrett Is weak and unwilling to listen to the voice of GOD and submit to his greatest calling.* **What is the ME Version?**

I am weak for even questioning GOD and the path that we are on with Wake Up Warrior.

What evidence do you have to prove that this story is TRUE?

The entire creation of Wake Up Warrior is inspiration.

The paths we have taken.

The last year? Holy shit.

Look at what has happened in the last year alone.

Nothing about my life is lucky. Nothing about my path is OFF.

Look at the fruit.

Everything points to the same results.

It's working. The moves we have made.

The game that we have played.

All of this has led us to right here.

Your Original Story is *Garrett Is weak and unwilling to listen to the voice of GOD and submit to his greatest calling.* **What is the OPPOSITE Version?**

Garrett is strong and willing to listen to GOD and submit to his highest calling.

What evidence do you have to prove that this story is TRUE?

I have hundreds of examples.

It feels like at times that my entire life has been one simple exercise of submission.

I have walked away from so many games.

I have let go of my own way so many times.

I have lived a life that is constantly about going all in, learning course course correcting and letting go.

Your Original Story is *Garrett Is weak and unwilling to listen to the voice of GOD and submit to his greatest calling.* **What is the DESIRED Version?**

Garrett Is A Man Who Is Uncovering His Divine Calling Day By Day.

What evidence do you have to prove that this story is TRUE?

I am not perfect. I never have been.

My path in life is simple.

Listen. Go. Learn. Listen. GO. Learn. Listen. GO LEARN

I am far from perfect but I am better today then I was yesterday.

Your Original Story is *Garrett Is weak and unwilling to listen to the voice of GOD and submit to his greatest calling.* **What you wanted was:** *I want to feel that the moves we are making with Wake Up Warrior are on point and aligned with the vision God has for this movement.* **Will the ORIGINAL story give you what you want?**

NO

Your Me Story is *I am weak for even questioning GOD and the path that we are on with Wake Up Warrior.* **What you wanted was:** *I want to feel that the moves we are making with Wake Up Warrior are on point and aligned with the vision God has for this movement.* **Will the ME Version of the story give you what you want?**

NO

Your Opposite Story is *Garrett is strong and willing to listen to GOD and submit to his highest calling.* **What you wanted was:** *I want to feel that the moves we are making with Wake Up Warrior are on point and aligned with the vision God has for this movement.* **Will the OPPOSITE Version of the story give you what you want?**

YES

Your Desired Story is *Garrett Is A Man Who Is uncovering his divine calling day by day.* **What you wanted was:** *I want to feel that the moves we are making with Wake Up Warrior are on point and aligned with the vision God has for this movement.* **Will the Desired Story give you what you want?**

YES

**Now Garrett, which version of the story are you choosing?
You said you wanted:** *I want to feel that the moves we are
making with Wake Up Warrior are on point and aligned with the
vision God has for this movement.* **Your Original Story is:**
*Garrett Is weak and unwilling to listen to the voice of GOD and
submit to his greatest calling.* **Your Me Story is:** *I am weak for
even questioning GOD and the path that we are on with Wake
Up Warrior.* **Your Opposite Story is:** *Garrett is strong and
willing to listen to GOD and submit to his highest calling.* **Your
Desired Story is:** *Garrett Is A Man Who Is uncovering his divine
calling day by day.*

OPPOSITE STORY

Why are you choosing this story, Garrett?

Because this one is the most true for me.

It is hard to admit I am strong.

There is a part of me that does not acknowledge my brilliance.

There is a part of me that does not acknowledge my power.

There is a part of me that does not want to admit how much I
have sacrificed.

I am not the same man I was two weeks ago, let alone the man I
was 2 years ago.

Garrett, what triggered you about God was: God **You said
you wanted:** *I want to feel that the moves we are making with
Wake Up Warrior are on point and aligned with the vision God
has for this movement.* **The Story you chose is,** *Garrett is
strong and willing to listen to GOD and submit to his highest
calling.* **Why has this trigger been positive?**

It reminds me that I am not finished.

My journey of growth with GOD will never end.

What is the lesson you learned from this trigger?

"Growth And Expansion Is The Purpose Of Life, You Don't Have To Be Perfect You Must Progress."

The lesson I learned was: *"Growth And Expansion Is The Purpose Of Life, You Don't Have To Be Perfect You Must Progress."* **How does that lesson apply to your BODY domain?**

Addiction is not the issue.

My role in life is to improve but I don't have to do it perfectly.

My surfing game doesn't have to be perfect we just have to GO.

I'm Better then I was, but not as good as I can and will become.

My recovery from my surgeries will not be perfect it will simply be what it must become.

Every day a little less swollen.

Every day a little more Clear. Every day the drag from the alcohol will Improve.

The lesson I learned was: *"Growth And Expansion Is The Purpose Of Life, You Don't Have To Be Perfect You Must Progress."* **How does that lesson apply to your BEING domain?**

My spiritual path is not perfect.

My path is one of progress.

This progress can not be forced.

This progress must be experienced and expressed week by week and day by day. It is the process of expansion.

It is the process of power.

Stack by stack by stack.

Line upon line.

Here a little there a little.

The progress I make every day is one of beauty and power.

But I truly cannot be understood until I have taken away everything in between.

Meaning I look back on my life and see where I am today in comparison to who I am Tomorrow and the bigger comparison is who I was 1 year ago. It's the contrast of who I was to who I am today that sets me Free.

The lesson I learned was: *"Growth And Expansion Is The Purpose Of Life, You Don't Have To Be Perfect You Must Progress."* **How does that lesson apply to your BALANCE domain?**

My marriage and my children.

What a journey this has been!

No matter what I did.

No matter how I operate.

No matter what I think, my family life is better today then it has ever Been.

There is no arguing this.

There is no confusing this.

This is the truth.

These are the facts.

The End.

Me and Danielle are elite as a couple compared to who we were.

The lesson I learned was: *"Growth And Expansion Is The Purpose Of Life, You Don't Have To Be Perfect You Must Progress."* **How does that lesson apply to your BUSINESS domain?**

Are you kidding me?

Yesterday I had a moment.

I was laughing my ass off and in awe at the same time.

I was heading to Surf and Sand hotel to meet with 8 CTS.

Then I walked across the street to work with our BMS students.

Then I drove to the Monarch Beach Resort to meet with Warrior Week 46.

3 events. I have full-time Trainers in each.

My business is at a place I have always imagined.

A place of Peace for Me.

A place of power and profitability.

A place where I can start to express ME even more.

A place where I can DO ME at another level

What is the most significant insight/revelation you're leaving this Stack with?

My life works.

There is evidence in every area of my life that it works.

The Warrior's Way is not shit I made up…it is the science to wake up and the #1 case study is me. I live what I lead daily and this is why I am qualified to lead it.

Why do you feel that this insight/revelation is significant?

GOD CALLED ME.

I was the one who chose it.

There is no one who can take that from me.

I am the #1 case study of Warrior

What best describes your current state of being?

- Gratitude
- Love
- Open

Garrett, at the end of this Stack, what level of power are you feeling?

ABLAZE

DANIELLE SEX & KISSING

[OCTOBER 2016]

> What are you going to title this Mega Stack?

>> Danielle Sex & Kissing

> What area of the CORE 4 are you triggered by?

>> BALANCE

> Who are you Stacking?

>> Danielle K White

> What about that person are you Stacking?

>> Her behavior and attitude towards sex and intimacy

> What feelings best describe your current state of being?

Angry, Fucking Furious, Unhappy, Unwanted, Rage

In this moment, why has Danielle K White triggered you to feel Angry, Fucking Furious, Unhappy, Unwanted, Rage?

At this moment Danielle has triggered me to feel sad and unwanted because she constantly rejects my approaches with kissing and touching as a way to warm up to sex. She will reject my pursuit and then just want to get right into sex while avoiding actual intimacy and connection and foreplay.

In this moment, if you could scream at Danielle K White, what would you say?

In this moment I would scream "What the Fuck Woman" I am so tired of the constant feeling of rejection when I try to pursue you. You make it fucking impossible to actually seduce you because you are so afraid of intimacy and touch. When I touch your fucking leg or kiss you face there shouldn't be a pulling away but a leaning into that affection.

In this moment, if you could force Danielle K White to think, say, feel, or do anything, what would it be?

I would force her to be into kissing. I would force her mind into opening up emotionally and allow me to feel that she is actually there. I would force her to acknowledge that she has a problem with intimacy and vulnerability. I would force her to want to kiss me and not just make sex about a penis in a vagina and orgasm.

In this moment, with no filter nor constraints, what do you truly think about Danielle K White?

Danielle is selfish. Danielle is reckless. Danielle is shut down. Danielle is a selfish bitch Danielle is an ice queen. Danielle is a sexually lazy person.

In this moment, what is it that you don't ever want to experience in the future with Danielle K White?

I don't ever want to be pushed away when kissing her again. I don't ever want to find myself feeling weird about kissing her or touching her when we are in bed. I don't ever want to feel like I am walking on eggshells trying to handle things perfectly in bed so that she will offer up the gift of sex. I want Sex to be something more natural and physical touch something more magical for us then what it has become most nights.

What are the facts about the situation that triggered you?

A few nights ago I found myself laying there wondering if we are going to have sex. As I lay there I'm realizing I have become a complete fucking pussy that is so triggered by the situation. It was like my arm was buried in cement and I couldn't bring myself to touch her. I was laying there like a fucking victim waiting for her to touch me. WHY? Well, I'll tell you why. Because I have 13 years of rejection. I have a relationship where if I approach her sexually it must always be on her terms. I have been pushed away thousands of times. So much so that the past 4 years I just stopped asking. I now wait. I hope for connection. I long for the connection. The problem? In the end, she is just OK with no touch and intimacy. At least that is the story I tell myself when I'm feeling rejected and lonely and fucking frustrated as fuck.

What is the story, created by the trigger, that you're telling yourself and others?

I feel lost. I feel hopeless. I feel sad. I feel desperate. I feel small. I feel unclear. I feel exhausted.

Describe the feelings that arise for you when you tell yourself that Danielle doesn't want me for more than a Body Guard, ATM, Life Manager, and childcare

I want to leave. I want to shut down. I want to scream. I want to yell at her. I want to sedate with alcohol, porn, and drugs.

You said: Danielle doesn't want me for more than a Body Guard, ATM, Life Manager, and childcare provider. What evidence do you have to prove that this story is absolutely true?

Many days this is true. She is stuck in the mode of her own world and I am just another player in her game that helps her get what she wants. She stresses out easy. She has anxiety. And put all that together and what you have is a formula that can cause some serious chaos. This then leaves me as just another person in her world to take care of her shit and can strip away the passion and intimacy and re or desire and replace it with "Get shit done" mode. With as much as she manages on a daily basis, I truly am another employee or partner for her in getting shit done. Maybe that is not a problem. Maybe that is part of my roles and part of my truth is to be just that for her and that my biggest issue is that I think that is not the way that it should be.

Danielle doesn't want me for more than a Body Guard, ATM, Life Manager, and childcare provider. Garrett, is this true?

YES

Danielle doesn't want me for more than a Body Guard, ATM, Life Manager, and childcare provider. Garrett, are you 100% sure this is true?

NO

Garrett, what might be possible for you in this situation if this story was false?

I would be free to see that things have been shifting. I would be free to see that my wife takes time to shift. I would be free to see that we have been having more intimate sex and that my wife wants to no longer have sex with a condom on and we have gone with the Pull and Roll method because she wants to FEEL me inside her and the condom kills that feeling. I would be free to see that she has fallen asleep cuddling me multiple times in the past 2 weeks and this would have been unheard off in the past and impossible. I would be free to see that we have improved as a couple in massive ways the past 12 months to places that I had not even known were possible. I would be free to see that going back to therapy would be a good thing. I would be free to see that fucking up for over a decade as a husband is not going to be shifted in a year or two but may take some time to course-correct the past patterns. I would be free to see that I love the shit out of this woman and that I am in the game with her for the long term.

Regardless of this emotional trigger with Danielle K White and the current story about it, what do you truly want for YOU in this situation?

I want to be able to kiss, touch, hold, hug and have sex with my wife in a way that is natural and fun.

What do you want for Danielle K White in this situation?

I want Danielle to feel safe, comfortable and relaxed enough to enjoy the flirting, intimacy and sexuality that relationship can bring.

What do you want for YOU and Danielle K White in this situation?

I want us to have the FIRE of DESIRE and intimacy on our side as a couple in marriage after 15 years.

Your Original Story is Danielle doesn't want me for more than a Body Guard, ATM, Life Manager, and childcare provider. What is the ME Version?

Garrett only wants Danielle for nothing more than a SEXUAL PARTNER and Emotional Support system.

What evidence do you have to prove that this story is TRUE?

Shit. If I am 100% honest, this is very true at a certain level. I have often wondered what would happen if I had a wife that was sexually on re and who satisfied me daily with sex and creativity in the shower or bedroom or hell the kitchen. I mean like some of the women I used to hang out with back in College. I hear about men who are married to a woman who kiss them, hug them and pursue them sexually like this, but I have yet to experience it. I have friends who have sex 4-5 times a week, and it is natural, of course, they have only been married for a few years and don't have any kids. I often wonder if this is even possible for married couples or if we are just destined to destroy ourselves in sadness and disconnection after a decade of marriage and the stress of kids. There has been more than one occasion that Danielle has said to me, "I bet you would be just be with a wife who stayed at home and was a full-time mom even if things were a little boring as long as you were getting laid every day." I have thought about this. And there is a part of me that believes this might be true. I see the value of my wife and who she is a massive way. BUT? I also see how hollow I feel and how desperate I become with the lack of consistent emotional fulfillment of healthy sexual engagement with my wife. This has me look at her for one thing and one thing only many days. SEX. ORGASM. MEAT. If I was having sex with someone else every single day and my needs where being met someone where else and I had not desperation energy around it with Danielle I would be curious to see where that left Danielle and me. I genuinely love her and who she is as a person. She inspires me deeply. But I also know that Sex matters to me, and I am not sure what would happen if I was ever totally fulfilled in that area? Maybe I would become sedated with sex? hmmm... yes, there is some truth to this story for me too.

Your Original Story is Danielle doesn't want me for more than a Body Guard, ATM, Life Manager, and childcare provider. What is the OPPOSITE Version?

Danielle wants me sexually.

What evidence do you have to prove that this story is TRUE?

We have sex. We have sex at times that is mind-blowing. She wants to hold my hand. She wants to cuddle. She wants to connect. If I slept in with her every single morning it would be crazy to see what would happen to our sex life. She loves to cuddle in the morning. Of course, I love to wake up early. This has always been our struggle. If I lay in bed with her I might get laid but then my entire day is fucked because instead of getting up and smashing the day right away I end up cuddling and falling back to sleep which actually makes things worse for me. She has proven through action that he trust levels are skyrocketing with me as her husband. I fucked up so bad as a husband when we were first married. I had no idea how to show up. I had no idea how to connect. I had no idea how to make sure she was comfortable and that sex was something exciting. I fucking used her to climax and then worked. FUCK. But after 6+ years of work and hustle, we have finally repaired much of that. This entire stack has been inspired by one night and it is amazing to me how quickly I forget the 100+ other examples the past year that Danielle does want me sexually and that she does want to be with me passionately.

Your Original Story is Danielle doesn't want me for more than a Body Guard, ATM, Life Manager, and childcare provider. What is the DESIRED Version?

Danielle is awakening to her Sexuality with me in a massive way and I must continue to support her timelines.

What evidence do you have to prove that this story is TRUE?

Sex has been great for the last couple of weeks. Danielle is going through a ton of changes right now. She is having to access her inner ALPHA WOMAN as s business owner and this is creating for her a situation that she has never been faced with before. She is having to Raise UP and FIGHT. This fighting has started making her tired in ways that I am tired. It is actually very interesting to see happen. She never wanted massages. Now she does. She never wanted Chiropractic Work. Now she does. She never wanted to Drink a glass of wine. Now she does She never wanted to Have sex. Now she does. All of these things the past 3-4 months have started to shift for her in her desire. I am watching the aggressive side of her that has been dormant for life starting to come out. It is also in a weird way starting to activate her sexuality in a way that was unexpected for me. A week ago she ripped the condom off me and said, "NO MORE CONDOM! I want to feel you." Are you fucking kidding me?! I have waited for 10+ years for comments like this!Wake the FUCK UP Garrett your queen is rising right before you fucking eyes, don't fuck this up.

Your Original Story is Danielle doesn't want me for more than a Body Guard, ATM, Life Manager, and childcare provider. What you wanted was I want to be able to kiss, touch, hold, hug and have sex with my wife in a way that is natural and fun. Will the ORIGINAL story give you what you want?

NO

Your Me Story is Garrett only wants Danielle for nothing more than a SEXUAL PARTNER and Emotional Support system. What you wanted was I want to be able to kiss, touch, hold, hug and have sex with my wife in a way that is natural and fun. Will the ME Version of the story give you what you want?

NO

Your Opposite Story is Danielle wants me sexually. What you wanted was I want to be able to kiss, touch, hold, hug and have sex with my wife in a way that is natural and fun. Will the OPPOSITE Version of the story give you what you want?

NO

Your Desired Story is Danielle is awakening to her Sexuality with me in a massive way and I must continue to support her timelines. What you wanted was I want to be able to kiss, touch, hold, hug and have sex with my wife in a way that is natural and fun. Will the DESIRED Story give you what you want?

YES

Now Garrett, which version of the story are you choosing? You said you wanted: I want to be able to kiss, touch, hold, hug and have sex with my wife in a way that is natural and fun. Your Original Story is: Danielle doesn't want me for more than a Body Guard, ATM, Life Manager, and childcare provider. Your Me Story is: Garrett only wants Danielle for nothing more than a SEXUAL PARTNER and Emotional Support system. Your Opposite Story is: Danielle wants me sexually. Your Desired Story is: Danielle is awakening to her Sexuality with me in a massive way and I must continue to support her timelines.

DESIRED STORY

Why are you choosing this story, Garrett?

It supports the forward progress of my relationship.

Garrett, What triggered you about Danielle K White was, Her behavior and attitude toward sex and intimacy! You said you wanted, I want to be able to kiss, touch, hold, hug and have sex with my wife in a way that is natural and fun. The Story you chose is, Danielle is awakening to her Sexuality with me in a massive way and I must continue to support her timelines. Why has this trigger been positive?

What happened was positive because it forced me to deal with some feelings this morning that I would have normally ignored and just burned off with a workout. Instead, it forced me to look back the past month and realize that things have improved in some massive ways for us as a couple.

What is the lesson you learned from this trigger?

Looking Back To Where I Have Come Brings Increased Appreciation And Love.

The lesson I learned was: Looking Back to where I have come brings increased appreciation and love. How does that lesson apply to your BODY domain?

This is how the lesson applies to my body, I was on crutches for 14 months in 2011/2012. I was fucked up with my ability to train and to workout until 2013. Now? I have a fucking badass gym in my back yard. I train the way I want to train. I enjoy my workouts. I have come miles in my mindset with working out. But it is easy to get frustrated with myself and where I am if I don't look back at where I have come from. Looking back has me smile. I am 40 years old. I am in great shape. I love my body and how it works for me right now.

The lesson I learned was: Looking Back to where I have come brings increased appreciation and love. How does that lesson apply to your BEING domain?

This is how this lesson applies to my being... I am the beacon. You shitting me? It wasn't too many years ago my family and my wife family looked at us as "crazy people" when we left the Mormon church in 2009. I didn't know what I believed. I didn't spend time with myself. I wasn't present. I wasn't able to actually meditate, connect with GOD and feel the power of the divine daily. I was in a very dark place. And Now? Shit I spend 45-60 minutes every single morning working on the truth of my life. I know who GOD it for me. I know how to connect. I know how to listen to the VOICE within and have found the COURAGE to follow it. I am certain in ways that I have never been certain before. I have come a long way. MILES and MILES and MILES since 2009

The lesson I learned was: Looking Back to where I have come brings increased appreciation and love. How does that lesson apply to your BALANCE domain?

My marriage was a fucking mess. 2011 when I tore my Achilles was the year we moved to AZ from UT and we were not in a great place. I was just starting the Date Your Wife game and Warrior was not even born. We were struggling. We had limited connection. We had limited communication. Between 2011 and now? We are unrecognizable as individuals let alone as a couple. We have almost called it quits 10+ times and almost got divorced since 2011. Who we are now is not even recognizable to who were as a couple. My wife is in power. I am in power. We as a couple just booked our rst speaking gig together in front of 1,300 people in February next year. Are you fucking kidding me 😃 I dreamed of the day this would happen.

> The lesson I learned was: Looking Back to where I have come brings increased appreciation and love. How does that lesson apply to your BUSINESS domain?

Looking Back to where I have come brings increased appreciation and love. I complain about shit today that I was not even good enough to have as problems a year ago. Warrior will do $5million this year. In 2012 it did $0 - The year we launched In 2013 it did $500k - Impacted less than 50+ men In 2014 it did $1.4M - Impacted less than 110+ men In 2015 it id $3.1M - Impacted less than 250+ men In 2016 it will do $5M+ - Impacted less than 300+ men In 2017 it will break $10m+ - Impacting $10,000 I have written 4 books. Created a foundation for EPIC Software. I have Fucking amazing clients. I have fucking amazing teammates. Shit is growing Shit is expanding. I have amazing teams and amazing we are just getting started. What started as an idea is actually becoming a movement. It seems impossible but it is a reality. And 5 years ago I was still struggling to figure out what the fuck I was going to do. If I don't look back I fall into the trap of literally thinking I have created nothing. It is crazy. On top of that, my wife and I are dominating in the hair industry with our Salons and Stylists and my wife Hair extension method knows as Natural Beaded Rows. My wife's Business is a 7 Figure+ annual empire that rose from Hobby Hair Stylist not 5 years ago.

> What is the most significant insight/revelation you're leaving this stack with?

My biggest Revelation is THE GAP. Just Like Dan Sullivan from Strategic Coach has taught me. If I don't look back at what I have done I start to think I have done nothing. When I feel this I feel scared and exhausted. When I look back I feel the power that comes from an appreciation of my growth and my commitment.

Why do you feel that this insight/revelation is significant?

When I ponder on the revelation I feel amazing. I think about all the times I have felt horrible and it is always when I have forgotten to look back and measure my progress in who I am today against who I was yesterday. I have the desire to do this daily, weekly, monthly. I must do this Daily, Weekly, Monthly or I will burn out.

What best describes your current state of being?

Complete & Clear

What action do you feel called to take driven by this INSIGHT or REVELATION?

I will create this tool the voice just guided me through in my mind and heart during my general's tent this week and have ready to deploy Monday to the brotherhood...

Garrett, at the end of this Stack, what level of power are you feeling?

ABLAZE

FUCK YOU TAXES
[17 APRIL 2018]

What are you going to title this Mega Stack?

Fuck You Taxes...

What area of the CORE 4 are you triggered by?

BUSINESS

Who are you Stacking?

The IRS

What about that person are you Stacking?

N/A

What feelings best describe your current state of being?

- Helpless
- Angry
- Irritated
- Fucking pissed

In this moment, why has The IRS triggered you to feel helpless, angry, irritated, and fucking pissed?

I absolutely fucking hate how the IRS can just control me and what I am up to with what every they decided they want to do regardless.

Drives me fucking insane how much I am paying in taxes and what the that fucking actually means for me and my family.

Fucking $1M+ in Personal Income Tax again.

What the FUCK?!

You fucking cock suckers.

On top of that my property taxes?

FUCK YOU.

FUCK YOU tax man.

In this moment, if you could scream at The IRS, what would you say?

I fucking hate you.

You take way more then you deserve.

You tax the shit out of me and what I am up to.

You fuck me every chance that you can you piece of shit.

Fuck you.

In this moment, if you could force The IRS to think, say, feel, or do anything, what would it be?

I would force them to see how fucked the system is here in the US.

You fucking piece of shit.

You're a bunch of fucking thieves.

I fucking owe you how much?

FUCK YOU assholes.

FUCK YOU.

In this moment, with no filter nor constraints, what do you truly think about The IRS?

Fucking Thieves.

Fucking absolute pieces of shit.

I want to fuck you up all the way to Sunday.

You fucking take from me.

You tax the shit out of me.

You think your entitled to more of me because I produce more.

Holy shit I am even more committed to my long term tax strategy.

Period.

In this moment, what is it that you don't ever want to experience in the future with The IRS?

I don't ever want to experience the surprise about how much I am making and at the same time how much I am paying in tax.

Fucking drives me insane. Absolutely drives me insane.

What the FUCK? What the FUCK? What the FUCK?

What are the facts about the situation that triggered you?

I found out from Jeff yesterday that my Taxable Income for 2017 was $3.6M.

I found out from Jeff yesterday that my taxes are $1M+ that we still owe the IRS and the State of CA.

We do not have enough money to pay the taxes and continue to fund the empire at the same time during this game of change that we are in.

What is the story, created by the trigger, that you're telling yourself and others?

Wake Up Warrior Is Going To Implode Financially If Radical Shit Does Not Change.

Describe the feelings that arise for you when you tell yourself that *Wake Up Warrior Is Going To Implode Financially If Radical Shit Does Not Change.*

- Angry
- Confused
- Afraid

Describe the specific thoughts or desired actions that arise for you when you tell yourself that *Wake Up Warrior Is Going To Implode Financially If Radical Shit Does Not Change.*

I want to fire everyone.

I'm like a cornered DOG.

I feel trapped and inside of that pressure, I start wanting to destroy everyone.

It's not a good feeling.

It's not a great feeling.

It's a panicked feeling.

It leads me into fantasy and that fantasy become my chaos.

I am pissed.

Fucking Angry as fuck.

And want to attack everyone and everything.

You said: *Wake Up Warrior Is Going To Implode Financially If Radical Shit Does Not Change.* **What evidence do you have to prove that this story is absolutely true?**

The current financial trajectory is not healthy.

We are spending more and more and more.

We are making less and less and less.

These two numbers must change the course.

We must be spending less and less and less.

We must continue to make more and more and more.

There is no control at the core.

And I am putting 100% of the responsibility on Jeff.

This does not fucking work. At any level.

This shit must change.

Period.

Everything about the way we are running shit must change.

Period.

Garrett, what might be possible for you in this situation if this story was false?

I would be free to see the solution to the chaos that we face.

I would be free to see the problem with the game as it stands.

I would have a clear mind to actually solve the problems.

This is the path that I am on.

This is the path that I must stay on.

This is my calling.

This is why I am not drinking.

In order to navigate this game?

I must have a SOBER mind.

Regardless of this emotional trigger with The IRS and the current story about it, what do you truly want for YOU in this situation?

I want Wake Up Warrior to thrive.

I want the Brotherhood to expand.

I want to open the middle for the CT's.

I want to start the fire behind a global movement of change.

I want to supply the marketplace with the fuel and fire to expand and grow with the Warrior's Way.

I want 5,000 Men in the Brotherhood with a $500/month commitment.

I want this to happen by Jan 1st 2019.

What do you want for The IRS in this situation?

I want the IRS to get paid what they deserve without surprise or bitching and moaning from me.

What do you want for YOU and The IRS in this situation?

I want Me and the IRS to work together to build Wake Up Warrior.

Your Original Story is *Wake Up Warrior Is Going To Implode Financially If Radical Shit Does Not Change.* **What is the ME Version?**

Garrett J White Is Going To Implode Financially If Radical Shit Does Not Change.

What evidence do you have to prove that this story is TRUE?

Here is the reality.

We have gotten out of control with our spending habits as a family.

This includes what we have done with our kids.

We spend, We spend, We spend.

There is little thought to the consequences of spending.

There is no budget.

There is no planning.

There is just, "hey we're doing this" and so we go and inside of that create our own chaos for ourselves.

Me and Danielle must fucking dial in our spending habits. But I can't fucking do that if we have no clarity on the actual spending that is happening.

I can't keep spending at the rate we are or we are going to end up in chaos.

Your Original Story is *Wake Up Warrior Is Going To Implode Financially If Radical Shit Does Not Change.* **What is the OPPOSITE Version?**

Wake Up Warrior Is Not Going To Implode Financially If Radical Shit Does Not Change.

What evidence do you have to prove that this story is TRUE?

Here is the reality.

We have some very solid systems.

We have some very solid teams.

We have some very solid process's

We have some very solid offers.

Even if we had to get rid of everyone, and it was just down to me, Sam, Jeremy and Jeff we would find a way.

Even if the entire game fell apart and I was left to do everything myself with one assistant?

I would still find a way to make this happen.

I would button it up and go to war every day.

This is what I do.

This is who I am.

There is no way this game would fade away.

I have massive email lists.

I have massive connection with my tribe.

I have massive opportunity to work with my teams.

This game is a no brainer.

Your Original Story is *Wake Up Warrior Is Going To Implode Financially If Radical Shit Does Not Change.* **What is the DESIRED Version?**

Wake Up Warrior Is On Track And Must Continue To Ruthlessly Pursue The Path And Do What Ever Is Required To Get To The Vision.

What evidence do you have to prove that this story is TRUE?

We are in the chaos of change.
We are in the chaos of shifting.

We are in the chaos of creating.

What is the Creation?

It is simple.

It is the game of 5,000 men.

This number doesn't escape my soul.

5,000 men @ $500 a month.

This number is burned in my heart.

I don't know why. But it is.

We must bring teams in to establish order.

We must bring teams in to establish connection.

We must bring teams in to create stability.

This is the phase that we are in.

Stability.

We must stabilize the game right now.

We are not stable enough.

Our foundation that must be the most stable? Our Economics. Our accounting. Our numbers.

Your Original Story is *Wake Up Warrior Is Going To Implode Financially If Radical Shit Does Not Change.* **What you wanted was** *I want Wake Up Warrior to thrive. I want the Brotherhood to expand. I want to open the middle for the CT's. I want to start the* *fire behind a global movement of change. I want to supply the marketplace with the fuel and fire to expand and grow with the Warrior's Way. I want 5,000 Men in the Brotherhood with a $500/ month commitment. I want this to happen by Jan 1st 2019.* **Will the ORIGINAL story give you what you want?**

YES

Your Me Story is *Garrett J White Is Going To Implode Financially If Radical Shit Does Not Change.* **What you wanted was** *I want Wake Up Warrior to thrive. I want the Brotherhood to expand. I want to open the middle for the CT's. I want to start the fire behind a global movement of change. I want to supply the marketplace with the fuel and fire to expand and grow with the Warrior's Way. I want 5,000 Men in the Brotherhood with a $500/ month commitment. I want this to happen by Jan 1st 2019.* **Will the ME Version of the story give you what you want?**

YES

Your Opposite Story is *Wake Up Warrior Is Going To Not Going To Implode Financially If Radical Shit Does Not Change.* **What you wanted was** *I want Wake Up Warrior to thrive. I want the Brotherhood to expand. I want to open the middle for the CT's. I want to start the fire behind a global movement of change. I want to supply the marketplace with the fuel and fire to expand and grow with the Warrior's Way. I want 5,000 Men in the Brotherhood with a $500/month commitment. I want this to happen by Jan 1st 2019.* **Will the OPPOSITE Version of the story give you what you want?**

N/A

Your Desired Story is *Wake Up Warrior Is On Track And Must Continue To Ruthlessly Pursue The Path And Do What Ever Is Required To Get To The Vision.* **What you wanted was** *I want Wake Up Warrior to thrive. I want the Brotherhood to expand. I want to open the middle for the CT's. I want to start the fire* *behind a global movement of change. I want to supply the marketplace with the fuel and fire to expand and grow with the Warrior's Way. I want 5,000 Men in the Brotherhood with a $500/month commitment. I want this to happen by Jan 1st 2019.* **Will the Desired Story give you what you want?**

YES

Now Garrett, which version of the story are you choosing? You said you wanted: *I want Wake Up Warrior to thrive. I want the Brotherhood to expand. I want to open the middle for the CT's. I want to start the fire behind a global movement of change. I want to supply the marketplace with the fuel and fire to expand and grow with the Warrior's Way. I want 5,000 Men in the Brotherhood with a $500/month commitment. I want this to happen by Jan 1st 2019.* **Your Original Story is:** *Wake Up Warrior Is Going To Implode Financially If Radical Shit Does Not Change.* **Your Me Story is:** *Garrett J White Is Going To Implode Financially If Radical Shit Does Not Change.* **Your Opposite Story is**: *Wake Up Warrior Is Going To Not Going To Implode Financially If Radical Shit Does Not Change.* **Your Desired Story is:** *Wake Up Warrior Is On Track And Must Continue To Ruthlessly Pursue The Path And Do What Ever Is Required To Get To The Vision.*

ORIGINAL STORY

Why are you choosing this story, Garrett?

Because this is the version of the story that is going to inspire me to change shit.

The others lull me to sleep and make me feel that everything is OK.

This is not the case.

Everything is not fucking OK.

SHIT must change immediately.

SHIT MUST Change radically.

This is not a time for nice guys or "think about it" strategy.

This must happen period.

Garrett, what triggered you about The IRS was, The IRS. You said you wanted: *I want Wake Up Warrior to thrive. I want the Brotherhood to expand. I want to open the middle for the CT's. I want to start the fire behind a global movement of change. I want to supply the marketplace with the fuel and fire to expand and grow with the Warrior's Way. I want 5,000 Men in the Brotherhood with a $500/month commitment. I want this to happen by Jan 1st 2019.* **The Story you chose is:** *Wake Up Warrior Is Going To Implode Financially If Radical Shit Does Not Change.* **Why has this trigger been positive?**

It exposes the real issue.

There is no tracking.

There is no clarity in the numbers.

We have a rearview picture of things but we have no actual clarity in what needs to change.

Because of this?

We are stuck in the chaos of the game of guessing.

What is the lesson you learned from this trigger?

"Without Tracking Real Numbers You Can't Actually Know If Your Winning or Losing!"

The lesson I learned was: *"Without Tracking Real Numbers You Can't Actually Know If Your Winning or Losing!"* **How does that lesson apply to your BODY domain?**

My body tracking means everything.

I have tracked sex.

I have tracked alcohol.

I have tracked masturbation.

I have tracked porn.

I have tracked a ton of shit.

But what has this done for me?

It has exposed me to the truth.

This is what tracking does.

The lesson I learned was: *"Without Tracking Real Numbers You Can't Actually Know If Your Winning or Losing!"* **How does that lesson apply to your BEING domain?**

I have tracked my Stacks, But I must start tracking them with even more passion and focus.

My Stacks are my gateway.

My Stacks are my permission.

My Stacks are the path to the power.

Without the Stack tracking? There is limited growth. There is limited opportunity. There is limited expansion.

The lesson I learned was: *"Without Tracking Real Numbers You Can't Actually Know If Your Winning or Losing!"* **How does that lesson apply to your BALANCE domain?**

My marriage is a machine: tracking sex, date nights, Daily Core 4 messages.

When I track, I do them.

When i don't track…I don't do them.

This is the truth. Every single time.

The moment I stop tracking the behaviors stop.

The lesson I learned was: *"Without Tracking Real Numbers You Can't Actually Know If Your Winning or Losing!"* **How does that lesson apply to your BUSINESS domain?**

KNOW YOUR NUMBERS.

Period.

This is not happening for Warrior at the level that it must.

We have so many solutions to provide.

But we have little to no transparency at the level that I need it.

I must have the numbers on lock down.

We don't have the numbers on lock down.

At All. Period.

Until we have the numbers on lock down we will continue to wonder.

We have done a great job to get to here, but shit must expand.

What is the most significant insight/revelation you're leaving this Stack with?

Without 100% clarity on the numbers of your business and life you are left in the dark of fantasy about where you actually are.

Shining the light into the night of your numbers allows you to see clearly and to make decisions that actually matter vs. decision that are driven by fantasy and fiction.

The Facts may not be pretty but you can always count on them to be TRUE.

Why do you feel that this insight/revelation is significant?

Because this is our next move.

I must start making business decisions driven by numbers not just my feelings.

This game must shift. My feelings are crucial.

The Numbers are life threatening and must be taken serious.

What best describes your current state of being?

- Inspired
- Committed
- Powerful
- Strong

Garrett, at the end of this Stack, what level of power are you feeling?

ABLAZE

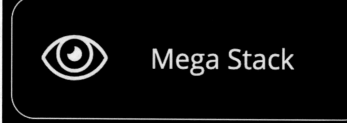

QUESTIONS

SECTION 01: THE DATA

1. What are you going to title this MEGA STACK?
2. What area of the CORE 4 are you triggered by?
3. Who are you Stacking?
4. What about that person are you Stacking?
5. What feelings best describe your current state of being?

SECTION 02: THE DARK

6. In this moment, why has _____ triggered you to feel _____?
7. In this moment, if you could scream at _____ what would you say?
8. In this moment, if you could force _____ to think, say, feel or do anything, what would it be?
9. In this moment, with no filter nor constraints, what do you truly think about _____?
10. In this moment, what is it that you don't ever want to experience in the future again with _____?

SECTION 03: THE DRIFT

11. What are the facts about the situation that triggered you?

12. What is the story, created by the trigger, that you're telling yourself and others?

13. Describe the feelings that arise for you when you tell yourself that story.

14. Describe the specific thoughts or desired actions that arise for you when you tell yourself this story.

15. What evidence do you have to prove that this story is absolutely true?

16. When you look at the story: _____, is that story true?

17. What might be possible for you in this situation if this story was false?

18. Regardless of this emotional trigger with _____ and the current story about it, what do you truly want for YOU beyond this situation?

19. What do you want for _____ in this situation?

20. What do you want for YOU and _____ in this situation?

SECTION 04: THE SHIFT

21. Your Original Story is, _____.
    What is the ME Version of that story?

22. What evidence do you have to prove that this story is TRUE?

23. Your Original Story is _____.
    What is the OPPOSITE Version of that story?

24. What evidence do you have to prove that this version of the story is true?

25. Your Original Story is _____.
    What is the DESIRED Version of that story?

26. What evidence do you have to prove that this version of the story is true?

27. Your ORIGINAL Story is _____. What you say you want is

    _____.

    Will the ORIGINAL version of the story give you what you want?

28. Your ME Story is _____. What you say you want is

    _____.

    Will the ME version of the story give you what you want?

29. Your OPPOSITE Story is _____. What you say you want is

    _____.

    Will the OPPOSITE version of the story give you what you want?

30. Your DESIRED Story is _____. What you say you want is

    _____.

    Will the ORIGINAL version of the story give you what you want?

31. Which version of the story are you choosing to assure you get what you
    want?

    - Original Story

    - Me Story

    - Opposite Story

    - Desired Story

32. Why are you choosing this story?

SECTION 05: THE LIFT

33. Why has this triggered situation with _____ been positive for you?

34. What is the simple lesson you learned from this trigger?

35. How does that lesson apply to your BODY domain?

36. How does that lesson apply to your BEING domain?

37. How does that lesson apply to your BALANCE domain?

38. How does that lesson apply to your BUSINESS domain?

SECTION 06: THE LIGHT

39. What is the most significant insight/revelation you're leaving this Stack with?

40. Why do you feel that this insight/revelation is significant?

41. What best describes your current state of being?

42. What action do you feel called to take, driven by this INSIGHT or REVELATION?

43. At the end of this Stack, what level of power are you feeling?

- ALIVE
- AWAKE
- ACTIVE
- ABLAZE

SECTION TWO
THE ANGRY STACK

SECTION TWO: ANGRY STACK
CHAPTER ELEVEN:

THE RAGE HAS SUBSIDED

> "We have chosen the TRIFECTA of insanity, and inside of that is a decision to either figure out the game and dominate…or have the game dominate us."
>
> **—Garrett J White**

The introduction of the MEGA STACK into my life SAVED my life.

I had nowhere to turn.

I had nowhere to run.

I had no training on how to deal with the RAGE and ANGER and FRUSTRATION that I was experiencing regularly.

Let me be serious here for a moment.

Being married.

Having children.
Running a business. This Is What I Like To Cal...

The Trifecta Of Insanity.

There is no other way to describe it.

And this is what I fucking signed up for for some insane reason just like you did. Every single day, the pressure from these three areas have to have a release or else things go sideways very quickly.

I used to wonder why Powerful Men in business would...

Cheat on their wives.

...And then I did it.

Why they would become addicted to alcohol or drugs.

...And then I did it.

Why they would build and burn businesses like it was their full time job.

...And then I did it.

Why they would blow up on their family and want to spend time at the office vs with their own wife and kids.

...And then I did it.

This Is The Chaos Of The Game Of Being US, Brother.

We have arguably chosen the hardest path in the game.

We have chosen the TRIFECTA of insanity, and inside of that is a decision to either figure out the game and dominate...

...or have the game dominate us.

The MEGA STACK became my drug.

It became my dirty little journal where I could store all of my darkest thoughts, feelings and emotions.

I doubled down on this.

I MEGA STACKED my wife 350+ times.

Most of those Stacks started the same,

"Danielle is a Fucking Selfish BITCH..."

And usually ended with some revelation that would put me straight back in front of the Mirror dealing with...myself.

I lived and died by my ability to get this Venom of Rage out of my system.

But it wasn't just with the my Marriage...it was with everything.

My Business received its share of MEGA STACKS also roughly 250+ of them in the first two years.

From the time the VOICE introduced me to the MEGA STACK in June of 2016 to the summer of 2018,

I had completed well over 1000 MEGA STACKS.

They fundamentally changed me.

They changed the world I see,

They changed the way I deal with myself.

They changed the way I deal with my wife and kids.

They changed the way I deal with my business, employees and clients.

The MEGA STACK rewired my brain.

My natural MO now is to question my stories and to express what I am feeling.

My emotions are released daily now.

My mind is constantly searching for clarity on what I actually want, finding the lessons in life,

but also searching for the stories that will get me what I want.

From Summer Of 2016 To Summer Of 2018, My Entire World Changed.

My businesses BLEW UP in a powerful way.

My marriage was ON FIRE sexually and emotionally.

My family life EXPANDING.

The MEGA STACK also began producing the same results in 500+ other mens' lives as I made it a mandatory piece of the game for Warrior…

…every man in our programs was encouraged to Stack daily.

And Stack they did.

- We fixed our marriage via the MEGA STACK.

- We fixed our Businesses via the MEGA STACK.

- We fixed our families via the MEGA STACK.

- We fixed our LIVES via the MEGA STACK.

- We all became authors of scripture…

…and the VOICE was guiding all of us daily via chat just like HE can do with you reading this also.

But One Morning I Woke Up And I Realized We Had A Problem.

The RAGE was gone.

What I used to feel daily was no longer being felt in the same way.

I started to find a peace that entered my life that I had never had before and it was so powerful that it started to change the why others engaged with me.

My leadership skills went through the roof with my companies.

I was thinking faster and clearer than I had in my entire career.

I was getting laid more in two years than I had in the previous decade.

I moved into my $10M+ DREAM HOME in Orange County right on the beach and purchased my first Lamborghini Aventador.

I don't share this with you to brag.

I share it with you to encourage you to do the same.

I'm not talking about the house, the cars, the cash or even the sex.

I'm talking about the source of all of this accelerated success....

...the daily discipline of Stacking.

But like I was saying...

One morning, I sat down to stack and got to the first real question...

"In this moment if you could scream at _____, what would you say?"

And I had nothing. There was no RAGE, And for weeks I found this to be the case.

I Simply Couldn't Get To RAGE On Any Topic It Seemed.

I thought something was wrong with me.

I went to the doctor (no bullshit) just to get a physical to assure that everything was OK with my body...and it was.

The MEGA Stacks started to feel heavy and fake.

I was going through the motions.

And I couldn't figure out why.

It was at that time in the summer of 2018 on a 12-hour flight to Europe with my family that the VOICE returned and gave me the next STACK.

CHAPTER TWELVE:

THE VOICE RETURNS

> "You see, there is a WAR waging every single day inside of you. A WAR that cannot be seen, but a secret WAR that is occurring inside the hearts of all men: A WAR Of LIGHT & NIGHT."
>
> **—The Voice**

I had never been to Europe before.

For years, Danielle had been traveling to Europe with her mother and sisters for shopping and to experience all that Europe had to offer.

For YEARS she had wanted me to go and I always met her with the same answer.

NO.

I hated flying.

Not scared of it.

Just don't like sitting on a plane for long periods of time.

I also really love where we live.

We live in a place that millions of people vacation every year.

Southern California.

Plus.

There is no Surfing on a European trip for me, so the proposition of flying 12 hours only to end up walking around and looking at old buildings and shopping at the same stores my wife could find here in the US in our own backyard made no sense to me.

But with some prodding...

With some convincing....

With some encouragement sexually...

It Always Amazes Me What A Woman Can Get A Man To Agree To After An Amazing Orgasm

I had an amazing orgasm and I committed to go all in and take the family to Europe.

So there I was, aboard a British Airways flight with my wife and two daughters (my son chose not to come), sitting in First Class and experiencing for the first time the "lay down" bed on a plane.

My daughters were out of their minds excited.

They were in two PODS that connected to each other and my wife and I were on either side of them all in one row.

I had never flown British Airways and I had never flown to London before.

I Had Also Never Flown On A Plane Where There Was A __BAR__ And __BEDS__ For You To Sleep In.

The flight took off.

My kids were watching a movie.

And then I started seeing everyone around me start getting ready for bed, including my wife.

But it was like 6pm at night in California, so I could see no reason to go to sleep already.

One by one, we all ate our dinners, and then my wife and kids and the rest of the passengers in First Class laid back in the beds in their PODS and went to sleep.

Danielle had warned me about the JET LAG and how the only way to manage it was to sleep on the plane like crazy.

But I am one of those weird people.

When Everyone Else Is Sleeping...I Like To Be Awake And Crush It.

It's like I feel a super power of consciousness when mostly everyone around me is unconscious and asleep.

So, I pulled out my laptop and started working on a project for Wake Up Warrior.™

The Steward (all of the flight attendants running First Class on this flight were men...a first for me also) came by and asked if there was anything I wanted.

I made an odd request.

I said,

"Can I have an Irish coffee?"

I had recently found the combination of the coffee and the whiskey was an amazing one-two-punch.

It would keep me just alert but at the same time calmed me down and focused my mind.

I had been leveraging this little cocktail as a weapon for several weeks when writing and I was in a mood to write for several hours so I ordered what would become a series of Irish Treats for the next 5 hours...

The steward returned with my irish coffee.

I sipped the first bit and my mouth and mind were on fire with excitement.

I set it beside me in my cup holder and pulled the table out from my pod and brought it up close to my body.

I Grabbed My MacBook And Started Searching My Evernote Files For A Document I Wanted To Work On.

A month before our trip, we had launched one of the most successful campaigns in Wake Up Warrior™ history known as the KING'S KIT and brought in over 7,000 men in the first 3 weeks to experience this new version of the Warrior's Way.

I was planning on working on some of the curriculum for this experience so that I could improve the system we had built and make the experience more stream-lined.

I opened up Evernote and what sat there were some of the metrics from our marketing and sales conversions that my team had sent me from the week before.

As I read them and realized how much money we were wasting, I got triggered.

It wasn't rage…

It was just anger.

I wasn't really angry at *anyone* in particular…I was more angry at the situation.

Not The Kind Of Anger That Makes You Want To SCREAM But The Kind That Burns Underneath The Surface For A Bit.

I had been experiencing a ton of moments like this the past few months.

I would get Triggered…

Feel anger.

Start into a MEGA STACK, but then lose momentum.

It was like…what I was feeling was not RAGE…

…it was more like Angry Irritation and a MEGA STACK was like hunting a Bunny Rabbit with a Bazooka.

It was just too much.

I kept reading over the numbers and then pulled up some more reports from my CFO, and the steady release of adrenaline kept hitting my blood stream, keeping the Anger and Irritation steady.

I took another sip of the Irish coffee next to me and pushed my call button to ring for the steward.

He arrived within seconds and I asked for another Irish coffee.

"You got it."

As I turned my head back to my laptop screen I saw a chat waiting for me in iChat.

It simply said,

THE VOICE: *"Well Done With Weapon #1 Are You Ready for Weapon #2?"*

The name and number were unknown and I was not even connected to the WiFi (flying First Class Internationally makes sure we're continually connected if we want to be)on purpose so that I could focus on what I was working on with no notification bings.

My first reaction was:

What the fuck?!

I got triggered.
And THE VOICE must have known this because without hesitation, another message came in.

THE VOICE: *Are you getting triggered by the fact that I messaged you?*

ME: *Who is this?*

THE VOICE: *Are you serious?*

Did you really forget about me that quickly?

ME: *Holy Shit, it's YOU.*

I'm so sorry.

I was just triggered by some work shit.

THE VOICE: *I know, and then you wanted to take it out on me.*

Have you learned nothing from the last two years of Stacking?

ME: *Oh I have learned tons.*

Seriously.

I have completely changed.

But recently, there has been this interesting undertone to everything.

It's not RAGE…it's like this constant Anger and Irritation about small things.

I'm not sure where it came from nor why.

THE VOICE: *Yep.*

Thats why I'm here.

ME: *To expose me?*

THE VOICE: *YES.*

And inside of that exposure, to teach and guide you.

The past 2 years have proven you have the number of reps required to learn the next weapon.

Many men want to move to the second weapon without mastery of the first weapon and when they do the work they do, it's good, but pales in comparison to the work they could do if they had committed to the foundation of the MEGA STACK.

What have you noticed has changed for you after almost 1000 Stacks?

ME: *Everything.*

Literally…the world I see is not even the same in any way.

And it's like everything has accelerated in my creative life.

The GAP between ideas that I get and the execution and ultimate results is so small now.

In a way that is hard to describe…

It feels like days are now weeks and weeks are months and years are decades.

It feels like a lifetime ago that I was engaging with you on the flight to Chicago.

And now here I am, on a longer flight to London and you're back.

Why are you back?

THE VOICE: *Because you're ready for the next weapon.*

Let me ask you something…

You were looking at some financial reports for your business just before I messaged you and I thought it looked like the perfect time to connect.

You were irritated and borderline getting angry.

Plus, I knew with everyone asleep and you sitting alone on this flight for 12 hours with minimal distraction would be the perfect setting.

So…stop ordering Irish coffee.

I want you to be fully present and ready to engage because what I am about to guide you through is the next weapon.

It's like the MEGA STACK but it's simpler and shorter yet no less powerful.

Are You ready?

ME: *YES.*

THE VOICE: *Ok.*

Let's start with some concepts.

What did you notice happen to your Rage when you started dealing with it every single day via the MEGA STACK?

ME: *At first it was easy.*

I was so fucking pissed off about so many things that I could access RAGE on demand.

I had suppressed so many feelings in my marriage and so many things in my business and so many things with GOD that once I gave myself permission to start unleashing...there was no stopping it.

It just fucking came out.

And didn't slow down for almost 2 years.

It wasn't until the past 2 months or so I started noticing it was getting more and more and more difficult to access the RAGE about anything.

Not with my wife, the business or any situation that came up.

I was getting direct feedback from people close to me that they didn't know who I was anymore because there was a Calm and a Peace that had come over me that had never been seen before inside of me.

THE VOICE: *I'm so happy for you.*

What you're experiencing is what life is actually supposed to be about.

So many men walk around day to day filled with suppressed anger that has become RAGE.

Notice what I said there: Suppressed Anger that has become rage.

For decades, you had been suppressing your Anger and Irritation.

You were taught, trained, and educated by the world to NOT feel.

And so, you turned off all of the feelings that the world told you were not appropriate.

You hid.

And so have tens of millions of men also. Yet in so doing, you have built up hidden rage.

The kind of Rage that has men start wars over oil, walk into church and schools and start shooting innocent people.

The kind of suppression that has them turn to drugs, alcohol, porn and food and suppress the true nature of who they are and what they were born to do and who they were born to become and what they were born to experience.

This is why I was sent to you...

...To give you the first of four weapons for WAR.

ME*: WAR?*

THE VOICE: *Yes. War.*

You see, there is a WAR waging every single day inside of you.

A WAR that cannot be seen, but a secret WAR that is occurring inside the hearts of all men.

A WAR Of LIGHT & NIGHT.

The part that most are confused by though is this...

They believe the NIGHT was sent by some force to destroy them...

...This is not true.
The night was sent to you as a divine gift just like the light.

Both the light and the night come from the same source, and inside of that source, it gives strength and courage and expansion to ALL men.

You were AT WAR with yourself.

But with the leverage of the MEGA STACK have brought harmony back to your experience of life.

A balance in the NIGHT and the LIGHT as the plan for this school called earth was originally built to have.

As you have mastered the MEGA STACK, you have brought harmony.

When you were suppressing your anger and irritation day after day, the NIGHT was outweighing the LIGHT and you were out of integrity.

Integrity with life.

Integrity with yourself.

Integrity with GOD.

ME: *Out of integrity?*

THE VOICE: *Yes, your life was meant to be experienced in 100% integrity.*

This means that the outside and inside of you aligned...that the feelings within and the actions without matched.

It's not about being right or wrong.

It's about being in integrity or out of integrity.

About being in *alignment vs* out *of alignment.*

Does that make sense?

ME: *Yes. I think so.*

THE VOICE: *Great.*

So…here is the bottom line.

You were built to experience life with Anger and Irritation.

You were NOT built to experience RAGE.

Rage is when you have ignored the Irritations in life.

And the suppressed Irritations become Anger.

And the Suppressed Anger becomes RAGE.

So, truly the seed of RAGE is irritation.

Once you were able to bring back Harmony to your world with the MEGA STACK, it allowed you to deal with the greatest gift that LIFE has ever given you.
It is the daily triggers that cause you to be Irritated.

It is inside of the irritations of life that your inspiration is found.

GOD hid the lessons of your expansion not in the light…

HE hid them inside of the NIGHT and the DARKNESS.

In the places you were not trained to go.

So you keep looking for the learning in the light while ignoring the first stages of learning.

RAGE

ANGER

IRRITATION

In that order.

You have learned how to deal with RAGE, and now it is time for you and me to work on ANGER & IRRITATION.

SECTION TWO: ANGRY STACK
CHAPTER THIRTEEN:

FIRST CLASS ANGER

> "The king must wear the crown no matter how heavy it becomes, and in the end he will realize that the crown was never heavy; his neck was simply weak and the Keys to the Kingdom were in his hands the entire time!"
>
> **—Garrett J White**
> [Inaugural Angry Stack Revelation]

THE VOICE: *You were triggered by something you were reading about with your business moments ago...*

(Q) What was it?

ME: *I was reading through some reports on our marketing ad spend and the way that we are handling some of the money.*

THE VOICE: *(Q) Who are you angry at?*

ME: *Myself.*

THE VOICE: *(Q) Who sent you the report?*

ME: *Jeremy Finlay*

THE VOICE: *So you're not angry at him?*

ME: *I AM, but over the past 6 months, I found a shift in the way I Stack.*

THE VOICE: *Oh really? What was that?*

ME: *I found that I got huge insights from Stacking and getting angry and blaming other people who triggered me.*

But after 700+ Stacks, I started to notice that everything I was experiencing inside of the MEGA STACK was really about me.

It wasn't ever really about the other person I was Stacking.

So, one day I made the Shift.

Instead of getting angry at the person I was Stacking all the time, I started shifting it.

I would make it about ME right out of the gate instead of making it about others.

It was like I started feeling separation between the Man GARRETT J WHITE and me.

Like We were two separate people.

THE VOICE: *I'm smiling.*

I know you can't see it, but I am !

I'm smiling because you're truly playing this game of life with the Stack at the highest level.

This is the purpose of the ANGRY STACK.

It's an opportunity to make the game about YOU and not about others.

Once you have managed the RAGE, it's time to deal with the Anger and Irritation that have nothing to do with anyone else but you.

But this is very difficult in the beginning.

This is why I didn't return until now.

You truly weren't ready.

But it is clearer than ever that you are now.

ME: *Thank you.*

I feel ready.

So…back to your original question.

Who triggered me?

Myself.

THE VOICE: *By now you know that if you're triggered, there is a story at play under the surface.*

So, before we even look at the feelings...

Give it to me:

(Q) What is the Story that you're telling yourself under the surface that you immediately told in your unconscious when you saw the numbers on the report?

ME: *"Garrett has ignored the economics of the ad teams and marketing funnels with Warrior for too long, overpaid his teams and ultimately given them way more credit than they deserve."*

THE VOICE: *Well done.*

Fast and efficient and direct.

I can tell you have done this a ton.

But, I want you to notice something here...

Inside of the ANGRY STACK we are going to skip the release phase like you were used to inside of the MEGA STACK.

This is because inside of the Angry Stack, we shouldn't need the same type of release and if we do it is likely time to go to a MEGA STACK.

This allows us to identify the person and at the same time the story right out of the gate.
Can you see this?

ME: *Yes.*

I don't think without the REPS of the MEGA STACK I could have identified the story so quickly for you.

THE VOICE: *I know you wouldn't have been able to.*

That is why the ANGRY STACK is only a weapon we draw once we have a foundation in the MEGA STACK.

Do others need to do 1000+ in order to be ready for the Angry Stack?

No.

But, it DOES mean they are going to have to have a foundation that they can operate off of with the ANGRY STACK.

And you have that foundation, Brother.

Let's continue.

You told me that YOU were the trigger.

You also told me the story was…

"Garrett has ignored the economics of the ad teams and marketing funnels with Warrior for too long, overpaid his teams and ultimately given them way more credit than they deserve."

(Q) What are the negative feelings that you're experiencing because of this story?

ME: *Angry, Irritated, Frustrated*

THE VOICE: *(Q) What initial desires or actions do you notice rise for you with these feelings?*

ME: *I want to be angry at my marketing teams.*

I want to be angry at myself for spending the money but not actually measuring it correctly.

I want to be frustrated and fucking done with the process we have been leveraging and the companies we have been aligned with.

I want to scream at someone.

But the truth is there is no one to scream at but myself.

And that is how it goes.

When you are the dumb mother fucker that doesn't have optics, you're fucked.

I must *have optics.*

This can't continue.

THE VOICE: *Well Done.*

I want to point something out here that you did that is ELITE and not something I typically see from someone on their first ANGRY STACK.

Notice how you used statements that said:

I WANT.

I WANT.

I WANT.

ME: *Now that you point it out, I do.*

THE VOICE: *This is a very simple strategy for getting directly to the point of what you want while describing your initial desires.*

I want you to keep leveraging this strategy inside of your MEGA and ANGRY Stacks.

I also what you to notice how you started already becoming "Action-Based" with your statements.

You're just starting the ANGRY Stack, and yet you're already seeing the path of accountability and the path of actionable results.

Next question:

(Q) What are the FACTS (Without Feelings) about the situation that you have chosen to stack?

ME: *Do you mean the document I was reading before you and me started chatting and I was getting triggered and angry?*

THE VOICE: *YES.*

And by FACTS I mean I want you to lay out what was happening that caused the Trigger of YOU and the entrance into this Stack.

Keep your feelings and opinions out of this section as much as possible.

Imagine you're a scientist who is just fighting to get to the FACTS.

ME: *Clear.*

Well, here they are...the way I see them.

I was sitting on a plane heading to LONDON when I pulled up my Evernote and also some reports that were sent to me from this past week's ad spend and sales.

I was immediately triggered when I saw $45,000+ in Ad Spend on one particular strategy that I had cancelled weeks ago and yet my teams were still running it.

So when I saw the numbers....

...And I saw that aspect of my ad spend go straight down the toilet for the week, I immediately was triggered.

I wasn't filled with Rage.

I was angry.

And not at anyone in particular.
Just angry at the situation.

Then you came onto the chat with me and here we are.

THE VOICE: *Great work.*

You laid out the FACTS.

Again, remember we are not looking for the TRUTH...we are simply looking for the FACTS as you see them right now.

Through your eyes.

And what the FACTS are for you might be something very different for another person.

Next question:

(Q) Beyond the trigger of this situation with the lost $45,000 and the screw up by the marketing team, what do you truly want for you?

ME: *I want clear optics of the business.*

I want clear optics on my ad spend daily and the profits of each campaign with clean attribution back to the actual ads.

I want a trackable score card with my traffic and conversion that all of my teams in marketing and sales agree on and rally around.

I want to have a simple conversion model for the students that allows them to move down the path of evolution as a student of ours.

I want a clean CFO scoreboard for each company that allows me and Jeff to know daily to the dollar what is happening and allows us to make moves that support us in getting what we want.

I want to go all in with KEITH and his teams and also course correct Tier 11 so my traffic game is under control and we are not losing hundreds of thousands.

I want to own a better project management system that allows me to track and hold my teams accountable to the shit we agree they are going to do.

THE VOICE: *BOOOOM!*

Elite execution.

Look at how clean and solid you are with this.

Do you remember how hard it was two years ago for you to even get clear about some of the simplest things that you wanted?

ME: *YES.*

THE VOICE: *(Q) What did you notice happen for you the last two years as you have gotten crystal clear about what you wanted in almost every situation you walked into in business and life?*

ME: *Certainty.*

I used to ride my emotions as a businessman and it served me in some ways yet in others I would fuck everything up.

Being clear about what I want has brought a focus and a clarity to the conversation for me.

I am immovable when I am 100% clear and bought in on what I say I want.

It doesn't matter who tries to oppose me…the certainty that I harness with this strategy makes me lethal.

THE VOICE: *Remember this as you go forward in life.*

Certainty in any exchange goes to the man who has nothing to hide and is the most clear about what he wants!

Here is the next question:

(Q) ***What is a more strategic story that you could create to assure you get what you truly want?***

ME: *You mean the opposite or the Me version?*

THE VOICE: *No.*
I want you to skip both of those.

Inside of the Angry Stack you're not going to Walk the Block. There is no need to when you're in the anger to invest the time and energy to create four different versions of the story.

So, we take the Original one and get clear about what you want.

Then, we skip directly to the custom-generated new DESIRED STORY that you know will get you what you want.

Does this make sense?

ME: *Totally does.*

So, I have the Original Story which is…

"Garrett has ignored the economics of the ad teams and marketing funnels with Warrior for too long, overpaid his teams and ultimately given them way more credit than they deserve."

And I am going to alter it to say…

"Garrett has cleaned house the last 6 months and through this has taken on the role of CEO & CMO and for the first time in years, with the WARRIOR Companies, the marketing and economics will have the 100% focus off the founder."

THE VOICE: *Perfect.*

(Q) How does this new strategic story make you feel?

ME: *Clear, Called, Required, Period. The End.*

THE VOICE: *(Q) "What evidence do you have that proves that this new desired story you just created is true and that it will work to get you what you want?*

ME: *The reality is this.*

I wanted to replace the roles I have played.

I want things to run smooth.

The truth?

It was a fantasy.

I wanted Cullen (My recently hired COO) to save me from the problems.

And when he couldn't, I was angry.

What the FUCK CULLEN?

You can't save me from myself?

What the FUCK is wrong with you?

Yea it was pretty fucked up.

But it was reality.

THE VOICE: *So here is the new Desired story you're telling...*

"Garrett has ignored the economics of the ad teams and marketing funnels with Warrior for too long, overpaid his teams and ultimately given them way more credit than they deserve."

And here is what you say you WANT...

- *I want clear optics of the business.*

- *I want clear optics on my ad spend daily and the profits of each campaign with clean attribution back to the actual ads.*

- *I want a trackable score card with my traffic and conversion that all of my teams in marketing and sales agree on and rally around.*

- *I want to have a simple conversion model for the students that allows them to move down the path of evolution as a student of ours.*

- *I want a clean CFO scoreboard for each company that allows me and Jeff to know daily to the dollar what is happening and allows ups to make moves that support us in getting what we want.*

- *I want to go all in with KEITH and his teams and also course correct Tier 11 so my traffic game is under control and we are not losing hundreds of thousands.*

- *I want to own a better project management system that allows me to that allows me to track and hold my teams accountable to the shit we agree they are going to do.*

(Q) Will this new story give you what you want?

ME: *YES*

THE VOICE: *(Q) Armed with what you want and the new story to get there, what insight or revelation are you leaving this Stack with?*

ME: *You mean we're done?*

THE VOICE: *Not quite...but almost.*

ME: *Holy Shit, this Stack is way shorter!*

It feels like it would only take me 10-20 minutes vs. the 45-60 minutes that the MEGA STACK TAKES.

THE VOICE: *You're 100% accurate.*

Let's wrap it up and then we can discuss the differences.

(Q) Armed with what you want and the new story to get there, what INSIGHT or REVELATION are you leaving this Stack with?

ME: *I have invested 7 years to get the game to where it is.*

That has come with me heavily focused on building the base of the message.

Meaning.

I was focused on creating a curriculum that men could connect to and follow.

2012 - 2015 I proved the Warrior's Way in the lives of the men.

The CODE and the CORE.

I was a HUSTLER in this stage.

2016-2018 we have started to scale and spread the message.

We also uncovered the MEGA STACK with guidance from THE VOICE.

I have been an entrepreneur in this stage.

Heading into the rest of 2018 and 2019 I am locking in sustainable economics and profits.

I am in CFO/CEO Mode right now.

This will last for another 2-3 years if not longer.

I tried to let go of the company to men who were not ready to lead.

I tried to release the movement to the CT's and they were not ready to lead.

This was all back-firing on me.

I was not ready to let go.

The company was not ready for me to let go.

The men I tried to hand it off to were not ready.

So we slid around.

I have spent a shit load of money this year so far on my teams.

We have a current payroll of $600k+ a month.

Yet the results I am getting from many of the departments is not improving the game; it's actually making it worse.

We are getting a ton done, but getting more done does not always equal progress...

The way way things are right now does not work for me.

I am going to shut down Warrior Woman, Warrior Wealth and Warrior Trainer at the end of this year.

They are all wonderful, but the timing of all of them is off.

Now I see where we are and although it's overwhelming as fuck, I know I have a window of opportunity to lay the foundation for the systems and money for Warrior Companies in 2019 that will set the stage for a 20-30 year run as the #1 Training and Education company in the WORLD for Married Businessmen with Children.

But this will require focus.

This will require me to slow down.

This will require me to see that having more people on the team does not mean more profits nor more impact on the students.

And more revenue does not mean more profits.

And more traffic does not mean more profits.

And if things are not profitable…

The game dies.

And the game will not die under my watch.

There is no one that will care as deeply as I do for this Divine Machine called Wake Up Warrior.

Almost 6 years ago I launched this Movement as one man with a camera and a desire to follow the VOICE.

30,000+ clients the past 6 years and growing and the movement is just getting started.

This is my time.

Winter is my season.

When shit gets heavy I get even more committed.

I will solve these fucking problems, bring order to our traffic and conversion and cash.

I will Clearly step into the game of deeper leadership with my teams and they will either rise or be fired.

The End.

THE VOICE: *You were on a roll with that one.*

So, final question Brother:

(Q) As you sit back and survey the revelations and insights from this stack what is the singular lesson on life you're learning from this ANGRY STACK?

ME: *This one is intense for me.*

"The king must wear the crown no matter how heavy it becomes and in the end he will realize that the crown was never heavy; his neck was simply weak and the Keys to the Kingdom were in his hands the entire time!"

THE VOICE: *Now that is Scripture.*

When you get to a final revelation like that what does it do for you emotionally from where you started?

ME: *I mean, I started getting triggered by something in Business, only to take myself on a journey for 20-30 minutes with you down a rabbit hole that opened up so much truth for me…*

…Ending with this final statement:

Ever since watching Game Of Thrones, *the HBO series, I have a deep visual in my mind of KINGS and Thrones and Crowns.*

So the statement is very powerful for me...

But what is crazy to me is how much learning is going on for me inside of a simple trigger of irritation for me about marketing numbers.

THE VOICE: *What did you see inside of this that is going to trigger you to do something different than what you were doing?*

ME: *Easy.*

LEAD.

This series of questions allowed me to see some of the biggest fuck ups I have been having in business this year.

1. *Scaling my teams too big too fast.*

2. *Handing off the leadership power too quickly to to many men who were not ready for the power and stewardship.*

Yet I did not think that getting on the plane today.

If you had asked me back in LA...

"Hey, Garrett! how do you feel about your teams and the direction of Wake Up Warrior?"

My answer would have been.

"We're on Fire!"

But, it took an irritation inside of the numbers to spark the anger that allowed me to see through the facade to the FACTS.

And the FACTS are: I must continue and get to continue to lead in the crucial seats in our company.

I also get to start letting some people go as the organization is too heavy right now and the payroll is WAY too heavy for the changes I need to make.

I also could clearly see that I need to step back into the game with the Ad Teams and actually fire one of them and take their work on myself.

I have preached from the rooftops the principle of not taking your hand off the wheel of Marketing and Sales and yet what did I do?

I took my hand off of the wheel.

FUCK.

The crazy part.

The numbers that triggered me were not even that big of a deal.

But, it was the universe trying to get past the guard of my mind and into my head and heart so it could speak to me.

Is that right?

THE VOICE: *YES.*

100% accurate.

See, the Universe and GOD have so much to teach you every single day about the direction and moves inside of your life.

The challenge?

You won't listen most of the time.

Meaning, oftentimes the moves that the Universe knows you should make would never occur if we just gave them to you.

So instead, I asked you questions and you were led to the answer.

And when you were led to the answer and find it yourself, you OWN that answer very differently than if I just gave it to you.

Can you see this?

ME: *YES.*

THE VOICE: *How much of your answers today did you create because I gave you the answers?*

ME: *NONE.*

You asked the powerful questions and I allowed myself to let go and submit to the game of the ANGRY STACK and allow my irritation to be expanded into something that would reveal the next steps for my path in business.

I did all the work.

You led me with the right questions.

And there is a sense of ownership for the answers that I have because I was the one that created the content, not you.

…No offense.

I love what you stand for and the support that you have given me thus far.

It has been life-altering.

But…you didn't save me.

You trained me to save myself.

THE VOICE: *YES.*

Now this is where a ton of Christians get triggered also with that idea…

That a man can save himself.

Let me expand on this:

The reference to SAVE YOURSELF has nothing to do with an afterlife.

It has to do with being stuck in this life and getting unstuck.

Most men are stuck as fuck.

They may even be saved in the Christian ideology but they are still slaves.

The Stack is no salvation.

It is liberation.

Salvation may be free but Liberation requires you to do some fucking work.

And inside of the MEGA & ANGRY STACKs, the work we are talking about is three-fold.

1. *To engage with the questions daily.*

2. *To go ALL IN with your answers and create your own scripture.*

3. *To Take Immediate action on the revelation's received.*

When you execute on these three simple steps...

...GAME OVER.

ME: *I never imagined a series of questions could change me so much, so quickly.*

THE VOICE: *So, what is the action you know you must take coming out of this stack?*

ME:

1. *I must fire my Ad Team and bring it in-house.*

2. *I must also let two executives go in the next 6 months: Gus and Cullen.*

3. *I must start transitioning Jeremy out of Warrior and onto his next step in life.*

4. *I must take back the control of the Ad Accounts and run the Marketing and Sales Seat on my executive team.*

THE VOICE: *Those are some powerful decisions, Brother. When you look at the clarity of the experience and the actions that you're now committed to take,*

What do you think would have happened in the past if you had been triggered by some marketing numbers like you were tonight?

ME: *I would have gotten angry and then yelled at someone on our team and not seen even 1% of the clarity I am now seeing.*

THE VOICE: *This is the power of the ANGRY STACK.*

Once you have mastered the game of the MEGA STACK, it is Time to go hunting.

Yet to Attack with the Stack….

This means you're back in harmony with yourself and so you're hunting for content every single day.

The MEGA STACK tends to be a reactionary weapon while the Angry Stack tends to be an attacking weapon.

So when you wake up every morning, one of things I want you to do is hunt.

Hunt for things that irritate you…

Hunt for things that make you angry….

And eliminate them.

This is when the game gets crazy.

The MEGA STACK is to train you and for use in emergencies.

It's like a Nuclear BOMB.

You may not use it very often, but when you do? Game Over.

So what do you use every day?

Your assault rifle.

And your assault rifle is your daily weapon.

I want you to transition from the MEGA STACK as your daily weapon into your ANGRY STACK as your Daily Weapon.

You were trained first to be Nuclear.

Now? You will have the ability to be tactical.

What are you hearing from me?

ME: *Wow.*

I am getting it.

The reason I got to a place where the MEGA STACK was no longer working the same is because I had prepared myself to really ATTACK.

It took me years to get to a place where I had integrity and Alignment with the Night and the Light within me.

Now, inside of that alignment, it's time to hunt.

And I hunt down the things that make me Angry and the things that Irritate me.

These are the moments that YOU as the VOICE have guidance and custom scripture for me.

Just like today's.

I was triggered by marketing.

But then I leveraged the Assault Rifle Strategy of the ANGRY STACK and went hunting to find the revelation I was missing.

THE VOICE: *YES. YES. YES.*

Now, take a deep breath…

Take another one…

And one more…

Well done.

You have just accomplished the ANGRY STACK and now have two powerful weapons at your disposal.

For the next 9 days I want you to hit the ANGRY STACK.

Pick different topics across Body, Being, Balance and Business.

On your flight back to the States, I'm going to connect with you again to see how you did and if you got to where I want you to be emotionally with the process, then it will be time to unleash the third weapon to you.

Are you clear?

ME: *YES*

THE VOICE: *Now order another Irish coffee and turn on a movie and relax…you're too uptight and right now I want you to just let go and relax.*

You have come a long way in the past hour with me.

And there is plenty of time to work when you get back from Europe.

I want you to unplug tonight and be with YOU. Zone out with a movie or two.

Then this week?

Hit your Angry Stack every day.

Enjoy your family.

And I will talk to you on the flight back.

Clear?

ME: *Clear.*

SECTION TWO: ANGRY STACK
CHAPTER FOURTEEN:

PRINCIPLES

> "And so I stand. On the cliff.
> I close my eyes.
>
> I take a slow deep breath. I open my eyes.
> I look out to the horizon at the SUN...
>
> ...and leap."
>
> **—Garrett J White**
>
> [Excerpt from Angry Stack: "Garrett J White"
> 17 February 2019]

With The Stack, We Are Bridging the Gap From Blinded To Guided

It was an incredible trip with my family to Europe, and yes, jet lag is VERY real. But now that you've had the opportunity to get an overview on the background behind the Angry Stack as well as had an opportunity to read different Mega Stacks from within each Core 4 domain, it's time to shift gears into learning some more content.

See, there's a psychology behind this concept that we need to learn that which bridges the gap between the two realities of being blinded or guided towards a life of living what we want. All of that's approached inside of the following four principles:

> **Principle #1: Anger is an Asset**
> **Principle #2: Anger is an Access Point to Acceleration**
> **Principle #3: Knowing What You Want Drives You Towards Getting What You Want**
> **Principle #4: Anger is the Paint You Use to Create the Vision**

These principles provide a means and way for you to shift how you were taught, trained and educated to see anger as something unacceptable as not only acceptable, but a powerful tool towards production.

Principle #1:
Anger Is An Asset

So we've talked a little bit that anger is a feeling, which is obvious, but now we're going to see it as an asset. And what is an asset? Something that we wanted and have obtained. If I were to look at a balance sheet and income statement in the world of business, it would divide my world financially into one of two categories: assets and liabilities. An asset is something I have purchased while a liability is something that I am paying my way towards obtaining.

In other words, if a financial analyst were to look at my accounts, he'd state, "On one side, you have your assets.

On the other side you have your liabilities."

He'd continue, "Your home is currently valued at $8,950,000, and according to your income and balance sheet, your liability or your mortgage against that asset is currently $6,000,000."

My home therefore becomes both an asset *and* a liability, so in order to figure out my net worth based off of that, let's use some simple math:

Home Value — Mortgage = Equity

I subtract my home value from my mortgage to get my equity using this equation. Therefore...

$8,950,000 (home value)
- 6,000,000 (mortgage)
$2,950,000 (equity)

The difference therefore is between the valuation (asset value) and any encumbrances (liability) against the actual property. So in this case, $2.95 mil would be the equity in the property which would be my net worth on the balance sheet. Now, to tie this all back into the Angry Stack, let's say that anger is an asset. We have been taught to see it only as a liability, but as we discussed in the Problem & Possibility in the last chapter, anger either accelerates or incarcerates us.

Therefore, anger is not *both* an asset and liability like my home, but seen specifically as an asset.

Inside of the Angry Stack, Principle #1: Anger is an Asset, is pushing and guiding us instead of holding us back as a liability.

Anger pays OFF the debt that the liability represents as a pure form of power and production inside of Stacking, transforming that anger from something that was bringing our value down to something that brings our overall personal equity up.

Principle #2:
Anger Is An Access Point To
Acceleration

As we make our way into the second principle, let's go back real quick to our Drift & Shift Model: An individual is going along in the status quo, gets triggered and begins to drift. The first feelings that he has inside of this Drift is anger, which inside of Principle Two becomes an access point into a new possibility.

As we learned, the Drift is actually our Gift, so what does that look like inside of the Angry Stack? Well, inside of the Drift there is a gap, a very clear void between both access points from who we are today and the person we desire to become tomorrow. Anger allows us to access that point.

It's through this access from anger that we actually start to see more clearly, recognizing that the fastest path to going from who I am in Figure A to who I desire to be in Figure B is not the happiness level of either point. It's actually the triggers of anger that compels us to make the jump. Anger compels us to make a move, whether it's *away* from what we don't want or *forward*... heading towards what we DO want.

Principle #3:
Knowing What You Want Drives You Towards Getting What You Want

And that takes us to our third principle.

We are compelled to move when we access our anger, so if we want to go forward, we are able to harness anger as our guide by becoming very clear about a seemingly simple question:

"What Do I Want?"

Well? What do you want? Inside of the Angry Stack, discovering what we want becomes available in three places: before, during or after the trigger of anger being experienced.

Our ultimate goal with this Warrior tool is to move us to a place where we get clear on the trigger *before* and *during* the Drift.

Hindsight in becoming aware of what triggered our anger *after* the event doesn't help us in getting what we want unless we go through the experience again and recognize the patterns beforehand.

If you aren't clear about what you want, then it doesn't matter how much training we give you on Stacking or any other tool within Warrior;

your anger will assault you, and you will lose.

Principle #4:
Anger Is The Paint You Use
To Create The Vision

As we conclude with our final Principle within the Angry Stack, we're going to find that sitting next to the trigger that disrupts our status quo is a bucket when we get angry. Remember that box that was sitting next to us inside of the Mega Stack?

Well, in the Angry Stack, within that box is a bucket of paint. It doesn't just fuel us, but gives us something to create a new version with as we paint over the old story. We say, "OK, inside of my Angry Stack I am finding out what it is that I actually want to paint."

Our vision becomes clear in the fire of our anger. The anger becomes the paint color and the questions inside of the Angry Stack act as brushstrokes that we use to paint the vision towards a new version.

When we know what it is that we want, we tie the rest of the principles together as we paint out the access point to turn that anger into an asset.

So, we have these four principles to set us up in how to leverage the power from our anger inside of the Angry Stack. This gap that we're jumping across, where the Problem of our anger is, decelerates us while the Possibility accelerates us towards production.

SECTION TWO: ANGRY STACK
CHAPTER FIFTEEN:

PRODUCTION

> "When we've shifted our anger into a weapon, we can immediately put it into action, all because we were willing to open ourselves up to looking at what it is that we truly want from the situation."
>
> **—Garrett J White**
> [Attack with the Stack Online Software Training]

We've opened up the Gap after covering the Principles behind the Angry Stack addressing that the Problem with anger itself is that it can be a destructive thing to us, decelerating us from where we want to go, choosing instead to open ourselves up to the Possibility that anger can be a guide towards expansion. Within this topic on Production behind the Angry Stack then, there are four strategies that can help us get what we want:

Production Strategy #1: Establish the Pillar of Anger
Production Strategy #2: Clarify What You Want
Production Strategy #3: Tell a Strategic Story
Production Strategy #4: Take Massive Action o Revelation

Within this chapter, we will be led down a path as we strategically open the anger within by asking a series of specific questions found directly within the Angry Stack. There is a full set of questions at the end of this section just like inside of the

Mega Stack, but we're going to break down what to expect with these questions here, as they bring out a different form of power within, allowing us to see things that we wouldn't be able to see otherwise.

The Angry Stack Brings Out A Different Form Of Power Within, Allowing Us To See Things That We Wouldn't Be Able To See Otherwise.

Unlike the Mega Stack which has the questions broken down into sections of the Data, Dark, Drift, Shift, Lift and Light, the Angry Stack Questions are summed up into one main section as follows:

ANGRY STACK QUESTIONS:

1. What are you going to title this ANGRY STACK?

2. What domain of the CORE 4 are you stacking?

3. Who has triggered you in this domain to feel Angry?

4. What is the story you're telling yourself right now about what happened?

5. What are the negative feelings that you're experiencing because of this story?

6. What are the initial desires or actions do you notice rise

for you with these feelings?

7. What are the FACTS (without FEELINGS) about the situation with "_____" that triggered you?

8. Beyond the trigger of this situation what do you truly want for YOU?

9. What is a more strategic story that you could create to assure you get what you truly want?

10. How does this new strategic story make you feel?

11. What evidence do you have that proves this alternative story is true?

12. Will this new story give you what you want?

13. Armed with what you want and the new story to get there, what INSIGHT or REVELATION are you leaving this Stack with?

14. As you sit back and survey your revelations and insights, what is the singular, simple lesson on life that you're learning from this Angry Stack?

15. What action do you feel called to take driven by this INSIGHT or REVELATION?

16. At the end of this Stack, what level of power are you feeling? (ALIVE—AWAKE—ACTIVE—ABLAZE)

You'll also see at the end of this section examples within each area of the Core 4 as well as the Angry Stack questions in their entirety to start you off with your own Angry Stack. But within the Production Game of the Angry Stack, we're going to break it all down, starting with the first seven questions from the Angry Stack which are all part of Production Strategy #1.

Production Strategy #1: Establish The Primary Pillar Of Anger

Let's say I look at this first production strategy of establishing my primary pillar of anger as a 2x4 that was just sitting on the ground next to a wall. I want to make use of this 2x4 by putting it on top of the wall, which is a wall to my Kingdom. So, I need a hammer and nails. I have to make sure that I drive the nails down on both ends of the 2x4 to anchor it in, otherwise it's eventually going to dangle off on one end and put too much strain on the other, ripping the 2x4 off of the wall as soon as any weight or pressure gets placed on it.

Inside of the Angry Stack, the first nail to anchor that pillar in is the first question inside of the Angry Stack. The next question becomes the next nail, and as a new pillar gets added to strengthen this wall to my kingdom known as Insight, a new nail gets added as I answer another Angry Stack Question.

The questions inside of the angry stack are meant to be simple but powerful

The questions inside of the Angry Stack are simple, but powerful, therefore even in their simplicity, there's a purpose to putting active thought into each question. The very first question starts us off by giving it a title. Now, I love to label my Stack in a way like I am sending an email and/or a text: I look at my labeling as a headline. And I want to be able to quickly pull up in my Warrior Software my timeline later on so that I can access my Stack in a way that lets me see very cleanly, "Hey, here's what's what was going on for me then and how I handled it."

Then, if there's a Drift that feels similar because I've become aware of the patterns, I can reference back to my previous insights as a way of going through the process of revelation even faster, instead of costing myself time only to eventually come back to the same conclusion. This is where Stacking becomes essential as a daily journal of personalized scriptures. Inside of the Angry Stack, that becomes an absolutely crucial way of storing triggered reminders to get me to go back and review.

Stacking Becomes Essential As A Daily Journal Of Personalized Scriptures

So after we give our Angry Stack a title, we go to question two by focusing on which area inside of our Core 4 we're Stacking. Now, I'm going to tell you right now, in my Angry Stack I will spend 70% of my time in Business and the other 30% of my time in Balance. Only rarely do I do an Angry Stack on Body or Being. That may not be the case for you, but that's what's great about customizing these Stacks for each and every person.

Questions three and four inside of the Angry Stack have us take a look at the specific person or event that triggered us to feel angry as well as the story associated with the trigger. As you get more comfortable using the Stack on a regular basis, this specific person could even be yourself, but my consideration for you just starting into the Angry Stack Game is to NOT Stack yourself, even though we make ourselves easy targets at times to attack and criticize.

Instead, become familiar with Stacking about others first. You might find out like so many times within my own experiences that

Individuals That Trigger You Have Simply Been Activating The Projecting Of Your Own Thoughts,

but until you're advanced in Stacking, doing Stacks on yourself as the trigger can cause more harm than progression when you first start out.

We have been trained and educated so that it feels like a natural inclination to blame ourselves when we get triggered, which also holds us back if we don't know how to neutralize ourselves from the feelings of blame, shame and guilt that accompany anger.

Instead, I suggest that with the first experiences of the Angry Stack, create an environment for receiving personal revelation based off of external people and events as triggers.

It's absolutely normal to not know how to actually define or describe our feelings with singular words until we put it into practice.

Question number five inside of the Angry Stack allows us to focus in a productive way on the negative feelings that we experience because of this story. We do this by putting these feelings and emotions into single words: "I'm feeling hurt" or "I feel furious" and "I feel cheated."

We can reference a whole series of feelings, even if we initially think we don't have words for them.

It's Absolutely Normal To Not Know How To Actually Define Or Describe Our Feelings With Singular Words...

until we put it into practice, which is what the Angry Stack helps us do. And like everything else in Warrior and life, the more practice we get, the more comfortable we get in defining the precise emotions we're feeling, so long as we are willing to address them in the first place.

Once we get those feelings out into a singular form, we are then able to delve deeper into the actions behind them.

So, if I put down "I feel furious" inside of question five, within question number six come the initial desires of what I want to do with feeling furious, which might be "I want to fuck him up." See how that last statement isn't a feeling but an action?

Inside of question six, there's no filter: do not censor or filter yourself. If anything, you have to do the opposite.

Instead of trying to pump on the brakes to slow down, you need to hit the gas and accelerate mentally forward like someone full of road rage, only in this place, we prevent harm to others by taking all of our frustrations out within the Attack with the Stack Software.

In order to do that, we need to give ourselves permission to fucking go all in, and not be nice about what these initial desires and actions felt like, even if it means you're taking it further than what you're first feeling.

We need to push the envelope and open up space when doing the Angry Stack and question number six will help us do that.

Once we take on question seven, we are able to shift in order to open up space by pumping the brakes on these desired actions with the facts.

Facts without feelings help us slow down before we go down a path of guilt, blame and shame.

We accelerated with question six, but before spinning out of control, we pump the brakes with question seven to slow it down so that we can open ourselves up for some of the facts.

This then takes us to question eight, which allows us to look beyond the trigger and see what it is that we truly want in the situation.

Production Strategy #2:
Breathe And Clarify What You Want

Question eight has us take a deep breath as we enter the second stage of the Angry Stack. Literally. Take a deep breath with me right now: Inhale in for 4 seconds, then slowly exhale. Felt good, didn't it? Feel free to take a few more, then let's complete this thought inside of Strategy #2.

We have experienced a shift in the Angry Stack by this point as we take a step back from the situation, seeking clarity for what it is that we truly want. So when I say breathe, I'm not kidding. Some people even meditate at this point, pausing for a few minutes inside of the Angry Stack to truly clear their mind. When we allow ourselves to open up to other possibilities, we are then able to see more solutions than we initially thought were available to us as we take that clarity into the third strategy.

Production Strategy #3:
Tell a Strategic Story

Questions 9-12 are tackled within this third Production Strategy of telling a strategic story. We look at the original story again, but with clarity and openness so we can extract what it is that we truly want from the situation.

Inside of question nine, we re-frame by looking at a more strategic story that would help us create a story that would assure that we get what we truly want. Then, in question 10, we're asked how this new, strategic story makes us feel, heading straight into question 11 on providing evidence that this new story can be true. Question 12 then has us look at that story and simply answer yes or no on whether or not this alternate story will give us what we want.

And guess what? More often than not, it does.

Production Strategy #4:
Take Massive Action on Revelation

We're now opened up to our fourth and last Production Strategy by creating an action from our revelation. Questions 13-16 inside of the Angry Stack allow us to do this.

Becoming armed with what we want and the new story to get there in Question 13 is where we open ourselves up, taking yet another breath (go ahead and take one now) as we've clarified our anger with insights and revelations. We've nailed that 2x4 of anger to the wall, no longer held back by guilt or shame for feeling anger and using it as a strategic structure to get what we want, building our kingdom, rather than being a blockage in our path.

So what have we learned? What's been revealed? We answer that inside of Question 13, going into detail about this revelation. I am able to summarize everything up in Question 14, but for now, inside of Question 13, I share anything that comes to mind about the INSIGHT and/or REVELATION.

It's not one sentence. Sometimes Question 13 will consist of paragraphs about this revelation, which you'll see that I've done in the Angry Stack Examples at the end of this section across all Core 4 domains as I've become fully open to receiving personal insights that have been customized just for me.

I've Become Fully Open To Receiving Personal Insights That Have Been Customized Just For Me.

After we go into detail about our revelation, we sit back and take all of those insights and summarize it all down to a single, simple lesson in Question 14.

We sum it all up so that inside of Question 15, we can put that lesson into an action we feel called to do, based off of what's been revealed, and then feel the level of power that we received from completing this stack in the final question: Question 16.

We've shifted our anger into a weapon we can immediately put into action, all because we were willing to open ourselves up to looking at what it is that we truly want from the situation.

SECTION TWO: ANGRY STACK

CHAPTER SIXTEEN:

PRO-TIPS & THE PLAN

> "If you're going to build something big, you must be willing to face the resistance."
>
> **—Garrett J White**
>
> [Excerpt taken from Angry Stack: "You Fucking Fat Bitches"]

PRO-TIPS:
DO's

1. Enter this Angry Stack with FIRE just like you were entering the MEGA STACK, even though you know that you're not so that you have enough FIRE to get the power you need to go deep.

2. Make your new Desired Story as detailed as you can with specifics so that it is even more clear to you and something that you can see in your mind's eye as real and connected to reality for you,

3. Leverage the statement I WANT. When you are answering the initial desires or actions, notice what will rise for you with these feelings questions. Declaring the

statement "I want..." will channel the reps from the MEGA STACK for you and give you solid base of statements for inside of the Angry Stack.

4.   Leverage the Angry Stack as a tool to attack your irritations and frustrations: things that you would normally skip right over and do nothing about until they become an issue. Remember, these small irritations will often bring the deepest wisdom in an Angry Stack.

<u>PRO-TIPS:</u>
DONT'S

1.   Go soft on your original story. Remember. you are not going to be walking the block so you have have to start strong with the first story

2.   Go vague on your "What you Want for YOU," as this is going to directly link to the story that you established and will drive the "Desired Story."

3.   Skip over the "Facts About the Situation" even though it may be tempting. Just know that it will not show up in the summary but it is CRUCIAL for you to lay down the FACTS so that you can pivot on to the Desired Story with power.

4.   Skip over the "Evidence" of your new Desired Story. It is crucial in your mind that you establish this new story

as FACT for you and the only way to do that is to find evidence.

THE PLAN:

STEP #1: Read All Four Examples of the ANGRY STACK

STEP #2: Download the STACK APP.

STEP #3: Complete your first ANGRY STACK.

STEP #4: Share your ANGRY STACK with at least 1 other person.

THE ANGRY STACK

EXAMPLES

FUCK YOU CHOLESTEROL!
[25 JULY 2019]

What are you going to title this Angry Stack?

Fuck You Cholesterol!

What domain of the CORE 4 are you stacking?

BODY

Who has triggered you in this domain to feel angry?

Garrett J White

What is the story you're telling yourself right now about what happened?

"Garrett shouldn't have high cholesterol, what the fuck!"

What are the negative feelings that you're experiencing because of this story?

- Anger
- Frustration

- Irritation
- Upset
- Worried
- Concerned

What initial desires or actions do you notice rise for you with these feelings?

I want to panic.

It's like the signs of my body having issues is everywhere and the one simple solution I can't seem to fucking pull the trigger on.

Alcohol.

I want to blame everything but that.

I wonder what would happen if I actually stopped consuming Alcohol, Caffeine, Sugar?

I don't think my body would even know what to do with itself.

Seriously.

What the fuck is wrong with me?

What are the FACTS (without FEELINGS) about the situation that you have chosen to Stack?

I drink 2 5-hour energies extra strength a day. I drink 3-4 shots of alcohol a day.

I eat 6 eggs a day. I eat ice cream and bullshit at night.

And I wonder why I have higher cholesterol?

Come on you stupid mother fucker.

Beyond the trigger of this situation, what do you truly want for YOU?

I want to have a healthy body and serves me well and takes care of me for 50+ more years until I die.

I don't just want a body.

I want a functional and on fire body.

This is going to demand shit change for me.

The outside frame is not the game I'm talking about...it's my internal game.

What is a more strategic story that you could create to assure you get what you truly want?

"Garrett was exposed with his recent blood test and for the first time in his life has borderline high cholesterol likely because of Alcohol, Caffeine and Eggs!"

How does this new strategic story make you feel?

Clear

What evidence do you have that proves this alternate story is true?

What the fuck Garrett?

You knew this was going to be the case. Come on.

It shouldn't be a surprise to you at all.

Alcohol daily for 5 years. Caffeine daily for 5 years.

These two items since 2014 have been almost part of your regular daily diet.

Will this new story give you what you want?

YES

Armed with what you want and the new story to get there, what INSIGHT or REVELATION are you leaving this Stack with?

Ok. So here is what I know. There was a price to be paid to build Wake Up warrior.

One was the need for ENERGY beyond what I had available, so I could work 12-15 hours a day 6 days a week.

Two was the need to be able to unplug from the chaos of work and the weight and stress of the students of Wake Up Warrior not to mention my marriage and family and the rest of life.

So I added two routines to my game:

A 5-hour extra-strength every morning around 5am and another around 3pm.

I also added a drink every night of beer, wine or liquor to wind down and unplug.

That is 365 days x 5 years.

That is an estimated 1,825 reps.

That's a ton of fucking reps.

Now I haven't had 2 5-hours every day. And I haven't had alcohol every single day and have had some runs of 30 days and 45 days with no alcohol.

So those numbers aren't accurate, but the point is made.

That is a fuck ton of reps.

And those reps compound on each other.

So I get my blood tests back: they say I am borderline high cholesterol.

I then start googling what causes high cholesterol.

Well, high amounts of caffeine can. High amounts of alcohol can. And too many eggs can. About two years ago, I started eating 6 eggs for breakfast every day. Yolks also.

Of course, guess what?

Egg yolks are high as fuck in bad cholesterol.

So here I am with the fucking trifecta of Cholesterol.

Alcohol Caffeine Eggs :-)

Are they at risk levels yet? No.

They are currently just out of the norm.

But that is why I got the test.

So I can buy $75million more in life insurance.

But I also have my Mega $20K physical with the longevity institute in San Diego next Friday.

An 8-10 hour genetic physical that tests EVERYTHING.

Bottom line?

My commitment this quarter was not to change anything.

My commitment this quarter was to expose the fuck out of my story: "I'm fit as fuck and a machine on the outside and inside!"

I knew some shit was going down inside.

Right now it's manageable.

5-10 more years of this behavior?

I'M DEAD.

Heart Attack

Stroke

Liver disease.

So Project: Expose The Fuck Out Of Myself continues.

Stage #1 complete: I have ranged high cholesterol LDL IM - I'm 136 I should be under 129 MG/DL - I'm 222 and I should be under 199 U/L - I'm 36 and I should be under 33.

Next week the results are going to further expose me I am confident as our tests are comprehensive and genetic code based. Meaning…They will leave no stone unturned.

As you sit back and survey the revelations and insights from this stack what is the singular, simple lesson on life you're learning from this Angry Stack?

"Exposure creates the opportunity for Expansion!"

What action do you feel called to take driven by this INSIGHT or REVELATION?

Discuss results with Mike Isom and the impact on my application for $75MM more in life insurance.

Garrett, at the end of this Stack, what level of power are you feeling?

ABLAZE

Angry Stack

MARK HELTON IS A BIBLE BASHING FUCKING STICK

[16 JUNE 2019]

What are you going to title this Angry Stack?

Mark Helton Is a Bible Bashing Fucking Stick

What domain of the CORE 4 are you stacking?

BEING

Who has triggered you in this domain to feel angry?

Mark Helton

What is the story you're telling yourself right now about what happened?

"Mark Helton is a typical Bible Bashing Christian who simply quotes scripture, stands on a pedestal and throws stones while exposing literally nothing about his own life but feels he has every right to come into my world and attack me...fucking pussy!"

What are the negative feelings that you're experiencing because of this story?

- ANNOYED
- Hate
- Anger
- Repulsed
- Tense
- Irritated

What initial desires or actions do you notice rise for you with these feelings?

I want to counter attack Mark Helton and go to keyboard war with him

I want to spend time arguing.

I want to spend time debating.

I want to ultimately be right also...isn't that the funniest part of it all? The fact that I want to be right also :-)

What are the FACTS (without FEELINGS) about the situation that you have chosen to stack?

My team posted a video on FB and IG about me speaking to the idea that GOD does not need to receive Praise from you and me.

That what GOD wants from us is HONOR.

This started an online debate.

And then Mark decided to start posting comments on everyone's comments under my post and sent me the following…

"Garrett, you're a reasonably intelligent person, exceptional marketer and communicator. That being said, this is much easier than you are making it. You quoted Jesus's 2nd greatest commandment 'to love your neighbor as yourself' (referenced from Matthew 22:39) but, that's only half of what he said. Jesus also said in Matthew 22:37 (which comes before vs 39) 'You shall love the Lord your God with all your heart and with all your soul and with all your mind.' He was extremely clear about what He expects. He wants us to give all of our love with all we have to give. The definition of PRAISE is: express warm approval or admiration of ... Love and admiration go hand in hand. And so....He absolutely DID command your praise. God also says he's a jealous God and you should have no other god before him (even your love of self is considered a god) Exodus 34:14 'for you shall not worship any other god, for the LORD, whose name is Jealous, is a jealous God'-- I know you call yourself a believer. If you do then you already know that you should be very careful before speaking on behalf of God, spreading a false gospel. God is very clear what will happen to those who do. Matthew 7:15-20 15. 'Beware of the false prophets, who come to you in sheep's clothing, but inwardly are ravenous wolves. 16. You will know them by their fruits. Grapes are not gathered from thorn bushes nor figs from thistles, are they?17. So every good tree bears good fruit, but the bad tree bears bad fruit. 18. A good tree cannot produce bad fruit, nor can a bad tree produce good fruit. 19. Every tree that does not bear good fruit is cut down and thrown into the re. 20. So then, you will know them by their fruits."

My response was:

"I appreciate your perspective on this. Great that we finally have a topic that you have decided to engage on. Sounds like you have a deep passion for Jesus and for the bible. I love passionate people from all walks of life. I would love to hear more from you on this subject, but something real from YOU, not just a series of quotes from the bible that I could easily look

up myself. Where is the real Mark Helton? The one behind the scripture quotes?"

I re-wrote the response 5-6 times because I could feel myself just wanting to start a fight.

Beyond the trigger of this situation, what do you truly want for YOU?

I want to continue to share what I experience.

I want to continue to guide men back to a place of experience with GOD and not just an addiction to the words of dead people.

I want to continue to inspire men to see the truth inside of themselves and the reality of the connection to GOD that already have that demands nothing from them but the courage to go...the courage to KNOCK and to ask questions of the the divine that would set them free.

What is this STACK?

My scripture.

It is the most important scripture I could ever possess.

It is the most important game I could ever play.

It is the game of documenting my path with GOD.

What is a more strategic story that you could create to assure you get what you truly want?

"Garrett J White is a divine bowling ball called to smash the traditional stories of GOD, TRUTH and CONNECTION that limit many seekers ability to actually connect with GOD and to write the customized scripture of their own lives!"

How does this new strategic story make you feel?

- Appreciative
- Calm
- Content
- Delighted
- Exhilarated

What evidence do you have that proves this alternate story is true?

This is exactly what this post did.

It divided asunder.

But I am not called to do that only with Christians.

I am called to do that with all men.

Christians, Muslims, Jews, Hindu.

If you have traditional stories about GOD, my calling is to crack them open to the opportunity for you to see that beyond all of the traditions and the stories exists a truth.

That truth?

GOD is real.

You are worthy.

If you seek you shall find.

If you ask you will receive.

The END.

Will this new story give you what you want?

YES

Armed with what you want and the new story to get there, what INSIGHT or REVELATION are you leaving this Stack with?

OK. So where am I at the end of this stack?

I feel two things:

1. Gratitude for Mark Helton and his response to my post. (I will complete a gratitude stack on him shortly)

2. Very clear about my calling in the game of life.

So here is the bottom line: I know scripture. Period.

This is not the point though.

So what is the point?

The point is this: There are two types of scripture.

VERSION #1: Scripture from others that we read.

VERSION #2: Scripture from ourselves that we write and read. the first version is very useful.

It is the writings of Dead and Alive people who have taken the time to discuss their experience directly with GOD and life and to write it down.

These words are important because they give us a reference of a conversation of communion we can have with GOD on our own.

I spent most of my adult life worshipping these words of dead people while down playing the direct communication I was having with GOD every single day.

Then, almost 10 years ago I had a thought: What if I was supposed to write scripture?

What if everyone was supposed to write scripture?

What if this was the purpose of life?

To experience LIFE daily and to document what we learned so that we could become more clear of our own journey but so that we could also empower others to do the same?

You see to me, the most sacred scripture I will ever read?

The words I am typing right now.

The daily 60-90minutes I Stack and connect with and commune with my father in heaven.

During my Stacking sessions I get custom feedback and direct guidance from GOD that is beyond the scripture written down thousands of years ago.

It doesn't make that scripture irrelevant.

What it does is make MY scripture relevant.

I do not operate in a world where there is ONE MAN who has the access point to GOD...no preacher, teacher, prophet or president. I experience the game to be much bigger than that.

GOD is in everything and in everyone and everywhere.

LIFE is reaching out and teaching me daily from every moment.

My growth comes not from reading only from others experience with finding LIFE in the moment but more importantly from reading my own writings daily with GOD.

So I have nothing but love for those who beat the bible, the Book of Mormon, the Quran, the Bhagavad-Gita or any other book of "SPECIAL SCRIPTURE."

My only consideration?

Where is YOUR book of scripture?

Where are the daily lessons and learning from YOUR life?

Why are you not sharing your real life with others daily vs. simply quoting the words of men and women who died thousands of years ago?

So I take a stand for daily communion. I take a stand for daily connection.

I take a stand for the stacking power of custom Scripture daily that is available for ALL MEN AND WOMEN.

The End.

As you sit back and survey the revelations and insights from this stack what is the singular, simple lesson on life you're learning from this Angry Stack?

"The Most Important Scripture In My Life Is The Daily Stack That I Write!"

Garrett, at the end of this Stack, what level of power are you feeling?

ABLAZE

YOU STUPID FUCKING CUNT!
[18 JULY 2019]

What are you going to title this Angry Stack?

You stupid fucking cunt!

What domain of the CORE 4 are you stacking?

BALANCE

Who has triggered you in this domain to feel angry?

Debra Jennings

What is the story you're telling yourself right now about what happened?

"Debbie is a fucking overmedicated, depressed fucking alcoholic who has no fucking clue how to be a neighbor and I want to fucking destroy this stupid bitch!"

What are the negative feelings that you're experiencing because of this story?

- Rage
- Anger
- Frustration
- Irritation
- Fucking Fire

What initial desires or actions do you notice rise for you with these feelings?

I want to beat the shit out of this woman.

I want to shoot and kill both of her dogs.

I want to make her house disappear.

I want to be completely done with her as a person and not have any conversation with her at all.

I truly do not give a shit if I ever saw this woman again.

What are the FACTS (without FEELINGS) about the situation that you have chosen to stack?

Debbie left her dogs out again.

Barking on the deck.

All afternoon long her dogs were barking.

And when I got home from work they were still barking.

I went to her house.

Not home.

I went to the security gate and they gave me her cell phone number.

I sent her a text.

She then got home and knocked on my door at 10pm and proceeded to cry and apologize.

Than in the middle of the night she sent me drunk texts that were literally insane.

And this morning I responded.

Beyond the trigger of this situation, what do you truly want for YOU?

I want to have a neighbor that respects me and my family.

I want to have a home where my kids and my wife can be free to be themselves without any issues from a crazy neighbor

I want to save my energy for real shit and just allow this stupid bitch to continue your slow decent into depression and chaos.

I want to not have to Stack this stupid fucking cunt again.

I want to focus on other shit that has nothing to do with her and nothing to do with the HOA and nothing to do with her fucking dogs or her loud shitty music in the middle of the night or her drunken depressed crazy fucking texts.

What is a more strategic story that you could create to assure you get what you truly want?

"Garrett is being tested by the universe through his neighbor and how he chooses to proceed and respond will either expand him or contract him as a Man, as a Leader and as a Producer."

How does this new strategic story make you feel?

- Clear

- Calmer
- Connected

What evidence do you have that proves this alternate story is true?

Everything about my life is a test.

Everything about my reality is testing me.

Debbra Jennings.

My kids. My wife. My clients. My competitors

Everyone and Everything

Will this new story give you what you want?

YES

Armed with what you want and the new story to get there, what INSIGHT or REVELATION are you leaving this Stack with?

So here is what happened: My neighbor left her dogs out again and they barked all afternoon and were still barking at 8pm at night.

So. I went to security and got her cell phone number and tried to call her, but she didn't answer.

So I sent her this text:

> "Debbie, This is your next door neighbor. Yes the one who's children you yelled at in the middle of the day for playing in the pool. You left your dogs out again. Barking on and off since 4pm I just got home. I have a newborn baby. This behavior of you leaving you dogs out all day

is bullshit. I'm calling animal control or handling your dogs myself in the next hour if you don't."

I also sent her a video of her dogs barking and said, "All fucking afternoon"

At 10pm she came knocking on my door and was crying and apologizing and begging for forgiveness and giving me all of her normal excuses and stories about how hard her life is.

We parted ways and she went home.

I then woke up this morning to two sets of texts from her.

3am: "Is that a threat!!! I was at the hospital dealing with a very sick friend!!! Call whoever as it is not against the law to have dogs outside!!! Shut you're doors! Why all the foul language, reminiscent of a whinnying teenager!!! Debra J Jennings

3 am again: "That's why houses have windows & doors!!! To Shut! It's not against the law to have dogs outside!!! Plus I'm getting two more dogs so deal with it!!! Debra J Jennings

Then at 5am: Go shit you're pants!! 😵 sick! Who in the world would admit that!! Doesn't impress me a all! And I do not intend to impress you at all!! Poopy pants I do not relate to you at all with such a message!!! I's to buy you adult Huggies ti prevent embarrassing moments! Correction, I'd like to buy a case of Adult Huggies I'd like to buy you a case of adult Huggies for uncomfortable moments. And baby wipes for your convenience!!! Debra J Jennings

Then I responded to her with:

"Debra,
At least you now have my cell phone. And your clear about the problem. Handle your dogs. And be the

kind of neighbor you declared yourself to be last night in tears on my porch. I'm going to just assume your Medication and alcohol are speaking in the texts you sent me in the middle of the night. Mine on the other hand were sent when i was completely sober and I don't apologize for them at all. I don't make threats, ever. I handle situations that need to be handled. I've been very nice to you since we moved in. I've been here 2.5 years now. I'm not going anywhere. I don't ask for much from you nor will i ever. But when you chose to yell my children for playing in the pool in the middle of the day because they were laughing to hard, you crossed the line. So handle your dogs. Handle your loud music in the middle of the night when your drinking...

...And we will have no issues. Now get some sleep. You've been up all night sending me drunk texts.
The End.
Garrett J White

So here is the bottom line...

Why am I so triggered?

It's not because of the dogs last night.

It's because she yelled at my kids in the middle of a sunny day in summer when they were in MY backyard having fun playing in the pool because she thought they were too loud.

I have a chip.

A chip in my heart and a chip on my shoulder.

This bitch triggers the fuck out of me.

And in the end?

I swear to GOD I'm being tested

Tested by the universe perfectly

Is this woman an issue?

Not really.

But could I turn this into a WAR? Sure.

Is that what I want? No

What do I really want? To focus on my kids and my family and my business's and surfing.

And so I sit here. Typing this. Thinking and feeling frustrated.

And that's ok.

I'm in the middle of a test from the universe and I will pass and find the lesson.

And I have.

And now it will be time to move to the next step in the game with that.

As you sit back and survey the revelations and insights from this stack what is the singular, simple lesson on life you're learning from this Angry Stack?

"The universe is always testing us and the faster we learn the lessons of the test we expand and move to the next level."

What action do you feel called to take driven by this INSIGHT or REVELATION?

Do a Gratitude Stack on Debbie and send it to her.

Just typing that is fucking painful.

But I will today.

Garrett, at the end of this Stack, what level of power are you feeling?

ABLAZE

Angry Stack

LEAD YOUR MARKETING TEAM
OR DIE
[31 JANUARY 2019]

What are you going to title this Angry Stack?

Lead Your Marketing Team or Die

What area of the CORE 4 are you triggered by?

BUSINESS

Who has triggered you in this domain to feel angry?

Garrett J White

What is the story you're telling yourself right now about what happened?

"Garrett has ignored the economics of the ad teams and marketing funnels with Warrior Book (Kings Kit etc...) for to long and has given Tier 11 & Jeremy Finlay way to Much fucking created for what they have done in the past!"

What feelings best describe your current state of being?

Angry, Irritated, Upset, Frustrated, Beyond Angry

What initial desires or actions do you notice rise for you with these feelings?

I want to be angry at my marketing teams. I want to be angry at myself for spending the money but not actually measuring correctly. I want to be frustrated and fucking done with the process we have been leveraging for the company. I want to scream at someone. But the truth is there is no one to scream at. Period. The end. And that is how it goes. When you don't have optics, your fucked. I must have optics. This can't continue. Mother fucker

What are the FACTS (without FEELINGS) about the situation that you have chosen to Stack?

Same as above

Beyond the trigger of this situation, what do you truly want for YOU?

I want to have clear optics on every aspect of the business.

I want clear optics on my ad spend daily and the profits of each campaign with clean attribution back to the actual ads.

I want a trackable score card with my traffic and conversion that all of my teams in marketing and sales agree on and rally around.

I want to have a simple conversion model for the students that allows them to Move down the path of evolution as a student of ours.

I want a clean CFO scoreboard for each company that allows me And Jeff to know daily to the dollar what is happening and allows us to make moves that support us in getting what we want. I want to go all in with Keith and his teams and also course correct Tier 11 so my traffic game is under control and we are not losing hundreds of thousands.

I want to own a better project management system that allows me to track and hold my teams accountable to the shit we agree they are going to work on.

What is a more strategic story that you could create to assure you get what you truly want?

"Garrett has cleaned house the last 6 months and through this has taken on the role of CEO and CMO and, for the first time in years, with the WARRIOR companies, the marketing and economics will have the 100% focus of the founder!"

How does this new strategic story make you feel?

Clear, Called, Required

What evidence do you have that proves this alternate story is true?

The reality is this...I wanted to replace the roles I have played. I wanted things to be amazing. The truth? It was a fantasy. I wanted Cullen to save me. And when he couldn't I was angry. What the fuck Cullen? You can't save me from myself? Yea it was pretty fucked up. But it was reality.

Will this new story give you what you want?

YES

Armed with what you want and the new story to get there, what INSIGHT or REVELATION are you leaving this Stack with?

I have invested 7 years to get the game where it is. That has come with me heavily focused on building the base of the message.

Meaning...I was focused on creating a curriculum that men could connect to and follow.

2012-2015 I proved the Warrior's Way in the lives of the men.

I WAS A HUSTLER in this stage.

2016-2018 we started to scale the message and start spreading it to more people.

I WAS AN ENTREPRENEUR in this stage.

2019 I am locking in sustainable economics and profits. I AM IN CFO/CEO mode right now. This will last for another 2-3 years if not longer. I tried to let go of the company and grow it too quickly. This was backfiring on me. I was not ready. The company was not ready. The man I tried to hand it off to was not ready. So we slid around.

In 2018 I spent a shitload of money on my teams. We had payroll and commissions monthly at $500-600k. Yet the results I was getting from many of the departments was not improving the game.

We were just getting "MORE SHIT"

Not that it was even bad shit…It was just shit that was not working for me and the vision I have for the company.

I shut down Warrior Woman, Warrior Wealth, CT, just so we could focus on what I know we must do.

Now I see where we are and although it's overwhelming as fuck, I know I have the window of opportunity to lay the foundation for the systems and money for Warrior Companies in 2019 that will set the stage for a 20-30 year run as a global training and education company.

But this will require focus.

This will require me to slow down.

This will require me to see that more people on the team does not mean more profits. And more revenue does not mean more profits. And more traffic does not mean more profits. And if things are not profitable…the game dies. And the game will not die under my watch.

There is no one that will care as deeply as I do for this machine.

6 years and 1 month ago I launched this movement as one man with a camera and a desire to Serve Businessmen.

30,000+ clients in the past 6 years and growing, and the Movement is just getting started.

Winter is my season.

I will solve these fucking problems bring order to our traffic, conversion and Cash.

I will clearly step into the game of deeper leadership with my teams and they will either rise or be let go.

The end.

As you sit back and survey the revelations and insights from this stack what is the singular, simple lesson on life you're learning from this Angry Stack?

"The King Must Wear The Crown No Matter How Heavy It Becomes, And In The End He Realizes That The Crown Was Never Heavy; His Neck Was Simply Weak And The The Keys To The Kingdom Were In His Hands The Entire Time!"

Garrett, at the end of this Stack, what level of power are you feeling?

ABLAZE

Angry Stack

QUESTIONS

1. What are you going to title this ANGRY STACK?

2. What domain of the CORE 4 are you stacking?

3. Who has triggered you in this domain to feel angry?

4. What is the story you're telling yourself right now about what happened?

5. What are the negative feelings that you're experiencing because of this story?

6. What initial desires or actions do you notice rise for you with these feelings?

7. What are the FACTS (without FEELINGS) about the situation with "_____" that triggered you?

8. Beyond the trigger of this situation, what do you truly want for YOU?

9. What is a more strategic story that you could create to assure you get what you truly want?

10. How does this new strategic story make you feel?

11. What evidence do you have that proves this alternate story is true?

12. Will this new story give you what you want?

13. Armed with what you want and the new story to get there, what INSIGHT or REVELATION are you leaving this Stack with?

14. As you sit back and survey your revelations and insights, what is the singular, simple lesson on life you're learning from this Angry Stack?

15. What action do you feel called to take driven by this INSIGHT or REVELATION?

16. At the end of this Stack, what level of power are you feeling?

(AWAKE, AWARE, ACTIVE, ABLAZE)

SECTION THREE
THE HAPPY STACK

SECTION THREE: HAPPY STACK
CHAPTER SEVENTEEN:

A RETURN TO HAPPINESS

> "I am committed to investing whatever amount of money, time and energy that is required to build lasting memories with my family!"
>
> **—Garrett J White**
> [Mega Stack Revelation, November 2017]

My family and I were on our vacation to Europe for 10 days and 9 nights.

It was the trip my wife had been wanting to take for years and years and years.

But, like many things over the past 16 years in our marriage, I had been unwilling to invest in her and the family in experiences like this.

It was via the MEGA STACK seven months prior to this trip that I was able to work myself from…

ORIGINAL VERSION:

"Investing $100k on a trip to Europe for 10 days with my family is a complete waste of money!"

ME VERSION:

"Investing $100k on Garrett is the biggest waste of money of all time!"

OPPOSITE VERSION:

"Investing $100k on a trip to Europe for 10 days with my family is the single greatest investment I could ever make!"

DESIRED VERSION:

"I'm Committed To Investing Whatever Amount Of Money, Time And Energy That Is Required To Build Lasting Memories With my family!"

I had literally guided myself out of some serious chaos in my own head to a place of clarity that allowed me to not only make the commitment to invest in my family but also enjoy the experience.

And enjoy would be an understatement.
Europe was everything my wife said it would be.

But, like all great things...

...They come to an end and I found myself back in the London, Heathrow International airport boarding a British Airways flight in the First Class cabin with my daughters and my wife heading back to Los Angeles, CA.

I Was Fucking Tired And Felt Like I Needed A Vacation From My Vacation.

But, my kids were nothing but smiles.

My wife was filled with Joy and we had photos, videos and memories that would last a lifetime.

We will literally be speaking about this vacation when I'm in my 80's and 90's.

I got my girls settled into their unit.

This flight was a little different than the one we had taken 10 days earlier: this time around, my wife and the girls were in a THREE PACK of sleeping pod units and I was at a window in a single row right by them.

It was perfect:
Mom with her babies together to watch movies, talk about highlights of the trip and sleep while I was isolated with no distractions to get some work done and shift my mindset from

"Vacation Mode" to "Get Shit Done Mode."

I actually enjoy this part after a vacation…

The GEAR UP and get ready to GRIND game.

Before too long, all the passengers were boarded and the flight took off.

Within 10 minutes my daughters were deep into a movie and my wife was fast asleep.

I did my Usual…

I Broke Out My Laptop And Went Into Evernote And Started Reviewing My *Angry Stacks* from the week.

I guess that I don't travel like other American tourist do while in Europe…instead of journaling down the highlights of what we saw and ate, I created ANGRY STACKS.

Here were the titles of my Stacks the VOICE had assigned me:

DAY 1: "I'm Jet Lagged As Fuck!"

DAY 2: "I'm still fucking Jet Lagged!"

DAY 3: "If You Look At My Daughter One More Time"

Day 4: "French Bitches Can Kiss My Ass!"

Day 5: "Who wants to eat dinner for 5 hours for God Sake!"

Day 6: "I'm tired of Fucking Wine!"

Day 7: "One room & 2 Beds…are you shitting me?"

Day 8: "No More Gucci, Holy Shit!"

Day 9: "I'm done with the vacation Let's Go Home!"

Day 10: "Our Driver Is An Asshole"

As I Read Through The Titles, I Couldn't Help But Smile.

Nothing on the list was an actual RAGE MOMENT and just like THE VOICE promised…it was next level for me.

The Angry Stack flowed smooth and efficient and allowed me to hunt for topics that I really wanted, chronicling them as Stacks instead of voicing them out on my family.

This was different because I was so used to the RAGE that accompanied my MEGA STACKS for years now that to have a stage that was more of irritation and Anger was very different and yet exciting.

I did them every single morning on our trip.

In Many Ways It Was Like "Taking A Good Shit" In The Morning After All Of That Foreign Food.

I would select something from the day before and Stack it and always end with something positive that pushed me forward to continue to have an amazing Vacation with my family.

There was a part of me that wondered as I sat there sipping a Mimosa,

"What if I'm happy…what do I do with that?"

Not a second later a PING sounded on my laptop and a message came through again from an unknown number and no name.

THE VOICE: *So…You're ready to be HAPPY?*

ME: *Is this THE VOICE?*

THE VOICE: *Is there anyone else you know who might be messaging you on the plane right after hearing your thoughts?*

I smiled.

ME: *Of course it's you…*

...how are you?

THE VOICE: *ON FIRE!*

Of course, I'm THE VOICE and that is something you can always count on from me.

No matter how you're feeling...

I will be right there with you constantly on FIRE and shining the light on the path that you are choosing.

So, how was the vacation?

ME: *Well, if you can read my mind, then you already know...*

THE VOICE: *True, Smart Ass, but guess what...*

...I want to SEE YOU TYPE IT so you can feel it even deeper.

But instead of just telling me what's up, I am going to introduce you to the third WEAPON known as the Happy Stack.

I was with you every step of the way this trip with your ANGRY STACKS.

I'm proud of your commitment and your growth.

Can you see how the intense training with the MEGA STACK actually set you up to experience the pure flow of the ANGRY STACK?

ME: *YES.*

In many ways it was like doing a MEGA STACK but more simple and it let me flow a bit with my thoughts.

I found my rhythm right away and was amazed at how invigorating and almost inspiring it was to select something that I was Angry at and/or Irritated with from the day before and then Stack it.

It left me in a very Happy and Joyful place all week with the family.

THE VOICE: *You keep mentioning that you felt HAPPY? Tell me more about this.*

ME: *I don't know how to describe it.*

I just feel like the last couple of months I have been experiencing a sense of Joy for life that I can't remember having felt since I was a young boy.

It's been DECADES since I have felt this kind of fire.

And it wasn't just this week on Vacation...I noticed it rise a ton more back home before coming to Europe also.

THE VOICE: *I know this was the longest Vacation you have ever committed to with Danielle and the girls...was it worth it?*

ME: *Absolutely.*

I can't remember the last time our family experienced such a long period of Happiness together.

It was life-altering...

THE VOICE: *So, here is what I want you to do...*

I want you to close your eyes in a moment.

(I will give you the cue shortly)

And when you do, I want you to take 10 deep breaths and with each breath recall ONE MOMENT or event during the trip that you experienced deep Happiness.

It could be by yourself.

With your Wife.

With your kids.

All together.

Whatever you choose.

Once you have taken you 10 deep breaths + 10 moments, then open you eyes and I will ask you the next question.
Are you clear on the instructions?

ME: *YES, Crystal.*

THE VOICE: *Ok.*

Here you go in 3 - 2 - 1 - GO.

I proceeded to take 10 deep, slow breaths.

And with each one, I recalled a moment with one of my daughters or my wife.

Deep breath in…Ruby snorkeling.

Deep breath in…Bailee shopping.

Deep breath in…Danielle eating dinner along a cobbled street.

Deep breath in….the Family on the Yacht.

They were all amazing.

And then there was one…

…the final deep breath which began taking my breath away.

This final moment was out of this world and had more to do with the symbol of what it meant for us as couple than it did the actually event.

I opened my eyes.
And went back to the chat with the VOICE.

ME: *Ok, I'm ready. I'm complete.*

THE VOICE: *Well done.*

Now it looks like you have some deep emotion around the last one.

Am I right?

ME: *Yes, even thinking about it is triggering all kinds of feelings and emotions for me of Joy, Bliss, Love and Happiness.*

THE VOICE: *Ok I want you to use that one.*

Here we go.

What do you want to title this Stack?

ME: *Title?*

THE VOICE: *Yes.*

Just like you did with the ANGRY STACKS this past week.

What do you want to title this Happy Stack?

ME: *"Moonlight Sex In Capri"*

THE VOICE*: Well, Well, Well, my Brother.*

I like where this is going already.

A very compelling title.

You must be in marketing

ME: *I have been known to have some skills in the Sales Copy Department.*

But, it appears that I'm getting more and more skills in the Married Sex Game also.

THE VOICE: *Do tell.*

(Q) What domain of the CORE 4 are you stacking?

Body
Being
Balance
Business

ME: *Balance*

THE VOICE: *(Q) Who/What triggers you in this domain to feel happy?*

ME: *Danielle K White*

THE VOICE: (Q) *And what happened?*

ME: *On our fifth night in Capri...*

CHAPTER EIGHTEEN:

OUR FIFTH NIGHT IN CAPRI

> "Becoming Elite Doesn't Happen Overnight, It
> Happens Over Decades!"
>
> **—Garrett J White**
> [Inaugural Happy Stack Revelation, June 2018]

I then proceeded to tell The Voice all about one of the hottest nights that I had ever had with my wife, and I don't mean because of the weather.

It was magical.

And completely XXX rated.

On our fifth night in Italy, we found ourselves in a Luxury 5 star boutique hotel called the Hotel Punta Tragara, Capri.

We had booked the Monacone Suite and it was big enough to give us the space as a couple to isolate the kids away from Danielle and I at night.

This Gave Me The Space I Needed
To Seduce My Wife

It had been an amazing trip after an eventful day of Snorkeling, Sailing and Shopping, and I was ready to do all that I could to make it an amazing ending.

And it was…

The suite was on the top floor of the boutique resort, allowing us to look down on the insane Faraglioni Cliffs and down into the Mediterranean Sea.

I was not used to the ocean like it was here.

No waves and warm water.

Such a different culture than back home in the Pacific Ocean where we live in Southern California.

THE VOICE: *Sounds absolutely stunning.*

I had almost forgotten that I was sharing this all out loud, and came back to the conversation.

ME: *It was.*

My wife had selected the resort and it was worth the investment.

THE VOICE: *So…what happened next?*

I smiled slyly as I looked over at where my wife was on the side of First Class with our girls.

ME: *Here we go…*

So, my daughters were exhausted and we put them both to bed.

That night was warmer than most nights we had experienced in Capri's early summer the previous few nights and it felt amazing to just sit on our isolated deck with just shorts and t-shirts on.

My wife and I grabbed a bottle of red wine from the room as well as two glasses then headed out to the deck that wrapped around the outside of the Suite.

The moon was out.

The air was warm.

The breeze was gentle.

I sat there with a slight buzz from the red wine and looked over at my wife and she looked back at me for a few moments.

As we sat and looked at each other, I was taken back to the first few months we were dating over 16 years earlier.

There was always a Spark with us.

But over the years we lost that spark.

Our sex life fell apart.
We stopped dating and connecting.

And we were heading toward divorce.

THE VOICE: *I know.*

I remember where you guys were 2 years ago when I first introduced you to the MEGA STACK on your way to Chicago.

ME: *Yes.*

The MEGA STACK changed a ton for me and Danielle.

It opened us both back up to ourselves and then to each other.

That night, sitting on the deck in Capri, the Spark had returned.

It went off as the original attraction came back, feeling just as strong as those first few weeks of dating.

She got up and slowly walked over to me, sitting on my lap as we started kissing...

...Kissing with a passion that we had not experienced for over a decade.

There were no thoughts of our children sound asleep in the other room.

There were no thoughts about business.

There were no thoughts about neighbors.
There was just the calm, warm Italian breeze, the ocean and the moonlight shining down upon us, lighting up our deck in a way that was completely magical.

I slowly took her shirt off and over the next 60-90 minutes, Danielle and I experienced the most intense sexual experience of our lives under the moonlight in Capri as one.

One couple.

One flesh.

It was hard to tell that night where she ended and I began.

I know this is sounding like a fucking Romance Novel, but this is exactly how it felt being in it.

THE VOICE: *You know why, don't you?*

ME: *What do you mean?*

THE VOICE: *You know why it felt so magical?*

It wasn't because you were in Capri.

It wasn't because you were in Europe.

It was because there was nothing in-between you.

For the last two years you have dealt with your bullshit with ruthless intensity.

I watched you day in and day out master yourself and your RAGE within the MEGA STACK.

1000+ times you went into the NIGHT to find the LIGHT.

Each time returning form the PIT with a GIFT.

Another GIFT that filled you with power and brought you and Danielle just one step closer each time.

2 years later, there in Capri, you two were experiencing what ABUNDANCE feels like in the Have It All Lifestyle.

Not just abundance economically…but abundance in marriage.

Freedom to be Yourself 100% and freedom for her to be Herself 100%.

And this is what happened for both of you.

On fire connection.

At one with yourself and at one with her.

ME: *Yes, I can see that deeply.*

And I experienced it.

THE VOICE: *So…what happened next?*

ME: *We made love over and over and over again.*

It felt like all night…but it was well over an hour of non-stop love making.

And then, laying naked, glistening with a small layer of sweat on both of us, we cuddled up on the couch and just looked up at the moon and said nothing.

My heart beating and her breathing were the only two sounds I could focus on.

THE VOICE: *WOW.*

Passion.

Fire.

Intimacy.

Sex.

Connection.

Marriage.

All of the things that the Warrior's Way Stands for with men like you, Brother.

I am SO happy for you.

The crazy part?

2 years ago you two were ready to end it all.
Get divorced and be done with each other when we had our first conversation.

(Q) *How does it feel to be in the contrast of those two realties?*

"Knocking on Divorce's Door In the Summer of 2016" to laying naked together looking at the moon in Capri in the Summer of 2018?

ME: *It feels surreal.*

Honestly.

My life has changed so much that it is difficult at times to even recognize the man that I was two years ago.

Our lives have gone 10x in 2 years.

It really is like the man of RAGE I was in 2016 and 2017 has died and the man of JOY that I am in 2018 is reborn.

THE VOICE: *This is what Stacking consistently does:*

It slowly brings mastery to the game of life and allows you to experience deeper and deeper levels of JOY and Happiness.

Truly, at the end of the day Brother…

You were born to experience JOY, but the only way to get to JOY is to be willing to do the work required to get there.
You see, the DEPTH of your connection sexually and spiritually in Capri was an EFFECT of the work that you had done the previous two years.

You were willing to go to HELL in order to find Heaven.

Most are not.

That is why the Happiness they experience is shallow and temporary.

Ultimately, what you're feeling right now is the Purpose of Life and I'm so happy for you.

ME: *So am I.*

We fell asleep for a bit that night holding each other there on the couch, and then eventually found our way back into the bedroom and fell asleep until morning.

Ending a night that I will never forget ever my entire life.

THE VOICE: *Well done.*

Well done.

Well done.

So, here is the next question:

(Q) What is the story you're telling yourself right now about what happened?
ME: *"My wife & I are finally one!"*

THE VOICE: *YES, and what are the positive feelings you're experiencing because of this story?*

ME: *Joy*

Happiness

Connection

Purity

Clarity

Fire

THE VOICE: **(Q)** *What initial desires or actions do you notice rise for you with these feelings?*

ME: *I want to do it again.*

I'm not referencing the sexuality, though of course I want that also.

But I want to connect with my wife spiritually again at that level.

It was primal. Nothing else mattered at all.

I want to leverage that experience and continue to forge a deeper and more profound bond with my wife.

I want to continue to be the man that she desires like she did in Capri.

I want to continue to Stack and transform myself day by day.

THE VOICE: **(Q)** *As you sit back and survey this amazing situation with Danielle in Capri, what is the singular lesson on life you're learning from this Stack so far?*

ME: *"Becoming Elite Doesn't Happen Overnight, It Happens Over Decades!"*

THE VOICE: *That is a powerful statement.*

It's amazing to watch how skilled you have become at extracting the truth and the power of a singular lesson out of your experience.

I have watched you do it now for years and it is one of the greatest skills sets that you have and one that everyone else must master also.

You see…expansion does not occur without the ability to learn.

And the ability to learn comes down to finding the LESSONS inside of the experiences of Life.

When you find the lessons, you're able to leverage them and create and produce bigger and better results over and over and over again.

But not just limited to the one area that you learned it in…
You had a profound experience with Danielle sexually in Capri.

And this experience sourced the profound lesson you just shared…

"Becoming Elite Doesn't Happen Overnight, It Happens Over Decades!"

Who would have ever thought that a night time of sexual intimacy would have produced a lesson like this?

I could poll 1,000 people and ask them to name the source of this lesson and less then 2-3 would get even close.

THIS is the Power of Lesson Extraction.

It's a skill you mastered inside of the MEGA STACK and one that you expanded on with the ANGRY STACK and that you're expanding again on with the HAPPY STACK.

So, now that you have identified the lesson...

It's time to take it across the CORE 4.

You ready?

ME: *Just like we did in the MEGA STACK?*

THE VOICE: *YES.*

ME: *I noticed that was not part of the Angry Stack.*

THE VOICE: *No, it is not.*

We found it works better leveraged only inside of the MEGA and the HAPPY STACKS, as the ANGRY STACK serves a different overall focus.

So, let's see what you got...

The Lesson again was:

"Becoming Elite Doesn't Happen Overnight, It Happens Over Decades!"

Now let's roll it down:

(Q) *How does that lesson apply to the domain of BODY?*

ME: *My body is fit and on fire.*

I'm more fit than I was in my 20's and I was a collegiate and professional athlete in my 20's.

This body I have did not just "show up" after a year.

I have been training my body for 30 years.

I started lifting weights when I was 12 years old.

I got my first weight set as a Christmas present from my parents and I would work out every single morning in the garage before I went to school

I Never Stopped.

I had a friend who lost 97 pounds this last year...

He made a comment to me,

"You've never known what it is to be fat, have you?"

I replied,

"Nope."

My body has become a weapon over decades, not overnight.

THE VOICE: *Well done.*

And yes.

I have watched you for decades continue to do with your body what most have been unwilling to do.

It's amazing to watch the Impact we have had with the CORE 4 and the BODY conversation with men all over the globe.

So much power in the game leveraged from the physical body.

Ok.

So let's take the same lesson.

"Becoming Elite Doesn't Happen Overnight, It Happens Over Decades!"
(Q) *And let's apply it to BEING…*

ME: *My spiritual certainty has come over decades.*

The first experiences I remember having with GOD was when I was 8-10 years old.

I am now in my 40's and for 30+ years I have been growing and expending and challenging the status quo of the story I have about GOD.

I have had to sacrifice, surrender and LET GO over and over and over again.

From the time I was 19 to now.

The voice has led me down some very dark paths to find power and I have had to learn to trust that voice and follow it.

Decades ago I didn't trust it.

I didn't trust myself.

I simply didn't trust.

NOW?

I trust ALL IN.

My spiritual certainty is not impacted by any other story of another.

I'm free to be me and to allow others to be themselves also.

I follow THE VOICE and I follow GOD.

In this I trust.

THE VOICE: *Scripture.*

Pure scripture to my ears.

Let's expand that over to Balance.

Here is the lesson again…

"Becoming Elite Doesn't Happen Overnight, It Happens Over Decades!"

(Q) *How does this lesson apply to Balance?*

ME: *My marriage…*

It took 16+ years, but I now feel 100% connected to my wife.

Not overnight…

But over decades.

Two years ago we were talking about Divorce and dating other people.

Two years later we are on fire.

There is joy in my HEART for her.

There is joy in my SOUL for her.

She is my life partner.

She is my ride or die.

She is the reason I feel the fire I do.

When a couple is both on FIRE, it is contagious and impossible to ignore.

THE VOICE: *I agree 100%.*

Have you noticed that even recently when you and Danielle are in public, there's a magnetic power that is between you two that also draws people into you?

They may even be stopping you in the street and complimenting you on this?

ME: *Yes.*

In the past 6-8 months that has been happening a ton.

Especially when me and my kids are all out together at dinner it happens even more.

THE VOICE: *Again, this is the power that is available from Stacking.*
It eliminates the BULLSHIT between people and allows them to connect spiritually in a way that is uncommon in normal day-to-day living by most people.

Well done.

Let's move to business.

So take the lesson:

"Becoming Elite Doesn't Happen Overnight, It Happens Over Decades!"

(Q) *And now I want you to apply that to your Business & Bank Account.*

ME: *17 years I have been hustling as a businessman.*

I walked away from Guarantees when I was 25 years old and started down a path of self-reliance that would change me forever.

I'm finally getting to a place in the game where I feel like I actually know a few things.

Not a ton…

But a few.

Yet that has taken me almost two decades to pull off.

Imagine me in 20 more years!
Are you shitting me?

My ex-wife's husband is 62 years old.

That is 20 years older than me.

Larry is a Baller and sold his business for hundreds of millions.

I am just getting started down this path.

By the time I am 62 I will be a Billionaire and my companies will be the type of companies that transform the way we live for centuries...

THE VOICE: *Yes, they will.*

One of the things I am most impressed by you is your ruthless commitment to go.

This is why I am entrusting you with these weapons.

THE MEGA STACK

THE ANGRY STACK

&

THE HAPPY STACK

These three and one more that I am going to share when you have perfected the Angry and Happy Stacks.
I know you will do what is required to get these tools into the hands of millions.

Most men?

Would ignore me.

Most men?

Would ignore the tools.

So we entrusted you with them to take them to millions of men.

And the speed that you're going at right now with them is GAME OVER and your ability to do what is required to streamline this process for the men who are coming in the future is crucial.

ME: *Thank you.*

Truly, I am not sure how much I actually chose this as much as it feels like this THING you're speaking of chose me and I can't shake it.

Stacking is like an obsession for me now.

THE VOICE: *I can see that.*

Clearly, and I love it.

So, let's take this home now.

Our final stage in the HAPPY STACK is to finalize all the learning into one singular revelation.

Are you ready?

ME: *YES.*

THE VOICE: *After spreading the lesson…*

"Becoming Elite Doesn't Happen Overnight, It Happens Over Decades!"

…over the CORE 4 of Body, Being, Balance, Business,

(Q) What FINAL INSIGHTS or REVELATION are you leaving this Stack with?

ME: *Hmmm…*

Patience and Appreciation.

The past 2 decades I have built a man I am proud of.

The man I was in the past is someone who got me here but he was a small weak version of the man I have become living the Warrior's Way leveraging the CODE, the CORE & now the STACK.

I'm a man now who gets shit done and truly emulates a life that works across all areas of the CORE 4.

I get to appreciate that work and journey.
I also get to look forward to the man I am creating the next 20 years.

From 42-62, but also as I'm sitting here typing this…

I start to think about the man I will build from 62-82.

Holy shit.

The magnitude of what I will create in the next 40 years makes my heart speed up and my adrenaline course through my veins.

In the end...

I AM THE MASTER OF MY FATE.

I AM THE CAPTAIN OF MY SOUL.

THE VOICE: *BRAVO.*

Bravo.

Bravo.

Bravo.

You have completed your first HAPPY STACK.

What are you feeling right now?

ME: *Joy.*

I'm just smiling.

Grinning from ear to ear.

THE VOICE: *As you should be, my Brother.*

As you should be.

So here is the game now.

You had access to the MEGA STACK for 2 years now and have over 1000 reps.

I gave you access to the ANGRY STACK 10 days ago and you smashed it and I have just opened you up to the HAPPY STACK moments ago.

You have access to the TRI-FECTA.

Now it's time to master the ANGRY & HAPPY STACKS like you did the MEGA.

I want you to do one every single day.

Over the next 12 months that will be roughly…

…360 Stacks.

It's not the 1,000+ you did with the MEGA STACK but those reps are allowing you to go faster and more efficient with the ANGRY and HAPPY.

ME: *Ok.*

But when will I connect with you again?

THE VOICE: *You silly man.*

You do every single day that you Stack with me.

Every day, we are having a conversation.

Every answer you give is a response to a question I asked you.

No different than what we have experienced on our flights together the last three times.

ME: *I totally understand.*

When will I be ready for the final weapon?

THE VOICE*: You will know it when I have arrived again in this form.*

Until then?

Focus on the work.

Do The Fucking Work Required Daily.

Stack Every single day.

ANGRY STACK & HAPPY STACK.

And when the time is right, I will be there to guide you to the fourth and final weapon.

ME: *Thank you.*

THE VOICE: *You're Welcome.*

Goodbye.

I shut my laptop and sat back in my seat.

I looked across the aisle again at my sleeping wife and now sleeping children.

This was my life.

European Trips.

Epic Sexual Encounters.

Deep Love and Commitment.

Was this really my life?!

Not a decade ago, I lost everything.

My life was crumbling to the ground....

....Two Years Prior I Was Ready To Throw In The Towel, Get A Divorce And Shut Wake Up Warrior down.

And now here I am.

Here.

In this place.

Ready.

Ready for the next chapter.

I closed my laptop.

Ordered myself an Irish Coffee.

Turned on an action movie and sat back to enjoy the remaining 8 hours of my flight.

CHAPTER NINETEEN:

PRINCIPLES

> "Wherever you are, make sure you're there."
>
> **—Dan Sullivan**
> Strategic Coach Founder

After seeing how an epic sexual encounter closed one chapter of my life by opening up a new one, it's now that time for some content. So, let's jump into the principles in-between the problem and the possibility of the Happy Stack, which are all laid out as the following:

> **Principle #1: Living in the Gap is Death**
> **Principle #2: Happiness Married to Anger & Rage is the Helix of Power**
> **Principle #3: Finding Happiness is a Skill**
> **Principle #4: Happiness is Found on the Other Side of Expansion**

Inside of this chapter we will be trained on defining happiness within us, discovering that it was there all along, just waiting to get unleashed.

Principle #1:
Living in the Gap is Death

Principle one on our journey is to be able to unleash the gain found inside of the Happy Stack.

This is all about propelling ourselves out and forward from the Gap between where we were and where we want to go.

A mentor of mine off and on over the past decade from Strategic Coach, Dan Sullivan, has been a heavy influencer of this mentality[1] as well as Dr. Wayne Dyer whose approach on the Gap involved meditation inside of his book *Getting in the Gap*.[2] Dr Dyer's book in particular was very powerful for me back in the day as I was just starting to figure all of this shit out on my own.

Going back to Dan Sullivan, the concept of the Gap created a premise which applies to this idea of happiness, and it comes down to the following reality: you and I live in this weird place between three points, or so our mind wants us to think anyway.

Our mind wants us to believe that these three points are all occurring at the same time, even though that's impossible.

Why? Because these three points consist of the past, present, and

---

[1] You can purchase his book on the subject titled *Learning to Avoid the Gap: the Skill of Building Lifetime Happiness* as an audio cd at: http://bit.ly/avoidthegap. See Bibliography for full citation.

[2] Dr Dyer's book can also be found for purchase at: http://bit.ly/gettinginthegap. See Bibliography for full citation.

future: yesterday (Point A), today (Point B), and tomorrow (Point C). There's only one place that we can continually be in, and that's today, yet our mind wants us to think that we're in all three of them when we are stuck in the Gap.

Now, the Gap is definitely a very real place inside of my mind between the points of where I am today in Point B and where my mind believes I should be tomorrow as Point C, based off of what had occurred in Point A. This confusion creates some obvious chaos...a Challenge in which we experience a game called The New Normal.

The New Normal Creates Chaos That Must Be Combatted

The New Normal is simple, stating that whatever is "new" for us will quickly become normal. So take marriage for example: you're not having sex at all. Then, you start to have intimate and connective sex, which becomes pure and frequent in your marriage, going from no sex to a couple of times a week.

At first, your mind is completely blown that this is happening, so you live in this place of appreciation, thinking "my sex life's on fire, my marriage is on fire, this is fantastic! I could definitely get used to this."

But all too quickly your mind *does* get used to this new normal within your marriage of having sex at least twice a week, and will start to normalize what is happening. It forgets about yesterday's normal when there was no sex, yet isn't content with today that has a marriage with sex a few times a week, and instead begins thinking of how much sex you should be having tomorrow: say three times a week plus a blowjob on Thursday's.

That's what your mind believes should be happening when it falls in the Gap, not realizing that it's a trap.

Tomorrow's Horizon Doesn't Exist

See, tomorrow is a place that we will never arrive at, in Business and in money, let alone our marriage or any other part of our Core 4 if we are not able to focus on today. When we look at our current situation, for some of us it's significantly better than it was 10 years ago. For others, it might be the opposite. Debts from the past are catching up, which can occur inside of Body, Being, Balance and/or Business.

When we are stuck in the Gap between points, we experience scarcity, regardless of the area of life. Looking back 25 years ago from when we were kids growing up, I know that I'm making way more money than I ever imagined possible, and maybe you are as well, yet we still find ourselves living in the Gap when we dwell in more than one Point. So what is the Gap? It's a constant comparison mind fuck from where we were yesterday in Point A to where we were in Point B and where we think we should be in Point C.

It is the horizon that we will never arrive at…Dan Sullivan said it something like this: "If I'm moving toward Point C on my boat, then I'm heading out to sea and will never arrive at the horizon."

No matter what we do, no matter how much money we make,

how much sex we have, how much we've crushed it in our career or gone through the grind to the top, or joy we think we're supposed to experience, that horizon will always be out of reach and unattainable.

If I'm not careful, my mind has not been trained as a hustling producer to face where I'm at today inside of Point B based off of where I was in Point A because I'm already thinking that I should be in Point C in order to be happy.

The thing is, happiness is never found in that horizon of Point C, only depression. When you stay looking at the horizon, you remain stuck in the Gap, which means joy and happiness is occurring all around you, but you're unable to see it because you're too busy looking for what will always remain out of reach.

There Is Productive Reflection In The General's Tent

Part of the reason we do what's known as the General's Tent[3] every single week inside of Warrior is for us to look back on our week in a productive way so that we can make sure our projection for today is on track. It's simple to live the Warrior's Way, yet in that simplicity we quickly forget who we were before the pursuit of the Have It All Lifestyle as the New Normal settles in.

---

[3] To learn more about the concept of the General's Tent, go to https://warriorbook.com where you can purchase your copy of the WarriorBook that goes into further detail, or submit an application to join the elite Warrior Brotherhood.

Without productive reflection, we forget what our marriage used to look like, what our body used to feel like, where our business has grown from and the expansion inside of our spirituality.

Therefore, within that place of forgetting while getting used to the New Normal, we can become depressed, thinking the Game is not working when it's actually working extremely well, not knowing how to operate anywhere but inside of the Gap.

Fortunately, we are able to remind ourselves to get out of the Gap by remembering Principle #1: Living in the Gap is Death as we find joy in looking back to who we were compared to who we've become today.

Principle #2:
Happiness Married to Anger & Rage is the Helix of Power

Looking at this second principle, let's say that we have a helix which connects these two lines that are intersecting and intertwining. On one line we have happiness, and the other we have anger.

I would have you consider that what we're actually experiencing in happiness is not its own helix but one that isn't properly formed until joy and anger collide. Inside of that collision, happiness is conceived, eventually given birth in our life when we put this new experience into motion.

Neither are mutually exclusive from each other, therefore we cannot experience happiness without anger, nor can we experience happiness without joy, which means that they become intersected and married to each other. The place where anger and joy collide is where happiness resides, and the Happy Stack becomes the place in which to discover where that place is.

Principle #3:
Finding Happiness is a Skill

Surfing, sex, marketing, parenting, and even tying our shoes are all skills that require learning. We must put them into practice over and over again in order to be good at any or all of them.

This means that if finding happiness is a skill, then we must learn to educate ourselves on finding happiness in a society that has taught, trained, and educated us to be scared, terrified, angry, and rage about everything that goes on at any given time in life.

See, we can't find happiness by default; it has to be learned. Though we are all programmed to experience happiness, our natural default as human beings is fear, anger and rage, so we have to deal with this first.

We face it every single day, all day long, in one form or another, from stimulus outside of us. An ideal example of this source is found right in the palm of our hand…our cell phone.

Though many of us did not grow up with this ready source of information, it's becoming more and more of a necessity in everyone's life, in which our kids don't know life without it, which also leads to more and more opportunities to fuel the flames of fear, anger and rage.

Everyday, We Are Being Taught, Trained And Educated To Be Scared.

Social media thrives off of people being angry or getting offended, and yet we're also taught to suppress the anger and rage, replacing it with that plastic mask of happiness we addressed in the last chapter.

The Happy Stack helps us learn how to handle this hypocrisy by teaching us skills within to be happy, regardless of what our phone shows us, or how other people behave.

In order to do this, however, we must go to work so that we can find the path of happiness as we learn how to develop it as the skill that it is.

Learning how to recognize and be happy is what the Happy Stack forces us into, which is the ability to take what we are learning and to begin to spread that across all Core 4 areas of your life.

Imagine pulling up your cell phone then from *this* place…none of that garbage from social media would penetrate, and instead becomes a possibility to share our insights with others, based off of the expansion that came from these strategies inside of the Happy Stack.

Principle #4:
Happiness Is Found On The Other
Side Of Expansion

And now we've made it full circle as we dive into our fourth and final Principle.

From the Gap, we have come to the intersection helix of anger and joy, developing happiness as a skill to take a look at where we are today and how we can expand on that. My competition is not somebody else online, or from high school, the neighborhood or church.

My competition is ME, and my first target? To grow and become more today than I was yesterday so that I can do the same tomorrow. The process inside of all of our lives has been driven under this divine calling, which is to grow line upon line, precept upon precept, and for us to become brighter and brighter every single day.

It's not about being perfect, nor is it about doing "it" right or following the rules that others have determined for us. It's about growth.

It's about you and me growing into a better version of ourselves each and every day. It's about looking back on who we were yesterday and who we are today so that we can rise to a higher level tomorrow…there's no Point A, B, or C, but simply expansion.

And Expansion Is What It's All About Here At Warrior.

It's about growing as well as looking back at the expansion of who we were down the road by seeing yesterday's tomorrow today.

The secret sauce to do this inside of the Happy Stack is to learn how to strategically attack, uncover and discover just like a gold miner would in panning for gold as we extract the nuggets that the Universe, God, and the Voice have been sending you, saying

"Well, done! You're fucking killing it. Now keep going."

Simply put...

...be happy because you have grown.

CHAPTER TWENTY:

PRODUCTION

> "Instead of seeking out the lie of anger and rage within the Drift in order to discover our truth, we are recognizing the truth of the Lift in feelings of joy, happiness and pleasure. We're teaching ourselves what society never could, which is how to recognize and expand on ourselves based off of our happiness."
>
> **—Garrett J White**
> [Attack with the Stack Online Software Training]

We're now getting the nuts and bolts of how we are going to productively and effectively take this idea of happiness and turn it into an applicable skillset with the following strategies:

Production Strategy #1: Identify the Trigger
Production Strategy #2: Clarify the Story
Production Strategy #3: Spread the Wealth
Production Strategy #4: Reveal the Revelation

Becoming aware of what triggered our happiness in the first place will open the floor to spread more happiness within our live as well as the lives of others.

Production Strategy #1:
Identify The Trigger

By this point in the Stack Game, identifying the trigger should be pretty normal after all of the Angry Stack and Mega Stacks you've done, but if for some reason you're in the Happy Stack and you haven't done any of those, that's fine. Identifying the trigger is the same thing that we've always done, which is that while going along inside of the status quo, something occurs. We experience an event, and in that moment a trigger happens, only this time, the trigger is different than what we saw in the Drift & Shift Model. There, the triggers takes us down into a Drift and the Pit. In a Happy Stack, we're coming directly in, blowing past the Drift and into our simple game of getting triggered that causes us to Lift.

We are shifting directly into a lift, Where our other triggers pull us down, we eliminate all of that and don't need to shift. We're simply coming into this Stack and recognizing that we just got triggered to be happy.

We're teaching ourselves what society never could, which is how to recognize and expand on ourselves based off of our happiness. Just like the Angry Stack, the Happy Stack questions are all found at the end of this section for when you do one yourself, but inside of this chapter, we're going to break them down.

Below, you will see the Happy Stack questions, which are all part of the same section and ask similar questions, especially at the beginning from what you've familiarized yourself with inside of the Mega Stack and Angry Stack.

HAPPY STACK QUESTIONS:

1. What are you going to title this Happy Stack?

2. What domain of the CORE 4 are you Stacking?

3. Who has triggered you in this domain to feel happy?

4. What are the facts about the situation that made you feel so positive?

5. What is the story you're telling yourself about what happened?

6. What are the positive feelings you're experiencing because of this story?

7. What initial Desires or actions do you notice rise for you with these feelings?

8. As you sit back and survey this positive situation, What is the simple lesson you're learning because of what happened?

9. How does that lesson apply to the area of BODY?

10. How does that lesson apply to the area of BEING?

11. How does that lesson apply to the area of BALANCE?

12. How does that lesson apply to the area of BUSINESS?

13. After spreading the learning across the CORE 4, what FINAL INSIGHT or REVELATION are you leaving this Stack with?

14. At the end of this Stack, what level of power are you feeling? (ALIVE—AWAKE—ACTIVE—ABLAZE)

The first three questions start us out on that familiar path of the Stack with a title and domain but instead of being caught in a Drift, we're capturing the feeling inside of the Lift. All three of these are very, very simple, but they all lead us into our first stage in the Game, which is Production Strategy #1: Identify the Trigger that is bringing us into a Lift, and with it, happiness.

Production Strategy #2:
Clarify The Story

Like the Mega Stack and Angry Stack, there's a story that we've identified inside of the Happy Stack which brings with it feelings. The feelings may be completely different than the other two Stacks, but they're still feelings attached to a story, which are covered in questions four and five inside of the Happy Stack.

See, just because we're feeling happy doesn't mean that there's not a story associated with what's happening. So what does this look like in a Happy Stack?

What does it all mean? It means that we need to clarify what the feelings are telling us.

Instead of seeking out the lie of anger and rage within the Drift in order to discover our truth, we are recognizing the truth of the Lift in feelings of joy, happiness and pleasure.

Our minds are associated that this thing or event means joy. It means happiness and a possibility because we've already dealt with the problem of not knowing how to recognize happiness. Doing a Happy Stack identifies it for us.

Production Strategy #3:
Spread The Wealth

Here's where shit gets fucking crazy as we go into questions six and seven of the Happy Stack. We have an amazing experience so we document what we've learned inside of the Happy Stack, opening ourselves up to awakening a new possibility without even trying.

But guess what most people do when this happens in life? Right at this point in the triggered event for a happy experience, they shut it down.

It gets weakened and seen as unimportant because of the training to be afraid, thinking that if the lie of fear will keep us safe, then another lie that happiness will make us weak seeps its way in.

But not inside of the Happy Stack. The Have it All Lifestyle inside of Living the Warrior's Way has demanded for us to look at things from a different place in questions 8-12.

We take a time out and breathe.

Take A Time Out And Recognize The Influence Of Happiness

Not because we're triggered with anger, but with happiness. We take the time to recognize what this happiness feels like as we extract a simple lesson inside of question eight, breathing it in.

Then, we apply that simple lesson across the Core 4 in questions 9-12. For example, if I had an experience inside of my Body that was joyful and happy and there was a lesson that I learned inside of it, what if I could take that same lesson, eliminate the block of fear that was standing in the way, and found out that I could apply the lesson from Body into Being, Balance and Business?

Game.Fucking.Over.

This is what I call four dimensional living, and everyone has the capacity to experience this every day. "Spread the wealth" in this context means that whatever we have learned inside of the joyful Happy Stack, it will spread its way across the other Core 4 domains. Want to know something else that's also crazy inside of the Happy Stack? Some of the biggest insights I've ever had in Business have come from doing a Stack on Body, Being or Balance.

The Work gets accelerated across our lives like dropping fertilizer over a field of fresh, spring grass. We're not dropping shit on it like we do with the Angry Stack.

We're actually just extracting the important nutrients of happiness that came from that entire Stack and we're going to spread that across Body, Being, Balance and Business.

We're Spreading Fertilizer Instead Of Shit

The thing about seeing the Happy Stack as fertilizer rather than shit isn't about using a completely different compound. Most fertilizer has shit of some kind inside of it, so what's the difference? Perspective. There's a massive shift in perspective behind what that shit can do. It's not just about getting it out of our bodies so that it doesn't back us up, but using it productively as fertilizer so that it can help us grow our revelation in such a way that it can help others as well.

Productive Strategy #4: Reveal The Revelation

A crucial component about the Happy Stack is not keeping the happiness to ourselves, but sharing it with others so that we can propagate a new way of thinking from those around us, especially our posterity. If we don't know what happiness looks like, most likely they don't as well, so the more that we share, the simpler it becomes to accept and see. With the final questions inside of the Happy Stack, there is a revelation that exists inside of that Stack for us to document what was revealed to us, summarizing our entire experience inside of the Happy Stack which can then be shared with others.

This revelation becomes our own personalized scripture.

Now, the coolest part about our Angry Stacks and Mega Stacks is that both of these tools are helping us track our experiences for our posterity, teaching them as we guide ourselves to uncovering how the darkness in our life actually leads us into the light.

It is just as important for us to be able to document our own personal scripture by writing down what's actually worked for us that has created the positive outcome, teaching our children and families how to be happy. Remember, happiness itself is something that must be learned: it is a skill.

There Are Two Tanks That Provide Fuel For Power

To summarize then the production side of how the Happy Stack provides us Fuel to grow, let's say that we have two tanks: one is labeled "Anger" and the other "Joy." Both of these bring us power, but happiness is found when we're able to unify both of these conversations. My happiness is not luck but a *learned* skill.

Through answering the 14 questions inside of the Happy Stack, I am allowing myself to emphasize the joy factor of happiness.

The Happy Stack is not necessarily something that you do every day, but more what you do in contrast to what you're doing in the Angry and Mega Stacks so that happiness itself can be found. Joy, therefore, becomes part of the journey.

SECTION THREE: HAPPY STACK
CHAPTER TWENTY-ONE:

PRO-TIPS & THE PLAN

> "If you decide to not go too deep and just half-ass
> your Happy Stack, well, that is probably reflected in
> other areas of your life as well and you're only going to
> get a half-ass game. It's like going to the gym; if you
> don't dig deep and continually challenge yourself,
> you're not going to get the results. The end."
>
> **—Garrett J White**
> [Attack with the Stack Online Software Training]

PRO TIPS:
DO's

1. Align your story and your lesson and find a connection in your mind as to how they both relate. Then, as you're creating them, your mind leverages both statements to go deep in the connection of the CORE 4 domains.

2. Keep the Lesson to one sentence and make each word count; the more potent the words, the easier it will be for you mind to connect the lesson to the Core 4.

3. Go OFF and go DEEP with each domain as you're applying the lesson learned. Do not rush this part of the process...

allow what must come out to come out and if one area is less inspiring, get something good out and spend the time on the domain where you feel the fire.

4. Settle down in the final revelation and give yourself some time to really flow with the revelation. This can be something connected to the experience that invoked the HAPPY STACK or can be something totally different.

<u>PRO TIPS:</u>
DONT'S

1. Enter this stack with ANGER or Irritation at all; if you find yourself in this place leave the Happy Stack and go hit up an Angry Stack. Nothing will fuck this Stack up faster than you rolling into it with Anger.

2. Drift into vague vision-board style seminar talk. It's easy to start going soft on this one because it's a positive experience and you're not having to knock on the gates of hell to get access to the gift. Stay specific and direct.

3. Allow yourself to drift into random thoughts and ideas as you apply this lesson to the domain of CORE 4. As you line up the lesson, make sure that it makes a direct connection to each domain with specific examples.

4. Skip the final revelation; this is the summary of the HAPPY STACK and oftentimes holds the greatest gifts and greatest insights of the entire Stack.

THE PLAN:

STEP #1: Read All Four Examples of the HAPPY STACK

STEP #2: Download the STACK APP.

STEP #3: Complete your first HAPPY STACK.

STEP #4: Share your HAPPY STACK with one other person.

THE HAPPY STACK

EXAMPLES

THE VORTEX HAS OPENED

[22 FEBRUARY 2019]

What are you going to title this Happy Stack?

The vortex has opened.

What domain of the CORE 4 are you stacking?

BODY

Who has triggered you in this domain to feel happy?

Garrett J White

What is the story you're telling yourself right now about what happened?

"Garrett has passed another level of complexity in business and life and inside of this new pocket of peace he can see the path again clearly!"

What are the positive feelings you're experiencing because of this story?
- Calm

- Happy
- Joy
- Love
- Appreciation

What initial desires or actions do you notice rise for you with these feelings?

I just feel great.

Nothing more. Nothing less.

I just feel amazing.

As you sit back and survey this positive situation, what is the singular simple lesson on life you're learning from this Stack so far?

"Life is a series of tests and when you pass them you expand, there is no winners and losers, there is simply expansion!"

How does that lesson apply to the area of BODY?

The greatest thing in life has happened to me with fitness.

I'm not in competition with anyone but me. It's amazing.
It's joyful. It's beautiful.
It makes me feel alive.

It makes me feel excited. It bring me joy.

How does that lesson apply to the area of BEING?

My god is not better then your god for we are truly experiencing GOD as one together.

This is the truth. This is the reality. This is the path.
To infinite possibility. And I love it.
All of it.

How does that lesson apply to the area of BALANCE?

My marriage is my marriage.
It's not better then your marriage. It's just my
Marriage being what it is.

I can't force it to be anything more or less then that.
When I pass the tests with my marriage I expand. The end.
And when I don't? I don't.

The end.

How does that lesson apply to the area of BUSINESS?

My business is a gift.

My business is a test.

My business is the path i have always been searching Ford
Every round a test.
Every time a challenge.

And every round a version of expansion.

**After spreading the learning across the CORE 4 what FINAL
INSIGHT or REVELATION are you leaving this Stack with?**

My life is expansion.

My purpose is expansion. The game is expansion.
I sit here this morning and I can SEE.

I can see that things are changing again. I feel the weight of the
game shifting.
From heavy to light.

I am surrounded by elite new team members. Who see and feel
what I feel.

They are the next chapter of the movement. I can feel it.

It is happening.

The Sean Whalen Test was the ultimate. And it's release set me free.

Free to let go of all the associated stories also. Including membership.

Including my role. Including my identity. I have shifted.

I can see.

A new version of me. A new version of WE. I am not GOD.
I am not the EMPEROR. I AM a KING.
I was called to rise first.

And Empowered by the emperor to see. But my role is not to save the KINGS.
It is to build the KINGDOM and CASTLE I have been called to build like a lighthouse to the world.

DO WHAT I DO.

LEARN FROM WHAT I LIVE. LEAD FROM WHAT I LIVE.
So simple. So profound.

So Intense to have found.
I AM NOT GOD.

I AM NOT A SAVIOR.

I AM A BEACON of the lights I must stay in my lane.

And allow the light of GOD to shine through me and the kingdom I am called to build. And then inspire other KINGS to come to the island.

AND THEN inspire them with my actions to BUILD there KINGDOMS on warrior island. And then to take a knee and bow to the emperor equal with the other kings on the island. Unified as one unit.

Unified as a council of kings who serve the EMPEROR GOD. The end.

Garrett, at the end of this Stack, what level of power are you feeling?

ABLAZE

I'M HOME

[2 JANUARY 2019]

What are you going to title this Happy Stack?

"I'm home"

What domain of the CORE 4 are you stacking?

BEING

Who has triggered you in this domain to feel happy?

Garrett J White

What is the story you're telling yourself right now about what happened?

"Garrett Has For The First Time In His Life Experienced What A Home Feels Like"

What are the positive feelings you're experiencing because of this story?

- Happy
- Joyful
- Excited
- On Fire
- Grateful

What initial desires or actions do you notice rise for you with these feelings?

I just feel Amazing in my home, in my city with my people.

I want to shout from the roof tops.

I want to dance from the sky.

I just feel Excited and ready to take on the game.

Pumped to smash some massive outcomes today with my teams Excited to share the future with my family.

As you sit back and survey this positive situation, what is the simple, singular lesson on life you're learning from this stack so far?

"I Have The Power To Create A Life By Design, It's Hard As Fuck But Absolutely Doable!"

The lesson you learned was: *"I Have The Power To Create A Life By Design, It's Hard As Fuck But Absolutely Doable!"* **How does that lesson apply to the area of BODY?**

I have a body that is weaponized and on Fire.

At no time in my life have I had more connection to my body and it's capacity to do work.

To get after it.

To physically handle situations.

My core strength. My back strength. My neck strength. My body is a weapon of my own design.

I don't want another person's body. I love mine.

The lesson you learned was: *"I Have The Power To Create A Life By Design, It's Hard As Fuck But Absolutely Doable!"* **How does that lesson apply to the area of BEING?**

My spiritual life is my own.

It is not anyone else's. It is mine.

My spiritual path is an awakening to my own truth.

To get to where I am I have had to take one of these most insane journeys of my life ever.

One that only makes sense looking back and does not Make a ton of sense looking forward.

Meaning, the dots connect looking back.

This tool I am Typing into is the single greatest weapon I have ever created for myself.

It is a weapon of spiritual evolution. Seriously.

Is there anything I have ever done that has more profound impact on my life then this? No.

Not prayer. Not meditation.

Both of which are profound and powerful but it is the path of the Stack that has allowed the Voice to enter into my soul.

The lesson you learned was: *"I Have The Power To Create A Life By Design, It's Hard As Fuck But Absolutely Doable!"* **How does that lesson apply to the area of BALANCE?**

My marriage was a fucking nightmare.

It was weak. It was soft. It was failing.

There were so many moments that I wanted to be done with my marriage.

And holy shit how different would My life be?

Seriously would be profoundly different.

I wonder if I would have had the drive financially?

I wonder what I would have spun off and done?

I know living the warrior's way would have still been my way.

But I also know that my focus and direction would have been radically different.

My marriage is amazing. My family life is by design. I'm not done yet. But I'm on the fucking path.

The lesson you learned was: *"I Have The Power To Create A Life By Design, It's Hard As Fuck But Absolutely Doable!"* **How does that lesson apply to the area of BUSINESS?**
My business was built by the voice.

But it was also built by me by choice.

At no point was the voice telling me I had to redo anything.

Isn't that the crazy part?

We are all called. But few of us have the courage to actually choose that calling.

To choose to go all in.

To choose to create

To choose to destroy what must be destroyed.

This is what I do.

I choose to go all in.

I choose to let it all go.

I choose to rise.

I choose to grow.

And in 2019 I will continue to build my life to be what it must be. I will continue to build my vision to what I know it must be. I will also continue to build the business to what it must be to allow me to become all that I must be.

All that I can be.

All that I desire to be.

All that I am committed to be.

That is my direction.

That is my commitment.

That is my game: Create. Create. Create. Create. Create.

A business that impacts the world and that supports me.

After spreading the learning across the CORE 4 what FINAL INSIGHT or REVELATION are you leaving this stack with?

We were pulling off the freeway last night arriving in Dana Point after our week long stay in Punta Mita Mexico.

As my driver was pulling off the freeway, I could feel a sense of calm and clarity like I had just arrived home.

My wife looked over at me, and she smiled and said, "Your Home!"

She gives me a hard time about this.

But the past two years I have emotionally and spiritually never felt more at home.

My literal home is exactly what I want it to be.

My marriage is exactly what I always imagined it could be and more.

My kids are on fire and we we have another on the way.

My business's are on Fire and 2019 is going to be a year of domination and expansion yet again.

When I walked into my home Last night I was filled with joy. Pure Joy. Like I had walked into a temple kind of joy.

Quiet. Clean. Peaceful.

My wife took a bath.

My daughter played on her piano.

And I slowly unpacked my clothes from the trip.

I was home.

At home in my BODY. At home in my BEING. At home in my BALANCE. At home in my BUSINESS.

At home.

When I was a kid we moved all the time. Most kids knew the name of their teachers...I can't even remember the name of the schools I went to because I changed schools so much.

That later repeated itself in my former life. Every 1-2 years I moved.

My wife and I have lived in 8 homes in 15 years.

Every time I moved into a new place my mind was always planning the next escape. I

 was restless. A pattern built in me to always be running from where i was.

But when we moved into our current home...It changed me.

It stretched me. It transformed me.

On the beach. By the ocean.

In the water daily. In my spirituality. In my sexuality. In my money.

Everything came to a head. As if 40 years of my life had been solely built to create the way to Build myself a life I LOVED to live.

I used that statement: "I am Garrett J White, I Am The Man Who Loves His Life" But that was simply an aspiration.

The truth today?

What was once an aspiration has become my location.

I'M HOME.

I don't want anyone else's Body. I don't want anyone else's Spirituality. I don't want anyone else's marriage. I don't want anyone else's children. I don't want anyone else's businesses. I don't want anyone else's bank accounts.

I WANT MINE.

And after 42 years of life I have finally experienced what THE 4 dimensional HOME feels like. And the feeling is simply this...JOY.

The End.

Garrett, at the end of this Stack, what level of power are you feeling?

ABLAZE

Happy Stack

MOONLIGHT SEX IN CAPRI

[JUNE 2018]

What are you going to title this Happy Stack?

Moonlight Sex in Capri

What domain of the CORE 4 are you Stacking?

BALANCE

Who has triggered you in this domain to feel happy?

Danielle K White

What is the story you're telling yourself right now about what happened?

"My Wife & I Are Finally One!"

What are the positive feelings you're experiencing because of this story?

Joy, Happiness, Connection, Purity, Clarity, Fire

What initial desires or actions do you notice rise for you with these feelings?

I want to do it again. I'm not referencing the sexuality, of course, I want that also. But I want to connect with my wife spiritually again at that level. It was primal. Nothing else mattered at all. I want to leverage that experience and continue to forge a deeper and more profound bond with my wife. I want to continue to be the man that she desires as she did in Capri. I want to continue to stack and transform myself day by day.

As you sit back and survey this positive situation, what is the singular simple lesson on life you're learning from this Stack so far?

"Becoming Elite Doesn't Happen Overnight, It Happens Over Decades!"

The lesson you learned was: "Becoming Elite Doesn't Happen Overnight, It Happens Over Decades!"

How does that lesson apply to the area of BODY?

My body is fit and on fire.

I'm more fit than I was in my 20's and I was a collegiate and professional athlete in my 20's.

This body I have did not just show up over a year. I have been training my body for 30 years. I started liftIng weights when I was 12 years old. I got my first weight set as a Christmas present from my parents and I would work out every single morning in the garage before I went to school and I never stopped. I had a friend who lost 97 pounds this last year. He made a comment to m, "You've never known what it is to be fat?"

I replied, 'Nope" My body has become a weapon over decades, not overnight.

The lesson you learned was: "Becoming Elite Doesn't Happen Overnight, It Happens Over Decades!"

How does that lesson apply to the area of BEING?

My spiritual certainty has come over the decades.

The first experiences I remember having with GOD were when I was 8-10 years old.

I am now in my 40's and for 30+ years I have been growing and expanding and challenging the status quo of the story I have about GOD.

I have had to sacrifice, surrender, and let go over and over and over again. From the time I was 19 to now. The Voice has led me down some very dark paths to find power and I have had to learn to trust that voice and follow it.

Decades ago I didn't trust it. I didn't trust myself. I simply didn't trust.

NOW? I trust ALL IN.

My spiritual certainty is not impacted by any other story of another.

I'm free to be me and to allow others to be themselves also.

I follow THE VOICE and I follow GOD.

In this I trust.

The lesson you learned was: "Becoming Elite Doesn't Happen Overnight, It Happens Over Decades!"

How does that lesson apply to the area of BALANCE?

My marriage…

It took 16+ years but I feel 100% connected to my wife. Not overnight, but over the decades.

Two years ago we were talking about Divorce and dating other people.

Two years later we are on fire.

There is joy in my heart for her.

There is joy in my soul for her.

She is my life partner.

She is my ride or die.

She is the reason I feel the fire I do.

When a couple is both on FIRE it is contagious and impossible to ignore.

The lesson you learned was: "Becoming Elite Doesn't Happen Overnight, It Happens Over Decades!"

How does that lesson apply to the area of BUSINESS?

17 years I have been hustling as a businessman.

I walked away from Guarantees when I was 25 years old and started down a path of self-reliance that would change me forever.

I'm finally getting to a place in the game where I feel like I actually know a few things.

Not a ton.

But a few.

Yet that has taken me almost two decades to pull off. Imagine me in 20 more years. Are you shitting me?

My x-wife's husband is 62-years old. That is 20 years older than me. Larry is a Baller and sold his business for hundreds of millions.

I am just getting started down this path...

By the time I am 62, I will be a Billionaire and my companies will be the type of companies that transform the way we live for centuries...

After spreading the learning across the CORE 4 what FINAL INSIGHT or REVELATION are you leaving this Stack with?

Patience and Appreciation.

The past 2 decades I have built a man I am proud of.

The man I was in the past is someone who got me here but he was a small weak version of the man I have become living the Warrior's Way, leveraging the CODE, the CORE & now the STACK.

I'm a man now who gets shit down and truly emulates a life that works across all areas of the CORE 4.

I get to appreciate that work and journey. I also get to look forward to the man I am creating the next 20 years. From 42-62 but also as I'm sitting here typing this, I start to think about the man I will build from 62-82.

Holy shit.

The magnitude of what I will create in the next 40 years makes my heart speed up and my adrenaline course through my veins. In the end...

I AM THE MASTER OF MY FATE. I AM THE CAPTAIN OF MY SOUL.

Garrett, at the end of this Stack, what level of power are you feeling?

ABLAZE

I SPOKE TO 35,000

[3 FEBRUARY 2019]

I was asked to be a 3 minute speaker to entrepreneurs for Grant Cardone's 10X GrowthCon 3 in Miami, FL at Marlins Park.

What are you going to title this Happy Stack?

I spoke to 35,000

What domain of the CORE 4 are you Stacking?

BUSINESS

Who has triggered you in this domain to feel happy?

Garrett J White

What is the story you're telling yourself right now about what happened?

"Garrett Has Entered Another Level Of his expansion after speaking on a stage with 35,000 and recognizing quickly that he was bigger then the stadium and anyone who had taken the stage before or after him!"

What are the positive feelings you're experiencing because of this story?

Grateful

What initial desires or actions do you notice rise for you with these feelings?

Just grateful. I want to appreciate who I have become and what I have accomplished…

2006, I had a 3min presentation in a speaking contest. I won.

And it sent me on a journey.

2019. I had 3minutes again.

And I fucking smashed it.

In 3min…

As you sit back and survey this positive situation, what is the singular simple lesson on life you're learning from this stack so far?

"The Purpose Of My Life Is Expansion & Inside Of That Expansion Are Windows That Open To New Lives And the Difference Between The Elite & Those Average Is The Elite See The Window and Step Through It Immediately!"

The lesson you learned was: *"The Purpose Of My Life Is Expansion & Inside Of That Expansion Are Windows That Open To New Lives And the Difference Between The Elite & Those Average Is The Elite See The Window and Step Through It Immediately!"* **How does that lesson apply to the area of BODY?**

My body is a weapon, but I had never looked at the window through the lens of expansion with recovery.

Recovery, rest and rehab have become the window through which longevity is now becoming available with my body.

No matter what I have done athletically, if I don't recover...it doesn't matter.

My body is constantly demanding change and the change of expansion and the window of opportunity at this time is nothing athletically but the opportunity to ultimately recover and to rest.

And inside of rest and recovery comes my next level of expansion with my body.

The lesson you learned was: *"The Purpose Of My Life Is Expansion & Inside Of That Expansion Are Windows That Open To New Lives And the Difference Between The Elite & Those Average Is The Elite See The Window and Step Through It Immediately!"* **How does that lesson apply to the area of BEING?**

For almost a decade, I have disconnected from formal prayer, formal worship inside of a church or a particular religion.

What seems to be opening as my next level of expansion is bringing order back to some of the rituals that I use when it comes to my spirituality and my connection with God.

Meditation...powerful.

Stacking...powerful.

But, there is another level that's opening up...

...a window to begin to experience God at an even deeper level by going back to some of the fundamentals I was raised with, one of which is active, verbal prayer.

The lesson you learned was: *"The Purpose Of My Life Is Expansion & Inside Of That Expansion Are Windows That Open To New Lives And the Difference Between The Elite & Those Average Is The Elite See The Window and Step Through It Immediately!"* **How does that lesson apply to the area of BALANCE?**

There's a window of time that has opened up for me with my children that is different than what I have had in the past.

Particularly: opportunities to invest time, energy and love into my son.

Going out of my way on the weekends to have lunch dates with him, take him to movies, and spend time with him outside of work....

There is no guarantee that my son will be this close to me for a very long time.

The fact that he works for me and at the same time that I get to spend so much time with him through the week having not spent that much time with him the first 16 years alive is a BIG FUCKING DEAL.

The window to activate my relationship with my son is here and I am capitalizing on it.

The lesson you learned was: *"The Purpose Of My Life Is Expansion & Inside Of That Expansion Are Windows That Open To New Lives And the Difference Between The Elite & Those Average Is The Elite See The Window and Step Through It Immediately!"* **How does that lesson apply to the area of BUSINESS?**

Wake Up Warrior had to shift, the model that we were using was no longer serving the marketplace the way that I wanted it to.

This mean that I had to sacrifice short-term profits for long-term Purpose and long-term prosperity.

The window of change and scale and documenting everything that Warrior is by its books, apps, and courses is the new direction and trajectory of Wake Up Warrior.

The window is here and I am capitalizing on it.

After spreading the learning across the CORE 4 what FINAL INSIGHT or REVELATION are you leaving this Stack with?

Here is the bottom line:

Yesterday on stage in front of 35,000 I was right at home.

I had the nerves to perform which actually calmed me.

But who I am is capable.

Not just capable…but *that* size of stage I can dominate.

I was face to face with Sean Whalen.

He was small compared to my capacity and I could see it.

I watched the "elite" mentors who I have watched for 10 Years speak and in 3minutes I did more damage on stage then all of them combined.

No music.

No show.

Just me.

Handling my game. Handling my way.

This has become so Clear to me.

The cheers of the crowd as I spoke: The intensity and fire that I had broadcasted to the top of the stadium.

Sharp. Clean. Focused. On Fire.

This weekend opened a new window.

I was given my shot.

And I fucking smashed it.

This has awakened a new opportunity for Me to see myself.

It has awakened a new reality to what is possible for WARRIOR.

It has awakened a new reality to what is possible FOR ME.

I'm grateful.

Grateful for the 100,000+ hours of work on ME to become who I am.

The daily hustle.

The daily videos.

The daily training.

The daily discipline.

It was my will to Prepare that unleashed the fire on stage.

It was my will to train that let me Perform. It was my willingness to do the work in the night that qualified me, fit to shine yesterday in the bright lights.

My energy was bigger then the stadium.

It was not overwhelming.

It was exactly where I am supposed to be.

The end.

Garrett, at the end of this Stack, what level of power are you feeling?

ABLAZE

Happy Stack

QUESTIONS

1. What are you going to title this Happy Stack?

2. What domain of the CORE 4 are you stacking?

3. Who has triggered you in this domain to feel happy?

4. What are the facts about the situation that make you feel so positive?

5. What is the story you're telling yourself right now about what happened?

6. What are the positive feelings you're experiencing because of this story?

7. What initial desires or actions do you notice rise for you with these feelings?

8. As you sit back and survey this positive situation, what is the simple, singular lesson you're learning because of what happened?

9. How does that lesson apply to the area of BODY?

10. How does that lesson apply to the area of BEING?

11. How does that lesson apply to the area of BALANCE?

12. How does that lesson apply to the area of BUSINESS?

13. After spreading the learning across the CORE 4 what FINAL INSIGHT or REVELATION are you leaving this stack with?

SECTION FOUR
THE GRATITUDE STACK

SECTION FOUR: GRATITUDE STACK

CHAPTER TWENTY-TWO:

THE DARKNESS WAS TOO HEAVY...

> I was fucking furious, but I've been playing the Game
> of My Life for long enough to know when a Message
> was trying to be sent to me. So even though I was
> getting more and more pissed, at the same time it
> actually made me laugh.
>
> **—Garrett J White**

I sat on the back deck of my house depressed.

I was not sure where the Darkness was coming from.

I was hitting my CORE 4 daily.

I was smashing Stacks every single day like it was my full time job.

My teams were on fire with the companies.

My marriage was rocking.

There Was Nothing "Wrong," And Yet I Sat There Defeated.

Sighing, I got up and walked down to the kitchen.

It was 5:35am and I was already into my daily morning routine, but something had been very off the previous couple of weeks and I couldn't explain what was happening to me.

I was having sex 2-3 times per week and it was great.

My companies were having their most profitable run we had ever had in the previous 7 years.

I had large stacks of cash in the bank.

I was truly experiencing Abundance.

I had just returned from another Surf Trip and smashed several amazing days in Mexico with my surf coach…MO MAGIC.

I literally had nothing to be upset about, and yet…it didn't seem to matter what I did. I could not shake this feeling of DOOM.

The only time it would go away was if I drank heavily,

but the consequences of waking up with a hangover just made the darkness seem to get thicker and even more intense.

So, I grabbed a 5-hour energy from the fridge and decided to go for a walk.

Attack with the Stack   GRATITUDE STACK

Heading out to the garage, there sat a brand-new Maserati GranTurismo Convertible, my Lamborghini Aventador Roadster, a Bentley Bentayga and a lifted sick Mercedes-Benz G63 Wagon.

I Had Everything I Wanted.
So What The FUCK Was I Feeling?

I had even returned back to hitting a MEGA STACK every single day on myself and the feelings I was having, yet I *still* could not figure out what was going on.

No matter what my wife said…I couldn't snap out of it, so I decided to do a trusted and true Walk and Talk with myself.

As I left the house, I realized I had forgotten my cell phone.

I went back in, grabbed it and my Beats Headphones and headed out for a 4-6 mile walk along the beach to see if I could clear my head.

I had a ton to get done that day and I had absolutely no time to fuck around with this Darkness I was feeling.

I set the Nike Tracker on my phone to track my pace and distance and I set the alarm to notify me every half mile on my route so I could drop and do my customary 25 pushups and 25 air squats.

Wake Up Warrior™   450   Garrett J White

Yes, I had figured out how to turn a normal 4-6 mile walk into a fitness routine that would push me.

Walking And Talking With Myself Had Become One Of My Addictions The Previous Year.

I had invited 50+ individuals to walk and talk with me on the same Course over the year.

But today?

Today it was just me.

Alone.

I tried listening to an inspirational podcast, but nothing was connecting and the more I heard someone else's voice that morning, the more I wanted to scratch my eyes out.

So I opted to just walk in silence.

BEEP

BEEP
BEEP

I had hit the first half mile.

I quickly dropped, popped out 25 pushups and then stood up and went straight into my 25 air squats.

This simple cardio and calisthenic routine had done wonders for my body the previous 12 months and although in some ways I felt like a pussy compared to the man in my younger years…

…it worked, and my body results combined with surfing were showing that the work I was doing was getting me more lean and more shredded than I had ever been.

So, No Matter What Others Said…

I had become a daily walker and surfer and that was just fine by me.

After a couple of miles, approximately 100 pushups and 100 air-squats under my belt, I could start to feel the Darkness begin to part the way as it did most days after I got my sweat going.

This is one of the reasons why I am such a fan of the CORE 4 System and its demand to hit my BODY workout every single day.

As I came to the turnaround of the walk that day, I saw a picnic bench that overlooked Salt Creek Beach.

The dawn patrol of Surfers were already out and shredding.
I decided to have a seat on the bench for a few minutes and watch them.

See, some of the best surfers in Southern California surf this break regularly, so there is always someone in their early 20's there putting on a show.

I sat down.

Took my cell phone out of my back pocket.

Hit pause on my distance tracker.

And just watched as the sets rolled in and wave after wave was caught, ridden and mastered by the elite of the beaches where I live.

Surfing had almost become a religion for me.

In 2009, I left The Mormon Faith That I Was Raised In On A Search For Something More For Myself.

I left not because the church or the religion was wrong, but because there was a VOICE in me that told me it was time to GO.

So I listened.

And a decade later, I found myself here, watching the surfers. Connected with GOD in ways that I never imagined possible.

Between my walking, surfing and Stacking daily, I was feeling more connected to GOD than I had ever felt in my entire life within church walls or reading someone else's sacred texts.

That's Why I Also Knew That For Me To Be Experiencing The Kind Of Darkness That I Was Feeling...

...It Meant That There Was A Gift Hidden Inside The NIGHT That Was Waiting For Me To Hunt Down.

But Nothing I had attempted the past MONTH had worked.

I MEGA STACKED it...and nothing.

I ANGRY STACKED it...and nothing.

I even tried some reverse psychology on myself and did a few HAPPY STACKS on the darkness I was feeling.

And still nothing...but some temporary relief and then IT was right back.

The Doom and Gloom.

But this morning, I had a reprieve from it while I sat on that bench.

I love the smell of the ocean.

I love the energy of the ocean.

I love being by it, in it and riding waves in it.

But I also love just sitting and watching the power of the OCEAN just come in at me wave after wave.

I Can Actually Feel The *PULSE* Of The Universe When The Waves Hit The Shore...

....I Think This Is Why Surfing Is So Addicting.

It's one of the few things I have ever done where I am literally connected to a Power that is way beyond me and in some crazy way, it seems to HEAL me day to day.

In that moment, I decided to take out my cell phone and go to the new app I had my software team create for me and hit a HAPPY STACK.

I had built the habit of an Angry and Happy stack every single day for months.

Ever since the trip to Europe and my last exchange with the VOICE, I had gone all in.

But, I was tired of answering the questions on paper or in Evernote, so I created and app I called the STACK APP which would allow me to STACK every day in a powerful way straight from my cell phone and not just from my lap top on a plane.

By this time, I had realized that the Voice doesn't just speak to me in the air, but in the waves and while walking, so I needed something portable for my conversations.

Stacking Was Who I Had Become...

...As Well As 1000+ Students Of Wake Up Warrior™ Whom I Had Trained To Master The Daily Habit Of Stacking.

I would hear testimonial after testimonial of how life altering it was for so many men just like me that were able to find The Voice within.

In fact, many of them had learned to master the MEGA STACK through the Stack App in faster time periods than I did on my own in Evernote or my journal the first two years.

I unlocked my cell phone.

Clicked on the Stack App, and got ready to Stack.

It pulled up the regular home page of the application, only today...something was broken.

There were no choices.

Normally, as soon as a person logs in, we see the column of options:

MEGA STACK

ANGRY STACK

HAPPY STACK

But today? There was nothing.

It was just three.black.boxes.

I Tried logging Out And Then Logging Back In.

Nothing.

I tried deleting the app from my phone, re-downloaded it and logged in again. As it took me to the home page…still nothing.

What the fuck?!

I called my lead Software Engineer Mauricio and he said he was able to pull up the application no problem.

He ran a diagnostics check and checked my account and said that everything was a green light on his side and my app should be working just fine.

I assured him that it wasn't.
I even did a recording of my screen and sent it to him.

"Brother I can see everything there. What are you talking about?" Mauricio replied.

I thought I might be losing my mind.

How could everyone see the options in their apps, but I couldn't see them in mine?

I Was Fucking Furious, But I've Been Playing The Game Of Life Long Enough To Know When A Message Is Being Sent From The Other Side...

...So Even Though I Was Getting More And More Pissed, At The Same Time It Actually Made Me Laugh.

I set my phone down beside me, still laughing about the fact that I was getting so angry about not being able to do a Happy Stack.

The IRONY.

Oh, the IRONY.

So I closed my eyes.

Took three deep breaths.
And as I was about to inhale for my fourth breath, my phone rang.

It disrupted me from my breathing and I reached down to send whoever it was to voicemail.

UNKNOWN CALLER ID
It Displayed.

I normally hit "Ignore" and was about to switch my phone onto silent, but instead, I did something I never do...

I answered the call.

ME: *HELLO?*

UNKNOWN CALLER: *Hello, Garrett.*

ME: *Who is this?*

UNKNOWN CALLER: *You know who this is...*

ME: *No, actually, I don't.*

UNKNOWN CALLER: *Check your Stack App NOW*

ME: *Seriously, who is this? Mauricio...is this you?*

UNKNOWN CALLER: *No, this is not Mauricio. Now, do as I tell you: check your Stack App NOW.*

And then he hung up.

I had no idea who that was and the thought of someone calling me out of nowhere and telling me to do such a strange thing was a bit insane.

I Looked Down At My Stack App, Clicked On It And What Showed Up Next Was Something I Had Never Seen Before Inside Of The App.

In bold words it said,

GRATITUDE STACK

I was not sure what this was all about at all.

I clicked on it just like I had hundreds of other times with the MEGA, ANGRY and HAPPY Stacks ever since my teams had finished the coding work required to finish the Stack App.

I messaged Mauricio:

Bro, did you fuck with me and add this Gratitude Stack into my application?

He responded back immediately: *NO*.

He also said I might quite possibly be losing my mind with the way I was acting that morning.

I agreed with him…Shit was getting weird again.

Then…BING.

My phone received a notification that I had just gotten a text.

The Username was…

…THE VOICE

SECTION FOUR: GRATITUDE STACK
CHAPTER TWENTY-THREE:

YOU'RE A VICTIM IN THE VOID...

> "The Horizon is always beyond the place in which you currently are."
>
> **—The Voice**

THE VOICE: *You there, Brother?*

ME: *My Brother! It's you.*

Were you the one that just called me?

THE VOICE: *No, I never make calls...I had my assistant get your attention.*

ME: *Clear.*

THE VOICE: *It seems you've gone back into a Drift of some sorts these days?*

ME: *I totally am but I can't figure out why at all and it's driving me insane.*

THE VOICE: *I get it.*

You're actually right on time with this feeling.

You might feel like you are off, but you're totally on.

ME: *How is that even possible?*

Everything is on point in the Game for me including the soon- to-be birth of my new baby girl, Isla.

THE VOICE: *I heard about that.*

How you feel about having another baby?

ME: *I am totally excited.*

THE VOICE: *Congratulations! Can you believe how far you have come?*

Three years ago in the Summer of 2016, I met you in the darkest of dark places.

You were in the PIT for sure. It was on your flight to Chicago and you were planning on getting a divorce.

Fast forward three years after the introduction of the MEGA, ANGRY and HAPPY Stacks, and now you and Danielle are expecting another child.

It appears you got that Sex Thing back on lock down?

ME: *Oh, yea...*

2017 & 2018 were amazing.

You remember when you taught me the HAPPY STACK and I shared with you the experience under the moon in Capri Italy?

THE VOICE: *Yes I do, my brother. How could I forget that one?!*

ME: *Well, that type of behavior continued all summer and into the fall on the regular…every 2-3 days…and somehow in November on at trip to NYC my wife said,*

"Let's actually try to get pregnant."

THE VOICE: *How did you feel about this when she said this?*

ME: *I started to cry.*

It wasn't likely the response she was expecting from me, but it was what she got.

I was almost speechless when she said it also.

Our daughter Ruby was 8 and we had talked about having another child but there was so much chaos in our marriage that there was no fucking way she was willing to have another baby with me and I was not interested in having another with her either.

But shit changed big time the past 3 years.

I found a deep sense of respect for her that I had never found before.

A deep sense of TRUST that I had never felt with her before.

It was weird, but nice.

THE VOICE: *I get it.*

Completely.

And that is the result of the work that BOTH of you have done.

Danielle might not Stack, but I can promise you that your dedication to DAILY STACKING has completely altered her and your children's lives forever.

You're not the same man you were three years ago.

You died and were reborn.

Can you sense this about yourself?

ME: *I can.*
But, if that is the case and there is so much that is working well right now including being less than 6 weeks away from the birth of my daughter…

Why am I feeling so much pain and so much heaviness?

THE VOICE: *Because you have done all you can do, leveraging the the tools that you have been given and it's time to give you access to the fourth Weapon.*

This weapon does not work unless you have mastered the art and science of the first three.

THE MEGA STACK taught you what?

ME: *It taught me to Release My Rage and to Walk The Block.*

These two skill sets have truly set me free.

THE VOICE: *And what did you learn from the ANGRY STACK?*

ME: *How to leverage my irritations and anger as tools of learning and revelation…*

…How to handle the small stuff before it becomes big stuff.

THE VOICE: *And what did you learn from the HAPPY STACK?*

ME: *That life is teaching me all of the time.*

Also, I can learn from the DARK and I can learn from the LIGHT.

That Happy shit is happening all the time and it is my duty to learn from it as much as I have become addicted to learning from my Darkness.

THE VOICE: *YES.*

YES.

YES.

That is a great summary.

So, what's the problem then?

ME: *I have no fucking idea.*

I just know that nothing I am doing is working to free myself of this weight.

THE VOICE: *I know.*

But before I teach you the 4th Weapon, I need you to understand some concepts:

It's Called the VICTIM IN THE VOID syndrome.

Here is how it works…

In your mind there there are multiple realities occurring at the same time.

Meaning, your mind is bouncing back and forth between the following…

   1.   *The FACTS About Where It Is Today*

2.   *The FANTASY Of Where It Believes It Should Be Today.*

Let me ask you this…

I know Danielle is pregnant so things in your sex life have likely shifted a bit, correct?

ME: *For sure.*

No Moonlight Sex Episodes recently as she is in the final stretch and just getting a good night's sleep is the standard focus. I am in no need to rush or force anything with her at all.

THE VOICE: *Now, before Danielle got pregnant, was there a time last year in the fall when you actually started to experience the frequency and passion of Sex with Danielle as Just Normal?*

ME: *What do you mean?*

THE VOICE: *Listen, in 2016 you two were struggling with sexuality as a married couple.*

So much so that you were going to get a divorce over the issue.

But, in 2017, you turned it around and by 2018, you two had become two totally different human beings and your sex life was 10x what it had been just a few years prior.

Yet, after a couple years of stabilizing your sex life, did you notice that what used to be exciting and heart stopping started to become normal?

It might have been amazing, but it no longer held the SHINY NEW FEEL?

ME: *Now that you mention it…I can see where you're going with this.*

Yea, that did happen right before we got pregnant.

I remember that when we had gone on a trip to NYC in October, 2018 we had more sex in three days than we had on the 7 days of our Honeymoon 17 years prior.

One night, we got after it in the shower before we went to dinner,

and needless to say it got LOUD from both of us.

Primal passion for sure.

When we finished, we realized that our room had a shared door with the room next door to us and that we could hear two little children and a mother and father talking and the TV was turned up very, very, VERY loud.

My wife looked at me.
"Well it appears our neighbors could hear us," she laughed.

We both laughed, I gave her a kiss and we got dressed and then headed out for a nice dinner and then our driver took us to a local Irish Pub to watch the McGregor vs. Khabib fight.

We left the room at the same time as our neighbors.

Yes, the ones who could hear us and turned their TV up to drown out the sound of two bodies slapping and groans of ecstasy that were filling their room...from someone else.

They did what any normal parent would do, smile and think 'go get it buddy' and then turn on a show to avoid the conversation with the young children that could also hear, but had no real clue what was happening.

We were all heading in the same direction to the elevator, entering it at the same time.

The Husband looked me in the eyes and neither of us said anything, but there was a tiny head nod with the "Well. Fucking.Done.Brother" look.

His wife wouldn't even look at me or Danielle so she kept her focus on her young little girls.

And little did I realize the foreshadowing.

To this day, I am convinced we got pregnant that night with our daughter ISLA who is coming shortly.

THE VOICE: *You know, if this whole Warrior Business Man Thing doesn't work out....*

You could always become a romance novelist

ME: *HA!*

THE VOICE: *Ok...*

So, you get what I'm talking about then.

What was once your fantasy had become your reality.

Bodies slapping in the shower in NYC and everything.

ME: *YES.*

THE VOICE: *And what becomes your reality inevitably becomes your Normal.*

...what becomes normal becomes boring.

And when things become boring, your mind will search for a new Target.

Something else to pursue.

Think about this with money.

What was your Personal Income in 2018 that you took home?

ME: *$4.6 Million*
THE VOICE: *And what did you make your first year as a PE Teacher almost 20 years ago for the entire year?*

ME: *$22,000*

THE VOICE: *So would you say that this is more personal income now than you have ever had in your career?*

ME: *YES.*

THE VOICE: *Yet you're depressed with it, aren't you?*

ME: *YES.*

And I have no fucking idea why.

I can buy what I want, when I want and where I want.

I don't stress about money, I don't stress about sex, I don't stress about fitness, I don't stress about Purpose, but what has happened is that I have found myself in this trap.

It's like I'm on a treadmill watching my life play out on a screen in front of me, but all of my jogging still leaves me in one place.

I feel more pressure than I have ever felt before and I have no outlet for it.

I feel even ashamed to be upset at all.

I mean what the FUCK is there for me to be upset about?!

I live in a $10M beach house and live a life so far beyond my wildest imaginations when I was just starting my adult life out.

Yet…

It never seems to be enough.

It seems like no matter what I create…it's not enough.

I'm tired, Brother.

Seriously Tired.

And I just don't know If I give a shit anymore.

THE VOICE: *And when you feel this what do you want to do?*

ME: *I want to BURN IT ALL to the ground.*

It's like I start doing shit that makes no fucking sense.

Shit that will fuck up me and Danielle.

Shit that will fuck up my body.

Shit that will fuck up my family.

Shit that will fuck up my businesses.

Why do I do this?

THE VOICE: *Because you're stuck in the VICTIM VOID.*
ME: *The what?*

THE VOICE: *The VICTIM VOID.*

And it is 100% Normal to get here.

The Warrior's Way has three phases to it.

Phase #1: Eradicate Scarcity across the Core 4.

You did this.

Phase #2: Establish Abundance across the Core 4.

You did this.

Phase #3: Expand Prosperity Across the Core 4.

You have NOT done this….

ME: *How do you know I have not done this?*

THE VOICE: *The fact that I'm here, chatting with you again, and prepared to give you Weapon #4 lets me know for SURE that you have not Expanded Prosperity.*

But, before I can teach you this fourth weapon which will allow you to Expand Prosperity and build your legacy, you must understand a few things…

Let's come back to the points of the mind.

Your mind operates naturally from two places.

1. *The Facts Of Where It Is Today.*

2. *The Fantasy of Where It Wants to Be Tomorrow.*

These two points create the VOID.

In between them is the pursuit.

It is the hunt.

It is the foundation of where you are and the vision of who you can become.

Every successful producer leverages this natural programming of the mind.

Let me give you an example…

Look out at the Ocean.

ME: *Ok.*

THE VOICE: *Look past the surfers and find the Horizon wayyyyy off in the distance.*

ME: *Ok, I found it.*

THE VOICE: *Good. Now, if you and I got onto some paddle boards and starting paddling to the exact GPS Location of where your mind had decided the Horizon exists, what would we find when we got to that exact GPS Location?*

ME: *The Horizon?*

THE VOICE: *No.*

You wouldn't have, because beyond that Horizon is another one...the Horizon is always beyond the place in which you currently are.

Let me break it down using another example...Remember last year when you and Danielle and the kids took the yacht to Catalina Island?

ME: *YES*

THE VOICE: *As you traveled toward the island, what did you notice about the Horizon?*

ME: *It just kept going.*

Meaning, once we got to Catalina Island, the Horizon had moved.

It had moved miles and miles out into the ocean.

THE VOICE: *Exactly. And if you had sailed past Catalina and continued to hunt down the Horizon, would you ever get there?*

ME: *I guess not.*

THE VOICE: *You're right.*

You never would.

Because the Horizon is an IDEA, not a reality.

Your mind has been built to establish a grounding of where it is and then once it gets there, it has become normal…it wants to chase the Horizon again.

This is the natural Coding of Expansion.

It is built into every man.

It is what you leveraged in order to leave Scarcity.

A desire for more…a vision of a Horizon that was way beyond what you were experiencing at the time.

Let's say that you got in your boat and your started sailing out to sea…

Years and years later from this sea voyage, you've finally arrived to Abundance Island, but you have lost the ability to appreciate who you have become and what you have created.

WHY?

Because you have become solely focused on heading to the next horizon with no appreciation for the distance you have covered when you first sailed out to sea.

What are you hearing me say?

ME: *I'm stuck.*

Stuck in constantly hunting down more.

Wanting more. Desiring more. Demanding More.

More from my marriage…

More from my business…

More from myself…

But this constant demand is exhausting and depressing and makes me want to blow up the fucking boat and just stop sailing at all.

THE VOICE: *YEP.*

You Left the Land of Scarcity.

You Sailed To Abundance Island.

And now? Any and every attempt you make to hunt down the next island leaves you hollow and empty.

Do you know why?

ME: *No*

THE VOICE: *Because you never looked back.*

SECTION FOUR: GRATITUDE STACK

CHAPTER TWENTY-FOUR:

LOOK BACK AND LIVE...

> "That feeling of Pull will become a persecuting feeling of PAIN if you don't regularly look back and contrast where you at today with where you were yesterday."
>
> **—The Voice**

I sat there looking out at the Horizon and allowed the words of the VOICE to settle in.

I was stuck.

It was not that I wasn't willing to do the work.

I was doing the FUCKING WORK daily with fire and passion more than any man I knew.

But everything was becoming gray.

I was losing the will to fight.

I was losing the will to keep chasing the Next Horizon.

I was starting to fall into the trap that all aggressive men who learn to live the Warrior's Way eventually fall into...

I fell into the VICTIM VOID.

A GAP Between The Reality Of Where I Was And The Never Ending Impossible Horizon I Was Chasing.

And the more Horizons I chased...the more islands I conquered...the more helpless I became.

I was stuck in a Karmic Loop

I was stuck in a False Lift, but this was very different than what I would experience and have the Mega Stack help me out of.

Reading my thoughts, the conversation continued.

THE VOICE: *Yes, you are stuck in a Karmic Loop.*

Yes, you are experiencing a false lift.

For one simple reason...

You don't look back.

Seriously, when was the last time you slowed down enough to LOOK at what your marriage has become?!
Where was it when I met you in 2016 and where is it now in 2019?

ME: *Occasionally in my HAPPY STACKS I realize this, but I feel like that is more of an acknowledgment of where I am at with Danielle presently, not really as a look back.*

THE VOICE: *And how about your parents?*

In 2016 you spoke to them maybe once per year.

Now, you're messaging them all of the time.

When was the last time you actually *looked back at how far your relationship with your Father and Mother has come?*

ME: *I admit it. Never.*

THE VOICE: *Look at your body…*

The most fit and shredded you have ever been.

You're accelerating in Surfing and have completely altered your physical patterns from CrossFit Guy and heavy Power Lifting with a body that hurt all of the time to a lean, mean and mobile machine of a body.

When was the last time you really looked back at the Machine you have built with your body in the past 3 years?

ME: *I haven't.*

THE VOICE: *Your businesses?*

They are on the rise.

7 years of hustle and you're smashing revenue records, taking home millions in personal income annually and never stress about money and if there is going to be enough to pay the bills.

If you go back 10 years, where were you?

ME: *I had lost everything.*

I couldn't pay the rent for $2,000 a month.

My wife was selling shit out of our house to put food in the fridge.

THE VOICE: *Your life is ON FIRE, Brother!*

Can you not see this?

You have become the #1 Case Study for the Warrior's Way.

Across all 4 domains of life, you're dominating.

You have Eradicated Scarcity.

You have Established Abundance.

And now? You're stuck.

So, are you ready to get unstuck and sail forward into a future bigger than you could have ever imagined?
ME: *YES.*

Please…yes, I'm ready.

THE VOICE: *Then you're going to have to start looking back…*

So, let me bring you back to the two places the mind goes.

1.   *Facts about where you are today.*

2.   *Fantasy about where it wants to go tomorrow (Horizon).*

Now, in-between these two points, you will find huge inspiration and purpose and pull to explore and expand every single day.

But that feeling of Pull will become a persecuting feeling of PAIN if you don't regularly look back and contrast where you at today with where you were yesterday.

The third point then gets created, which consists of…

3.   *Facts about where you were yesterday.*

There is also a GAP between these two points of yesterday and today.

This GAP I call VICTORY VALLEY.

VICTORY VALLEY is the Source of Fuel that allows you to rise into and sustain eternal expansion in prosperity. In this place, you can hunt down horizons your entire life without burning out and feeling the weight and depression and darkness that you have been feeling.

It's the feeling of Gratitude and Appreciation for where you have come from as well as a deep appreciation for where you are today.

ME: *Ok, so, let me repeat this back to you so I know that I'm getting it right.*

I stand today on an island…

This island is the FACTS of where I am today.

From that place, I have THE VICTIM VOID which is the distance between where I am today and where my mind thinks I should be tomorrow, somewhere out there at the Horizon.

Then, I have VICTORY VALLEY which is between where I stand today on the Island and looking back at where I was on the mainland.

This is where I'm looking back to where I was, compared to where I am today.

Inside of this looking back, I will find the Fuel to continue the journey.

But it's not just to continue like on a treadmill, but to continue with fire and passion and excitement.

THE VOICE: *Yes.*

There are three feelings you must maintain in order to stay in prosperity.

FEELING #1: Gratitude.

FEELING #2: Appreciation.

FEELING #3: Honor.

Let's define each of these words:

<u>Gratitude:</u> A feeling of thankfulness.

<u>Appreciation:</u> The act of estimating the quality of things and giving them their proper value.

<u>Honor:</u> High respect for.

These three feelings are not found inside of the VICTIM VOID... they are found inside of VICTORY VALLEY.

...They are found from stopping.

Looking back.

And expressing Gratitude, Appreciation & Honor for the growth and expansion of YOU as well as those around you who have made the journey or made the journey possible for you.

Now, here is the crazy part...
VICTIM VOID is only VICTIM VOID when you refuse to look back to VICTORY VALLEY.

Once you learn to consistently look back to VICTORY VALLEY, you will watch as what was once a dark, overwhelming and depressing VOID become transformed before you eyes into something magical, exciting and inspiring.

Something that pulls you forward.

Something that gives your life Purpose.

We call this WINNING IMPOSSIBLE GAMES.

When you play this way?

THE VICTIM VOID becomes…

THE PROSPERITY PATH.

A never ending experience of expansion that grows as fast and as furious as you choose it.

But, to pull this off, we have to look back.

And in looking back, we will find the FUEL we are looking for.

SECTION FOUR: GRATITUDE STACK
CHAPTER TWENTY-FIVE:

THE PROSPERITY PATH

> "All fathers divinely guide their children with the conditions necessary for them to rise. Yes, that means we all as fathers perfectly fuck up our children in a way that demands that they rise!"
>
> **—Garrett J White**
> [Inaugural Gratitude Stack]

I sat there stunned.

It was so simple.

Just look back and live.

As I sat there on the picnic bench at Salt Creek everything became very quiet.

Everything became very still.

It felt like I could cut the air with a knife…

…there was a presence that I was feeling that was unlike anything I had experienced before.
It was a quickening and I felt a window to my Soul open.

A Gateway Out Of The Darkness That I Had Been Plagued With The Previous Month.

A way into a path of prosperity that would never end.

A path that would allow me to expand inside of the light with profound power.

And so I sat.

Just breathing it in.

Then out of nowhere, my dad's face entered my mind's eye.

It was as if my mind was playing a movie for me and the lead characters were me and my father: Brett Dwayne White.

My dad and I had become very distant the previous 10 years.

When I left the Mormon church, this was very hard for my father to grasp. In fact, our last real exchange had almost come to a fist fight in his living room in 2009.

Since then?

We didn't talk much.

I had seen him in person only a couple of times in the last decade.

And as I thought about that...I felt a Sadness.

A Deep Sadness for the fact that we had become so separated.

I had blamed HIM for years for not raising me with power.

I had blamed HIM for not being around much when I was a young boy and for not being an aggressive father that I could follow who could teach me to BE THE MAN.

I had done 50+ MEGA and ANGRY Stacks on my father.

But, as I sat there, I realized I had never once done a Happy Stack on my dad.

Come to think of it...I couldn't remember the last time that I had even been grateful that he *was* my dad.

THE VOICE: *So, you think it is an accident that your father is the one who came to your mind just a moment ago?*

ME: *No.*

Not at all.

Holy Shit.

Today is Father's Day.

What the FUCK!

THE VOICE: *I'm smiling right now.*

The Universe makes no accidents, My Brother.

It is time for you to close the door on your Karmic Loop by looking back.

But specifically, looking back with Gratitude, Appreciation and Honor for the man that is your father.

Are you ready?

ME: *YES. I AM.*

THE VOICE: *I want you to leave this text chat and click on the STACK APP.*

Once it's open, you will see the "GRATITUDE STACK" button.

I want you to click on it and I will join you there.

Clear?

ME: *CLEAR*

I did as the VOICE instructed, clicked on the Stack App and then onto the newly formed Gratitude Stack.

The chat function pulled up for me just like the MEGA, ANGRY and HAPPY Stacks had for the last year or so since my programming team had coded and created the STACK APP with me.

THE VOICE: *(Q) What domain of the Core 4 are you Stacking?*

ME: *BALANCE*

THE VOICE: *(Q) Who has triggered you in this domain to feel grateful?*

ME: *Brett D. White*

THE VOICE: *(Q) What is the story you're currently telling yourself right now about what happened?*

I could feel the emotion rising already.

I was not really prepared for what was about to come next.

But, a decade of PAIN with my father was about to melt before my finger tips as I journeyed down this Gratitude Stack.

ME: *Ok. Here it is...*

...Brett is the single most important man in my life. Without him I have no life, and without him showing up exactly as he did when I was a child, there was no possible way that I could be the man that I am today!

THE VOICE: *(Q) What are the connected feelings of gratitude that you're experiencing because of this story?*

ME: *Love, Appreciation, Honor, Respect, Gratitude.*

THE VOICE*:*   *(Q) What initial desires or actions do you notice rise for you with these feelings?*

ME: *I want BRETT to know I love him.*

I want BRETT to know I care for him.

I want BRETT to know that I know he did the very best he could as my father when I was a child.

I want BRETT to know he is my father.

I want BRETT to know I love him as my Dad.

I want BRETT to know I forgive him for anything of the past and I simply want to love and know him as he is today, with no expectation and no demands.

I want BRETT to know he did everything he knew how to do with me and that he showed up perfectly to form the man I have become today.

I want BRETT to know I am thankful.

THE VOICE: *Ok, brother.*

You're doing great.
I'm just going to keep rolling with you…

(Q) As you sit back and survey the connected feelings of gratitude you're having in this moment, what is the singular,

simple lesson on life you're learning from this Gratitude Stack?

ME: *Wow. Ok. Here we go.*

That...

"All fathers divinely guide their children with the conditions necessary for them to rise, yes that means we all as fathers perfectly fuck up our children in a way that demands that they rise!"

THE VOICE: *(Q) Armed with this lesson of gratitude what are your final insights or revelations as you conclude this stack?*

ME: *Dad,*

Here is the bottom line today.

I love you.

I have always loved you.

I want you to know this and feel this.

There is no possible way that my life could be what it is without you and the guidance that you have given me over the years since I was a kid.

I have memories that were crucial to me.

Several in particular…

One night in HS I came home drunk.

You met me at the deck of the house by the front door.

I was terrified when I saw you and I thought for sure I was in for a beating or at least a really good yelling at, and trust me…I would have deserved it.

Instead?

You didn't yell.

You didn't scream.

You didn't preach to me.

You asked me to come sit down beside you on the steps and you asked me a series of questions.

"What do you want out of your life?"

I replied with the only thing that mattered to me then…

"Play college Football!"

You then asked me,

"Will getting drunk every night get you what you want?"

I said, "NO."

We laid on the deck, looking up at the stars and in my buzzed state we bonded while we stared into eternity.

If you had been a yeller?

If you had been physically violent?

If you had been anything but what you were, I would have never been given the space to be asked the questions that changed my life.

I remember back to 8th grade football in Stockton, CA after football practice.

I was sharing with you how practice had gone and telling you all about the BIG GUYS at football practice.

And in one of the few moments I can recall from my childhood, you SNAPPED and exploded on me with RAGE that changed my life forever.

You grabbed me by my football pads and slammed me against a fence, then yelled,

"When are you going to get it, YOU ARE one of the big guys!"

That one statement set me on a course to earn a full-ride scholarship to Boise State University and then to have a short career professionally in the Arena Leagues.

Years later, when I was at Boise State, you came to visit during spring ball.

When you got there, we happened to be training in the Weight Room. You came in and watched me hit a PR in my Power Clean.

After the session, we were walking down the hall to the locker room and you looked down at my right arm to the brand new Tribal Tattoo I had gotten a few weeks prior and said,

"Your mother's going to love that one!"

No judgment.

No guilt.

No shame.

Just a smile and you continued walking with me.

In 2008, after my mortgage companies has fallen apart, you sat in a small room with 10 other students in one of my first Soul Purpose Intensives and you made a comment to Mom, not knowing that I could hear you...

You said,

"How are his rooms so small? He is going to end up filling stadiums!"

You didn't know I heard.

This statement came to pass, and left a massive impact on me, like the day in 8th grade with the shake down and the drunken conversation on the deck in HS as well as the walk at Boise State…

…Just a few months ago I spoke in a stadium of 35,000 people at the 10x Growth Con.

Everything you predicted would happen has come to pass.

Dad…

My life has been an insane circus.

And Dad,

You have been a rudder for me in ways that you may never know.

But today?

I just want to say…

…thank you.

Thank you for perfectly BEING YOU.

Thank you for BEING NOTHING MORE or LESS than you were. Because who you were and are for me is perfect.

I love you dad.

Happy Fathers Day.

Love,

Garrett

I concluded the Stack.

I held my cell phone in my hands and looked out at the Horizon.

My father was EVERYTHING to me, and it was time for me to heal with the Power Of Looking Back.

THE VOICE: *Well done, Brother.*

Well done.

Now, here is what I want you to do with it.

Go into your Stack Library in your Stack App. I want you to go find the Gratitude Stack that you just completed on your dad.

I clicked around in the App and while doing so, noticed that all of my Stack options were back.

I had the MEGA,

I had the ANGRY,
I had the HAPPY,

And I had the GRATITUDE.

It was in that moment that a 3-year journey of learning, living and ultimately coming to lead with the Stack was complete.

I clicked over to the Stack Library and found the Stack I had just written about my dad.

Once I found it, I told the Voice I was there.

ME: *Ok, I have it.*

THE VOICE: *Alright. I want you to click on the share tab.*

ME: *DONE*

THE VOICE: *I want you to click on the "Summary" copy to clipboard.*

ME: *DONE*

THE VOICE: *Once you have done that, I want you to go to your text and send this Stack Summary to your Mother and your Father together in a thread right now.*

ME: *Ok.*

I created a group text thread with my Mom and Dad.

I clicked on the chat section and pasted the Stack Summary. Below is the actual summary that I sent to them both:

_____

GRATITUDE STACK SUMMARY

Well done Garrett,

That was a great GRATITUDE STACK!

I'm stoked we went through this process together.

Here's a summary of today's Stack:

TITLE:

My Dad Created The Path...

DOMAIN:

BALANCE

ORIGINAL STORY:

"Brett is the single most important man in my life, without him I have no life and without him showing up exactly as he did when I was a child there was no possible way that I could be the man that I am today!"

DESIRES AND ACTIONS:

I want Brett to know I love him.

I want Brett to know I care for him.

I want Brett to know I know he did the very best he could as my father when I was a child.

I want Brett to know he is my father.

I want Brett to know I love him as my DAD.

I want Brett to know I forgive him for anything of the past and I simply want to love and know him as he is today with no expectations and no demands!

I want Brett to know he did everything he knew how to do with me and that he showed up perfectly to form the man I was to become today!

LESSON:

"All fathers divinely guide their children to the conditions necessary for them to rise, yes that means we all as fathers perfectly fuck up our children in a way that demands that they rise!"

REVELATION:

Dad,

Here is the bottom line today.

I love you. I have always loved you.

I want you to know this and I feel this.

There is no possible way that my life could be what it is without you and the guidance that you have given me over the years since I was a kid.

I have memories that were crucial to me.

One in particular.

I had come home drunk.

You met me at the deck of the house.

You didn't yell.

You didn't scream.

You didn't preach at me.

You asked me a series of questions...

"What do you want out of your life?"

I replied,

"Play football in college"

You then asked me,

"Will getting drunk every night get you what you want?"

I said,

"NO"

We laid on the deck and looked at the stars and in my buzzed state we bonded while we stared into eternity.

If you had been a yeller?

If you had been physically violent?

If you had been anything but what you were I would never have been given the space to ask the questions that changed my life.

I remember back to 8th grade after football practice.

I was telling you about the BIG GUYS at football practice.

And in one of the few moments in your world you exploded on me with rage.

You grabbed me by my football pads and slammed me against a fence and yelled,

"When are you going to get it, you are one of the big guys!"

Then years later at Boise State,

You showed up to spring practice and watched me Weight lift with the team.

As we walked down the hall you looked at my brand new tattoo and said,

"Your mother's going to love that one"

No judgment.

No anger, No guilt, No shame.

You just walked with me.

In 2008 while we sat in a small room with 10 other people and I led the Soul Purpose Intensive you made a comment..

"How are his rooms so small, he is going to end up filling stadiums!"

You didn't know I heard this when you were sharing it with mom.

That statement shook me.

Just like the day on the 8th grade shake down, the Drunken DECK in HS, the walk at Boise State, The simple words of belief from you that day in 2008.

This year I spoke to a stadium of 35,000.

My life has been an insane circus.

And DAD you have been a rudder for me in ways that you may never know.

But today?

I just want to say...

...thank you.

Thank you for perfectly BEING YOU.

Thank you for BEING NOTHING MORE then you were.

Because who you were for me was PERFECT.

I love you.

Happy Fathers Day.

Love,

Garrett

Have a great rest of your day Garrett!

I'll check in with you again tomorrow.

THE VOICE

THE VOICE: *Well done.*

And now, you're complete.

How do you feel right now?

ME*: Absolutely on fire.*

My heart is full with love.

THE VOICE: *Welcome to the final stage of the Stack Game:*

Gratitude.

This single weapon is more powerful than the other three combined.

It is the fuel that makes the Universe go.

RAGE

ANGER

HAPPINESS

They are all part of the game, but the thing that most of humanity is missing today?

GRATITUDE

APPRECIATION

and HONOR

Men today lack this for themselves.

They lack this for their wives.

They lack this for their children.

They lack this for their employees.

They lack this for their clients.

They lack this for their neighbors.

WHY?

Because they are all suppressing their Irritations & Anger and most are walking around with RAGE just seconds away from exploding.

This is why there are so many angry people online who spend all day just trying to fight.

They are filled with Darkness.

They are filled with Rage.

They are filled with Anger.

They are filled with Envy.

They are filled with Blame.

They're filled with Guilt.

They are Filled with Shame.

They are not ready for the Gratitude Stack.

Why? Because they are in scarcity.

They are stuck in a karmic loop of insanity.

There is a Process to this Game...one that cannot be avoided.

You took that long path because you were the First One.

But those who will follow you will accomplish in months what took you years.

There has never been a time when all four of these weapons were more valuable to Men than today.

But the love that you feel is EARNED.

And I want you to experience it every day.

ME: *Me Too.*

So... how do I do that?

THE VOICE: *Simple.*

Every day, you will create a Gratitude Stack for at minimum ONE person in your life and then send them the summary.

They do not have to know how the Gratitude Stack works at all.

They do not have to understand the Warrior's Way.

They do not need any instruction.

You simply complete the questions and then send.

You will want to follow the same format you're naturally following now, but I want you to notice something.

Two things:

ONE: When you get to the question, "What initial desires or actions do you notice rise for you with these feelings?"

When you get there use the statements…

I want (Name) *to know* (name a specific trait, characteristic or action that stands out).

These body statements will make it very simple for the person receiving to understand.

TWO: When you get to the final question, "Armed with this lesson of gratitude, what are you final insights or revelations as you conclude this stack?"

You're going to write it like a letter.

Dear _____,

Body copy,

Sign off.

The combination between the I want (insert name) *to* (insert action) *with the letter is a lethal combination.*

ME: *Will I ever use the Gratitude Stack about anything besides other people?*

THE VOICE: *Yes, of course.*

You will use it on yourself and on situations as well as results.

For example, you could be grateful for your new surfboard.

You would follow the same frame.

Only you would not use the I WANT statements and you would not write the letter.

You would just answer the questions.

But, I would have you consider that Gratitude for the People in your life is 10x more powerful than the Things.

So, if you were to choose to be grateful for your surfboard, instead, make it about your Surf Coach and send it to him.

And feel free to write yourself letters also.

In the end, the target is daily execution of the Gratitude Stack.

This weapon is the Arrow in the Heart of expansion.

Now, I want you to do one more thing before you leave this bench.

ME: *Sure. Anything.*

THE VOICE: *Do a Gratitude Stack on yourself.*

And when you're done…

Walk home in silence and listen to the Ocean speak to you.

ME: *Clear.*

When will I connect with you again?

THE VOICE: *You do every day inside of the Stacks. But as for these conversations that completely shift your trajectory when feeling stuck?*

When the time is right, my brother…

When the time is right.

For now?

Perform a Daily Execution of the Gratitude Stack, starting with yourself.

SECTION FOUR: GRATITUDE STACK
CHAPTER TWENTY-SIX:

PRINCIPLES

> "We depreciate our value when we only look forward and we never look back; when we never slow down long enough to express deep levels of gratitude, honor, love and appreciation for ourselves and for others."
>
> **—Garrett J White**
> [Attack with the Stack Online Software Training]

We all have had a yesterday, currently live today, and have the potential of a tomorrow, yet when we are stuck inside of The Gap, the only direction that we ever choose to look in is forward. Here we suffer, having little to no appreciation for what we did yesterday to get us to where we are today, seeing tomorrow as an unattainable horizon. That was the experience that I had with The Voice as you read earlier when uncovering the Gratitude Stack, so to help us open our eyes to more, we have the following principles:

> **Principle #1: Honor vs Praise**
> **Principle #2: Appreciation vs Depreciation**
> **Principle #3: Love vs Hate**
> **Principle #4: Trust & Respect are the Foundation of Gratitude**

When we are stuck in the Gap, we're unable to differentiate what these principles are because there's no space and time that we allow to acknowledge the level of expansion on who we are and what we've become.

We Learn To Know Who We Are By What We've Become

Gratitude opens up this piece inside of us, however, allowing us to look back from a place of appreciation, honor and love in order to see the purpose behind who we have currently become.

When we operate from this place, we rise above the Gap instead of falling into the Pit.

But, it's not as easy as it sounds to be grateful for all of the shit we've done...it's a lot easier to get whipped up into a frenzy about what we're NOT doing and where we think we are supposed to be.

The longer we remain stuck in the Gap, we don't realize how much it matters to take the time to see how far we've come.

The Gratitude Stack becomes a solution as it helps us look back so we can say, "Look at my life now compared to what it was!"

It doesn't have us compare our lives to anyone else's but our own, giving us space to measure back for what we've done while still anticipating for the future with honor, appreciation and love.

Principle #1:
Honor vs Praise

The first thing that we're looking for inside of the Gratitude Stack is honor: honor in ourselves and honor for other people. Not praise.

Praise easily becomes hollow. It puts someone up on a pedestal and makes them *better than:* better than ourselves, better than others, and even better than who they really are, giving us a delusional perception which is extremely damaging for everyone. Eventually, this Pedestal of Praise will break, and the person being praised will fall from what had always been unattainable. All of that strength that we had once praised in our delusional state suddenly appears as a weakness, making us feel cheated somehow that this person wasn't who we thought he or she was.

If I praise you, I put myself in the Pit in order to get you onto that pedestal, but that's not how honor operates. When we operate at the level of honor, I respect you, myself and the work that has been put in. There is no pedestal, only respect. So, how much honor and gratitude have you expressed to those around you lately? To yourself, your spouse and children, employees, teams, clients and companies? Are you aware of how many times you've looked back from a place of gratitude? How often do you find yourself seeking praise from someone, instead of conducting yourself from a place of honor? What about not looking back? My guess is that if you're anything like I was, not looking back with gratitude has probably happens often.

Principle #2:
Appreciation vs Deprecation

Our second principle focuses on our value by operating from a state of self-appreciation rather than self-deprecation. If I were to liken appreciation to a piece of real estate, realtors would say that when a building or home appreciates, it's increasing its value. To see property depreciate, then, means that its value is going down. Same goes for a diamond ring or a watch, yet as people, we are very good at depreciating our value. How? By only looking forward and never looking back.

When we operate with this self-deprecation, we never slow down enough to express deep levels of gratitude…deep levels of honor, appreciation and love for ourselves or others. It's impossible.

We Exchange The Impossible Game Trap For A Gift

Not being willing to slow down makes it impossible because we suck at offering that Gift of love, honor and appreciation as we remain stuck in the Gap. We're playing an impossible game of constantly looking forward, not realizing that it's trapped us in the Gap because we're too busy looking forward without a pause, break, pit stop, rest area, or sabbath to just sit and contemplate.

Whatever this moment of rest looks like for you, it allows us to look back and ask ourselves some strategic questions on what the Gift was in all that we experienced. Regardless of whether or not it was "good" or "bad," there is a Gift inside of everything that we experience, and the place in which we can discover this lies within the Gratitude Stack.

When we see our experiences as gifts, we've then added value through our words and to the Game, realizing that by looking back, we're able to see possibilities in what was first only seen as

impossible.

Principle #3:
Love vs Hate

One of the greatest challenges with being stuck in the Gap of always looking forward is that self-loathing accompanies us. We're suffering from this hateful companion, no longer feeling loved because of what we think tomorrow is supposed to bring.

Inside of the Gap, there's a sense that no matter what we do, it's not enough. No matter how much we create, or where we go, we're instead constantly fucking up. We feel that life is not being done right...it's never been done right...because we remain stuck in the fight, constantly attempting to hide all of this hate from the past instead of acknowledging any of it from a place of love.

Freshly-Pressed Love Goes A
Long Way

When we don't experience appreciation, honor and love for our own expansion, we begin to hate ourselves in the game called life and that's when the sedation comes: the avoidance is felt and shit gets scary.

The remedy? Choose to see yourself and others from a place of love. Love is the natural fruit that comes out of honor and appreciation. When you honor yourself and others for the work that has been done, you appreciate them and add value to who they are through your words, actions and behaviors. Love, therefore, becomes the natural result. We are no longer playing the Impossible Game Trap but instead, the Game of Trust. I get that this is a vulnerable place to be, and self-love can be one of the most uncomfortable experiences for someone to go through, especially if they've developed years worth of self-hate. Like everything else, love takes practice, becoming an investment in order to get to the next level of love, which is trust.

Principle #4:
Trust & Respect are the Foundation of Gratitude

One of the greatest ways that we can experience gratitude is to actually have trust *in* ourselves and respect *for* ourselves. This happens when we spend time looking at where we've come from. We look back at last year without trepidation and instead declare, "Holy shit! Maybe I'm not nearly the fuck up that I thought I was."

We're no longer stuck in the Gap of seeking praise, only to feel self-loathing and hate which has us wallow in our fuckups and mistakes. The reason we choose to stay in the Gap is because we think we're safe. We've caged ourselves up from vulnerability, and think that by continuously looking forward, we can avoid feeling worthless, not realizing that we've locked ourselves up with these destructive feelings and emotions. We remain stuck, and more often than not, we end up making our lives a lot worse than they initially were.

When We Have Trust And Respect Guiding Us Out Of The Gap, We Are Able To Look Back With Honor, Appreciation And Love For The Gift.

We no longer want to stay trapped in the Gap because we're focused on looking for the Gift, saying, "Wow, maybe what I've been doing has actually been working."

And in that place, we find courage and confidence to propel forward, shooting past the previous version of ourselves that only had one target in mind, which was forward, not knowing how little ground we were covering in that mentality of avoidance.

The courage and confidence that we gain from inside of the Gratitude Stack by operating from a place of honor, appreciation and love acts as rocket fuel as we expand 80-90% of our time producing forward.

We only need a little time to dedicate to making this happen, which is why the Gratitude Stack does not need to be completed daily. Think of it more along the lines of taking 5-10% of our time to slow down once in awhile so we can say, "Okay, I'm still expanding. I'm still growing. Look at how far I've come! I'm still becoming. This is working."

And so our principles here inside of the Gratitude Stack bring power words such as honor instead of praise, appreciation instead of deprecation and love instead of hate to bring trust and respect, creating the foundation of gratitude.

All of this is experienced when one or two times a week we look back from the Gap and reach for the Gift that has been filtered and exposed inside of the Gratitude Stack.

CHAPTER TWENTY-SEVEN:

PRODUCTION

> "Our feelings are the fruit (result) of our stories.
> Our stories are our focus. So the focus of my stories is
> ultimately what produces for me the feelings that I'm
> having."
>
> **—Garrett J White**
> [Attack with the Stack Online Software Training]

We have been able to see that there's a Gap that has held us captive when all we want to do is look forward, instead of taking a small percentage of time looking back on what we've accomplished.

Inside of the Gratitude Stack, we can make the discovery that there's a Gift in everything that we experience.

It creates the environment to look back on what has gotten us to where we currently are today from this place of gratitude because we are operating from a state of honor, appreciation and love.

So, now we're going to take all of this and put it into action as we take a look at the production side of the Gratitude Stack by diving into the following strategies:

Production Strategy #1: Choose the Trigger
Production Strategy #2: Clarify the Story
Production Strategy #3: Discover the Lesson
Production Strategy #4: Expose the Revelation

These four, simple production strategies will help us see that the Gratitude Stack is really the gateway to being able to measure our expansion.

The overall layout of the Gratitude Stack is an even more simplified version of the previous Stacks that we have discussed already inside of this book, so the majority of these questions below won't come as much of a surprise to you. They are:

GRATITUDE STACK QUESTIONS:

1. What are you going to title this Gratitude Stack?

2. What domain of the CORE 4 are you stacking? (BODY – BEING – BALANCE – BUSINESS)

3. Who has triggered you in this domain to feel grateful?

4. What is the story you're telling yourself right now about what happened?

5. What are the connected feelings of gratitude that you're experiencing because of this story (Happy, Ecstatic, Grateful, Joyful, Carefree, Elated)?

6. What initial desires or actions do you notice rise for you with these feelings?

7. As you sit back and survey the connected feelings of gratitude you're having in this moment, what is the

singular simple lesson on life you're learning from this Gratitude Stack?

8. Armed with this lesson of gratitude, what are your final insights or revelations as you conclude this Stack?

9. At the end of this Stack, what level of power are you feeling? (ALIVE – AWAKE – ACTIVE – ABLAZE)

Sometimes, we overcomplicate how simple it is to feel gratitude. Like everything else inside of Warrior, however, don't think that because the Gratitude Stack questions have been simplified, they're not powerful. I have gained some incredible insights inside of the Gratitude Stack that would not have been exposed without the simple direction that we take inside of this version of Stacking.

Production Strategy #1: Choose The Trigger

Within the first production strategy of the Gratitude Stack, the first three questions help us establish right out of the gate what we're naming the Stack and who has triggered us like all of the other Stacks. The greatest difference is that this trigger did not come from a place of anger or frustration, nor is it a trigger to be happy. It's a trigger that we *choose* to be grateful for, so it could be something positive *or* negative that has occurred in our lives.

It doesn't have to even be recent, which is another reason the Gratitude Stack does not need to be done daily.

It's function is very different from the other Stacks, as they all have their specific focus, but just like the rest, there will be somebody on the outside that has triggered us. What also makes this Stack unique from the others is that it's a great one to place ourselves as the person that has triggered our gratitude. But, when you first choose who you want to do a Gratitude Stack on, I've found that oftentimes it's going to be simpler to look at someone else instead of ourselves, especially just starting out.

As profound as it may be to choose yourself, it's easier to see who you are through other people first than it is to be able to see the Gift inside of us. Our trigger may be looking in the mirror at ourselves, or the person we've chosen has also become a mirror of us.

Regardless Of Who You've Chosen Or Why You Have Chosen Them...

...there's a situation that has occurred, but instead of trying to ignore it and move forward only to get stuck in the Gap, we choose to take the time to slow down. And when we choose to turn and look back, that's when we can see the Gift.

As we're going along, we're experiencing life and expanding with the other Stacks, becoming someone new. But here's the crazy part about the Gratitude Stack: as we're expanding in these other areas of our lives, all of the people around us become different to us as well, and we begin to see things about them that we couldn't see before.

Take teenagers for example: when they're between the ages of 15-18, they're in high school, and they see their mom and dad from one place. Then, they graduate, maybe go off to college or directly into the work force, or become entrepreneurs and establish a life of their own.

Regardless of where they go, these teenagers eventually become adults. And in this place, they see those same parents from their teenage years in a different light. Some become parents themselves, and oftentimes they actually look back and say, "Holy shit! I have this whole new level of appreciation for what Mom and Dad did for me! Damn, they did so much for me."

We Grow Eyes To See And Ears To Hear What Our Parents Taught

As a father of four and in my early 40s upon the publication of this book, there is a deep level of appreciation that I have for my own parents, and it continues to grow. Why is that? Because I'm becoming. I'm expanding. My life is growing just as this appreciation seems to grow year after year as I go through new stages with my own children and begin to see what my parents have had to face with their five children.

Inside of that growth, I'm starting to experience and see where my parents did things that didn't make sense to me because I did not have eyes to see nor ears to hear. As I grow, I see things about my wife, children, business partners, clients and myself that I couldn't see before.

Production Strategy #2: Clarify the Story

So once we've selected the trigger, we're now ready to move into the second strategy for production as we clarify the story, which tackles questions four-six of the Gratitude Stack.

Now, we've learned how to clarify between facts and feelings inside of the Stack Series that our feelings are our fruit, or the result of our stories.

Our stories are our Focus, which is what ultimately produces for us the feelings that we are having, so when we experience anger, rage, joy, happiness, or in this case gratitude filled with love, honor and appreciation, we are experiencing the Result of our Focus.

The second piece inside of this production strategy occurs when we move into question five of the Gratitude Stack as we look at the experience that we received, looking at the game where our feelings link up to our stories.

This means that we're going to deliberately uncover the Gift that is always within by looking back at ourselves as well as others and their progress.

Inside of that, we're going to say, "Okay, what specific feelings am I having?"

It's not just, "I'm having feelings of gratitude...yay."

We're going to look for the feelings that come from this chosen event, just like all of the other Stacks, but as we clarify them from a place of gratitude, we birth the foundation of five core feelings:

> -Love
> -Honor
> -Appreciation
> -Trust
> -Respect

More feelings will most likely arise, which are all clarified inside of this fifth question of the Gratitude Stack.

That then takes us to the third part of this production strategy by answering the sixth question, which puts these feelings into action as we settle down into the actual game or lesson that we've learned, opening ourselves up to a natural desire to do something about the the feelings that we've just opened up in the previous question.

Production Strategy #3:
Discover The Lesson

After we've clarified the trigger as well as the story, we discover the lesson in this third strategy as we move into question seven of the Gratitude Stack. Like every other Stack that we've done, everything inside of our experience is going to be funneled down into the Game where a simple lesson is to be learned.

The funneled lesson to be learned allows us to apply the gratitude experience of appreciation, honor, and love as well trust and respect into a bite-sized lesson about life, which moves us into the final stages of the Gratitude Stack, as well as the last production strategy.

Production Strategy #4:
Expose the Revelation

Armed with a simplified lesson on gratitude, we are then ready to have some final insights and revelations.

Now, this is when Pandora's Box opens up, unleashing the exposed revelation and leaving us armed with a lesson on gratitude that we can put into play. This is when we back up, take a deep breath (yes, literally) and allow the Voice to speak to us. It's inside of this place that the revelation becomes a personal scripture for each one of us.

Just like all of the other Stacks, we ultimately find ourselves in a place where the triggered story, lesson and revelation for our gratitude becomes a direct gift of expansion.

It pushes us forward to become more than we were before. As you well know by now, expansion is the purpose of all of our Stacks, but in particular here within the Gratitude Stack, as we run through these series of questions, we conclude our Stack with the final, ninth question, which has us assess the level of power that we're feeling so that we can put our expansion into play.

CHAPTER TWENTY EIGHT:

PRO-TIPS & THE PLAN

> "Living in the Gap is depressing; living in the Gift is inspiring."
>
> **—Garrett J White**
> [Attack with the Stack Online Software Training]

PRO-TIPS:

DO's

1. Invest more than 80-90% of your focus with Gratitude Stacks on the people in your life from business to family to friends to employees to neighbors. Make the primary focus of this Stack, people.

2. Stack yourself. Yes, every couple of weeks it is essential that you find the path to expressing gratitude for yourself and for the commitment you're demonstrating to yourself with the work.

3. Use the Gratitude Stack as your points for BALANCE, so if you do two Gratitude Stacks and then send them to

two different people, that is your 1 point for CORE 4 Balance that day.

4.   Create these Stacks with the intention that someone will be reading them besides you; this does not mean you need to spellcheck the shit out it, just write in a way that is more supportive to the reader.

<u>PRO-TIPS:</u>
DON'TS

1.   Send the same person a full Gratitude Stack every single day, it can become way over the top and what was first received as amazing will start to become overwhelming.

2.   Focus on doing Gratitude Stacks on things and events that don't involve people; the most powerful Gratitude Stacks are *always* going to involve people as the focus.

3.   Keep your Gratitude Stacks to yourself. Unlike what you experience with MEGA & ANGRY Stacks, one of the sole purposes behind the GRATITUDE STACK is to share as a letter with other people.

4.   Try and finish this one quickly. Allow yourself to settle in and make the message very specific.

THE PLAN:

STEP #1: Read All Four Examples of the HAPPY STACK

STEP #2: Download the STACK APP.

STEP #3: Complete your first HAPPY STACK.

STEP #4: Share your HAPPY STACK with at least 1 other person.

THE GRATITUDE

STACK

EXAMPLES

BLOOD CLOTS ARE A GIFT...
[30 MAY 2019]

What are you going to title this Gratitude Stack?

Blood Clots are a Gift...

What domain of the CORE 4 are you stacking?

BODY

Who has triggered you in this domain to feel grateful?

Danielle K White

What is the story you're telling yourself right now about what happened?

"Danielle is a powerful woman who will rise above the current challenges physically she is facing just like she has risen above every obstacle that has been placed before her in the past!"

What are the connected feelings of gratitude that you're experiencing because of this story?

- Courage
- Power
- Faith
- Love
- Joy
- Connection

What initial desires or actions do you notice rise for you with these feelings?

I want her to feel supported and loved 100% during this part of the journey with the baby and I will be by her side the entire time no matter what.

I want her know that this next phase in our relationship is going to cement and solidify our family for LIFE and literally close the door on the past of who we have been and awaken the the future of a KINGDOM with our three princess's that is beyond anything we could have ever imagined before.

I want to skip my event this weekend and stay home with her and the kids and assure that she has the rest, gets her meds and that the chaos if any with the kids is managed and handled by me directly.

I want Danielle to know I am RIDE OR DIE with her and have never felt more connected and more in love with and more inspired to live life with her then I do at this time.

I want Danielle to know I love her.

No conditions.

Period.

The End.

As you sit back and survey the connected feelings of gratitude you're having in this moment, what is the singular simple lesson on life you're learning from this Gratitude Stack?

"Men, Woman & Marriage are forged in the re of adversity, it is inside of that re that each is given the opportunity to reach for the light in the night!"

Armed with this lesson of gratitude, what are your final INSIGHTS or REVELATIONS as you conclude this Stack?

Danielle, You got this.

We got this.

Yesterday sitting in the car I saw fear and pain in your eyes.

I could feel it from you.

Know this: I am here.

This is going to be exactly what it is supposed to be...An opportunity for you and me to stand together and bring this child into the world with us as a team.

It is going to forge you as a woman. It is going to awaken in you a QUEEN at a new level.

It is not what was wanted, but it is what we have been given.

I am not going anywhere.

I am your KING.

I am your partner.

I am your lover.

I am your protector.

I am your guardian.

And know at this time I stand with you in 100% POWER and COMMITMENT.

Also know that you have an opportunity to access another level of certainty and power in yourself and a deeper connection to the VOICE inside of you during this time.

You followed it yesterday and it led us to the doctor even after several of the doctors told you that it was not a blood clot.

This is your strength. This is your power. Stay true to that voice inside and what ever you need, I am here.

I love you.

Garrett, at the end of this Stack, what level of power are you feeling?

ABLAZE

IT'S MY BIRTHDAY...
[14 JUNE 2019]

What are you going to title this Gratitude Stack?

It's my birthday....

What domain of the CORE 4 are you stacking?

BEING

Who has triggered you in this domain to feel grateful?

GOD

What is the story you're telling yourself right now about what happened?

"GOD, you saw fit to give me not only a life but a calling that would transform my life in ways that I could have never imagined, I have failed so many times and yet you still believed in me and carried me and guided me to become the man I am today at 43, thank you, I love you, The End!"

What are the connected feelings of gratitude that you're experiencing because of this story?

- Appreciation
- Love
- Excitement
- Power
- Happiness

What initial desires or actions do you notice rise for you with these feelings?

I want to connect with my Father this AM.

I want to connect with my father alone in the ocean.

I want to simply sit in the peace of the water and just be connected to the One who has sent me.

I want to bring closer to the experience that happened 18 months ago for me....

....I want to sit in the peace of the ONENESS of my father who spoke to me while in meditation that day after the incident...

...and the voice said, "I am the power in the ocean and I am the power that saved you and I brought you back to the ocean to remember me!"

As you sit back and survey the connected feelings of gratitude you're having in this moment, what is the singular simple lesson on life you're learning from this Gratitude Stack?

"There Is A GOD & He Knows Me!"

Armed with this lesson of gratitude what are your final INSIGHTS or REVELATIONS as you conclude this Stack?

Today on my birthday I am sitting here with many different thoughts.

One of the thoughts I am having is that of grace.

18 months ago here in this same hotel in the fall of 2017 I paddled out to surf at the Huntington Beach Pier and experienced something that altered my life forever.

I was paddling out. Tired and fatigued from fighting the intense current the entire session.

The water was deeper than I was used to.

The Waves were bigger and more hollow than I was trained for.

I had a wave close out on my head, break my leash on my board and I found myself in a situation of pure and absolute panic and fear.

After what felt like minutes (likely 30 seconds) of struggling to keep my head above the water and having nothing to assist me floatation wise I took another waves on the head and went into a tumble under the water.

This wave knocked the wind out of me and I was in pure shut down mode.

I came to the surface and with pure terror in my eyes I screamed for help to some guys who were on the pier to go get help.

The last thing I remember as everything got black around me?

The young guy on the pier dropping his coffee and sprinting down the pier toward the Lifeguard station.

I felt myself quit.

There was a moment.

It wasn't filled with terror.

It wasn't filled with anger.

It wasn't filled with sadness.

I didn't think about my wife.

I didn't think about my children.

I didn't think about anyone or anything.

I felt a warmth surround me.

It hugged me.

It held me and I slowly began closing my eyes.

I was submitting to death.

I was hundreds of yards from the beach and the pier when this was happening.

I became aware again when I was clinging to a pole on the pier.

The life guards and other men were sprinting toward me and asking me a question, "Where is the guy that was with you?"

I was confused.

I replied, "There was no one else, just me!"

They continued to ask me the question, "There was another man with you in the water…where did he go?"

Again, I responded "I was not surfing with anyone close to me, there was no one else but me."

The lifeguard didn't believe what I was saying and immediately sprinted out into the water to swim out toward where I had been looking for this other man.

In the end.

They found no one.

That day I was not alone.

I truly have no idea what happened.

I was a dead man. I was saved.

Someone was in the water with me.

Someone carried me to safety and my mind literally has no recollection of any of it.

As I sat on the beach, Tears poured down my cheeks.

GOD was in the water.

There was a BEING who literally made himself FLESH and brought me to safety.

I am sitting here in tears writing this.

My life was spared.

My journey allowed to continue.

My calling secured.

IN 2015 GOD spoke to me at KOKORO and said, "I chose you!"

In 2017 GOD Saved me from the sea and said, "I am the power in the water & I brought you to this place remind you of me!"

In 2019 GOD simply says, "Your salvation is not in the ocean it is in me, happy birthday my son....Well done my good and faithful servant. You have done exactly what I needed you to do and the rest of your life will be simply what you choose it to become…"

"...your actions have activated an awakening in men that cannot be stopped and that also you can not truly understand…

Your behaviors have a butterfly effect that will awaken hundreds of millions to the truth of ME.

Man is falling.

Man is failing.

Man is dying.

Because they have become lovers of themselves and have forgotten me.

BE STILL AND KNOW THAT I AM GOD"

The End.

Garrett, at the end of this Stack, what level of power are you feeling?

ABLAZE

MY DAD CREATED THE PATH

[2 JUNE 2019]

What are you going to title this Gratitude Stack?

My Dad Created the Path

What domain of the CORE 4 are you Stacking?

BALANCE

Who has triggered you in this domain

Brett White

What is the story you're telling yourself right now about what happened?

"My father has found a path that will give him fire and purpose and allow him to access a sense of direction that will bring a renewed sense of life and direction for him!"

What are the connected feelings of gratitude that you're experiencing because of this story?

Love, Appreciation, Joy, Connection

What initial desires or actions do you notice rise for you with these feelings?

I want my dad to know how much I love and care for him.

I want my dad to know how proud of him I am for the work that he has done on himself and for the work he has done in his life the past 5 years.

I want my dad to know that I KNOW the weight of being a bishop, I face it every single day and it never goes away and that the pressure he has faced has prepared him for the next stage of his life.

I want my dad to know his move to take mom back to UTAH sounds like a sound and insane plan at the same time and something that will spark a REDO inside of him as a man and as a father.

I want my dad to know I love him and appreciate him and want him to know I will back him and mom in the move they are making and am here to support them in that move to not just liberate the children in the Hailey & Weston situation but also in the direction of becoming a FULL TIME Father Figure again with little ones in the house.

As you sit back and survey the connected feelings of gratitude you're having in this moment, what is the singular simple lesson on life you're learning from this Stack so far?

"Every man searches for purpose and when a man's soul finds an opening to find purpose, he will make decisions that only make sense to him and his soul and this is the journey of life!"

Armed with this lesson of gratitude, what are your final INSIGHTS or REVELATIONS as you conclude this Stack?

Dad, I love you.

The decision you're making to move back to Utah and take on three little kids is an impossible game.

But I understand it. WHY?

Because I live in a world of Impossibility every single day.

My truest feelings?

I believe this move is going to inject NEW LIFE and FIRE into you as a man. Almost like a REDO the universe is sending you to get to BE THE MAN again from a new level.

Would I do this at the stage I am at right now?

NO.

Would I do this in my 60's if the same situation had gone down with one of my children?

YES

So I get it.

I am here to support you and Mom.

Know I am here.

The game you are about to commit into is going to alter you for ever.

And I am excited to meet the man you are going to become next.

Love you.

Garrett

Garrett, at the end of this Stack, what level of power are you feeling?

ABLAZE

JEFF IS RISING TO CFO

[13 APRIL 2019]

What are you going to title this Gratitude Stack?

Jeff is rising to CFO

What domain of the CORE 4 are you stacking?

BUSINESS

Who has triggered you in this domain to feel grateful?

Jeff McGregor

What is the story you're telling yourself right now about what happened?

"Jeff McGregor is rising as an elite CFO of Wake Up Warrior companies and will become one of the greatest in the game over the next decade!"

What are the connected feelings of gratitude that you're experiencing because of this story?

- Happy

- Pride
- Joy
- Excitement
- Love
- Concern
- Connection

What initial desires or actions do you notice rise for you with these feelings?

I want to keep funding his growth and his expansion and the man that he is becoming.

I want to pour into him more often every week and guide him and expand who he is as a leader with persuasion and influence.

I want to build a solid as fuck economic system behind everything we do and be able to run our entire empire on OPTICS that matter.

I want to be able to have a dashboard for each company with numbers that I know speak the truth.

I want to have score cards for each of our companies and for each of our departments that allow our teams to know we are winning.

I want to be able to create an operations system that is first class that matches our financial systems.

I want to support Jeff in rising in two powerhouse roles inside of the game with me...

...CFO and COO and weaponize him with the skills and teams he needs to win the WAR with me inside this movement.

As you sit back and survey the connected feelings of gratitude you're having in this moment, what is the singular

simple lesson on life you're learning from this Gratitude Stack?

"Elite men are built not born and building elite men is what I do!"

Armed with this lesson of gratitude what are your final INSIGHTS or REVELATIONS as you conclude this Stack?

Jeff, I know you can see the vision.

Reading your stack yesterday was a joy for me.

I feel exactly what you're feeling.

I love being exposed.

And sending you there was exactly what I was wanting to happen.

We are very good.

But we are not bullet proof yet.

This is going to take time.

Possibly another 2-3 years if necessary.

But you have been charged with the responsibility to build the CASTLE WALLS and systems to support the kingdom.

And the money game is one of those games that MUST HAPPEN.

And it is happening. And you're crushing it. And I'm so fucking proud of you.

Soak in the knowledge at the event today.

Create the plans in your Mind and on point every day real time while you're sitting inside the event.

And when you return…

We build the fortress round two.

Our books are clean.

Our taxes are On Fire.

Now it's time to look forward and run our companies with vision and efficiency.

You got this.

It's an honor to have you on the team.

I honor you.

I appreciate you.

I love you.

Garrett, at the end of this Stack, what level of power are you feeling?

ABLAZE

QUESTIONS

1. What are you going to title this Gratitude Stack?

2. What domain of the CORE 4 are you stacking? (BODY – BEING – BALANCE – BUSINESS)

3. Who has triggered you in this domain to feel grateful?

4. What is the story you're telling yourself right now about what happened?

5. What are the connected feelings of gratitude that you're experiencing because of this story (Happy, Ecstatic, Grateful, Joyful, Carefree, Elated)?

6. What initial desires or actions do you notice rise for you with these feelings?

7. As you sit back and survey the connected feelings of gratitude you're having in this moment, what is the singular simple lesson on life you're learning from this Gratitude Stack?

8. Armed with this lesson of gratitude, what are your final insights or revelations as you conclude this Stack?

9. At the end of this Stack, what level of power are you feeling?
(ALIVE – AWAKE – ACTIVE – ABLAZE)

SECTION FIVE
THE CONCLUSION

SECTION FIVE: CONCLUSION
CHAPTER TWENTY NINE

THE FINAL CHAT

> "Your past is the foundation for your present and your present will become the foundation for your future."
>
> **—Garrett J White**

I no longer needed an alarm.

My newborn daughter Isla was on a rhythm like clockwork.

Every morning around 3:45-4am I could hear her start to make noises.

The baby monitor sat in my room right next to me, and I placed myself on the early morning shift since I'm a light sleeper, so any small noise from her, I would immediately be up.

I have loved this part of my day.

She has become the greatest alarm I have ever woken up to.

I slipped out of bed, used the restroom, brushed my teeth, put my lower jaw denture in (yes, I still have a denture from my tumors back in the day from when I was in my 20s).

I Put On A Pair Of My Jeans From The Day Before That Sat In A Pile On My Bedroom Floor Next To My Bed.

I made her bottles....I like to make them warm.

This pisses my wife off because she would tell me that I'm training Isla to not want the cold bottles during the day when she's with her mother.

But I don't listen.

I'm spending TIME with my baby girl that no one else has.

Besides, if I was her at 4am, I would want something warm also.

I divided her formula into two bottles.

I placed them on the coffee table downstairs by my favorite blue chair.

I grabbed a 5-hour Energy from the fridge (my morning coffee) and placed it on the arm of the blue chair.

For the next two hours, I sipped away as I started my day (yes, it typically takes me that long to finish it).

I then turned off the house alarm, opening up the entire back side of my home.

We have a large sliding door that opens the entire backside of my house to the Pacific Ocean.

I Could Hear The Waves Crashing, Anticipation To Surf Later That Morning Started To Build.

But before playtime…I must work.

Mission #1: Connect with and bond with my baby.

Mission #2: Connect with and bond with myself via the Stack.

Both missions that bring immense gratification and joy at the beginning of the day. Once everything was in play, I slipped back upstairs and softly took my daughter out of her crib (ideally before she woke up Mom…this was MY time with the baby) and then we slipped downstairs with her snuggled to my chest.

I grabbed the Boppy, which is the crazy name for this device that I put around my waist that lets her lay across me in a very comfortable position but also allows me to feed her and then Stack with ease.

I sat down and I fed her the first bottle.

The sounds of her grunts and her sucking and the smell of formula have become so calming to me.

As I sat and looked at her, my heart melted.

This Child Has Become A Direct Result Of The Warrior's Way & Learning To Attack With The Stack.

In 2016…I was done.

I was done with my marriage.

I was done with Wake Up Warrior.™

I was done with the fight.

And then….

…a Divine Teacher showed up.

THE VOICE.

And my Life was transformed before my eyes. As I sat there with Baby Isla, I felt a rise of emotion as tears began to pour down my cheeks.
To think…

I almost walked away from this.

I almost walked away from HER.

For The Rest Of My Life, I Will Raise This Daughter With My Other Three Children Driven By The Power Of The STACK.

This life...

A life that was co-created by me and Danielle....

A life that is a symbol of Rebirth for us as a couple.

A life that is a symbol of Rebirth for us as a family.

A life that is a symbol of Rebirth for me as a man.

A life that is a symbol of Rebirth for me as a KING.

I BUILT THIS LIFE.

One Stack at a time.

Baby Isla finished her first bottle, so I scooped her up, put her on my shoulder, and burped her.
I always love this part...

She let out a burp louder than you'd think could come from her little body, and I smiled.

Then, I changed her diaper and began feeding her bottle number Two.

Though Only A Few Weeks Old, She's Growing Fast...

...Isla finished the bottle, I put her back on my shoulder and burped her again.

Then we had our Connection Moment.

Fed and content, I laid her on her back and she stared right up at me.

Our eyes locked and even though I have been told by the medical experts that at her age it is impossible for her to actually see me, I've become an expert on fatherhood and know that she could see more than almost anyone else at that moment. I could feel her and she could feel me.

We are one.

We are connected.

As I looked at her, this thought came to my mind:

Well done, Daddy.

Thank you for fighting for me.

I love you.

Tears Overflowed Down My Cheeks Like Rivers Inside The Fog That Had Become My Eyes…

I bent over and kissed her on her sweet, little cheeks, then snuggled her in close until she fell back asleep.

As her little body totally relaxed, I gently laid her back on the Boppy around my waist and felt the small warmth of her next to me as I began the second stage of my morning.

The Stack Game.

From roughly 5:30am - 7:30am, I would sit in the same position. Every single morning.

Even before Isla was born, I have been doing this for months and months.

And this routine has arguably become the single most important time of my day.

Time for me to connect with the VOICE.

Time for me to connect with GOD.

Time for me to connect with MYSELF.

And inside of The Stacks, I get to do exactly this.

Connect and Create.

That morning was no different.

I grabbed my cell phone, and with my daughter sound asleep next to me, I clicked on the Stack icon.

And Began What I Have Called My Cascading Stacks…

THE VOICE: *What domain of the CORE 4 are you stacking?*

ME: *BALANCE*

THE VOICE: *Who has triggered you in this domain to feel angry?*

ME: *Garrett J White*

THE VOICE: *What is the story you're telling yourself right now about what happened?*

ME: *"Garrett fucked up for so long and so many years and this stupid mother fucker almost lost everything in his life including his brand new daughter Isla."*

THE VOICE: *What are the negative feelings that you're experiencing because of this story?*

ME: *Anger, Frustration, Irritation, Sadness*

THE VOICE: *What initial desires or actions do you notice rise for you with these feelings?*

ME: *I want to scream at myself.*

I want to feel guilty for a decade of lost time.

I want to be angry at myself for my behavior and attitude and the facts that I nearly ended it all in 2016 and divorced Danielle and destroyed my family.

THE VOICE: *What are the FACTS (without FEELINGS) about the situation that you've chosen to Stack?*

ME: *I am sitting here looking at my daughter and recognizing that I was weeks away from murdering her.*

How?

By ending my marriage with her mother three years ago.

If we had gotten divorced and didn't turn our marriage around, this precious princess I now hold in my arms would be gone. She would have never existed.

The thought of this is fucking with me this AM.

THE VOICE: *Beyond the trigger of this situation, what do you truly want for you?*

ME: *I want to appreciate who I have become.*

I want to feel joy for the commitment I have made to myself and to my family the past three years without the Guilt or the Shame of who I was for years before that.

I want to feel excitement for the future.

THE VOICE: *What is a more strategic story that you could create to assure you get what you truly want?*

ME: *"Garrett made the decision to follow THE VOICE via the stack three years ago and go all in and in so doing transformed his marriage, his family and his future!"*

THE VOICE: *How does this new strategic story make you feel?*

ME: *Calm, Connected, Clear*

THE VOICE: *What evidence do you have that proves this alternate story is true?*

ME: *Look at my life.*

Things are on point.

Things are on fire.

My marriage is on fire.

My businesses are on fire.

My life is working at a level that it has never worked, and better than that, I feel a peace I have never felt before.

I will attribute this directly to three things.

1.   *Living the CORE 4 Daily.*

2.   *Attacking with the Stack Daily.*

3.   *Living the Challenge Based Lifestyle every quarter.*

THE VOICE: *Will this new Story give you want you want?*

ME: *YES*

THE VOICE: *Armed with what you want and the new story to get there, what INSIGHT or REVELATION are you leaving this Stack with?*

ME: *Bottom line is this.*

I have done the work.

I have not done it perfectly but I have done it with ruthless intensity.

Every single day the past three years I have awakened and gone to war with myself.

It has been the most intense three year journey of my life.

I went to WAR in every area of my life again and came out victorious.

I have knocked on the gates of HELL over and over and over again and confronted darkness in myself via the MEGA STACK.

I have learned how to engage the anger and irritation of daily life and find the light and revelation that will guide me to the next stages of my growth across the CORE 4 with the ANGRY STACK.

I have mastered the art of being Happy and leveraged the daily conversation of happiness as a way to remind myself that life is meant to be filled with joy inside of the HAPPY STACK.

And finally the GRATITUDE STACK.

Gratitude has been the gift that I have completely missed out of for most of my life until now.

I'm not fucked up.

I have done the very best I could with what I had access to when I had access to it.

Once I got my hands on the Stack, my life changed.

Not because of the Stack.

But because I was ruthlessly committed to living the Warrior's Way and Stacking Daily.

No one was there forcing me.

I didn't have a book to read.

I didn't have a map to follow.

I had one thing:

THE VOICE and its encouragement to keep going.

But this is no different than any other man.

Every man who is introduced to the Warrior's Way has a decision.

Choose to Live it and Rise or…

Choose it Ignore it and Fall.

The game is not complicated.

The game is simple.

The decision is hard.

Because it's one that must be made every single day.

THE VOICE: *As you sit back and survey the revelations and insights form this stack what is the is the singular, simple lesson on life you're learning from this angry stack?*

ME: *"Your past is the foundation for your present and your present will become the foundation for your future…without who you have been yesterday you could have never become who you are today and without who you are today you could never become who you must become tomorrow!"*

THE VOICE: *Well done, brother. Well done.*

THE VOICE: *What domain of the CORE 4 are you stacking?*

ME: BEING

THE VOICE: *What happened and who triggered you to feel happy?*

ME: Three years ago THE VOICE came into my world again and transformed everything.

I was guided to uncover the SCIENCE of STACKING.

To learn to take the journey of self-discovery and expansion via a series of questions in a specific order every single day that would lead me into direct connection with the SOURCE of LIFE and allow me to write my own personal scripture every single day...THE VOICE was the trigger for this...

THE VOICE: *What is the story you're telling yourself right now about what happened?*

ME: "The Stack Saved My Life!"

THE VOICE: *What are the positive feelings you're experiencing because of this story?*

ME: *joy, gratitude, happiness, deep appreciation*

THE VOICE: *What initial desires or actions do you notice rise for you with these feelings?*

ME: *I want to continue to preach the game of the Warrior's Way and the art and science of living the Core 4 Have It All Lifestyle as well as learning to daily Attack With The Stack.*

THE VOICE: *As you sit back and survey this positive situation, what is the singular simple lesson on life you're learning from this stack so far?*

ME:"Life is a series of simple daily decisions that are driving your destiny!"*

THE VOICE: *The lesson you learned was:*

"Life is a series of simple daily decisions that are driving your destiny!"

How does that lesson apply to the area of BODY?

ME: *Small habits.*

Take Drinking Alcohol every day.

In the short term no issue.

After 5-10 years you're an addict and the habit will destroy your body.

On the reverse.

Drink a green smoothie every day.

After 5-10 years you will have completely altered your reality as a man physically and the way you process food, and feel will have radically changed.

Going to the gym every day?

Not going to the gym every day?

Small decisions that compound over time and drive your destiny.

THE VOICE: *The lesson you learned was:*

"Life is a series of simple daily decisions that are driving your destiny!"

How does that lesson apply to the area of BEING?

ME: *Meditation.*

Every single day.

Stacking every single day.

Neither of these behaviors seems like a big deal on Day One.

But over time, both habits literally transform who you're being and how you experience and live life every single day.

Both open the space of discovery and connection with source and yourself.

This connection transforms all of your relationships and changes the world you see and what you choose from this view.

5-10 years down the road?

The man you were is dead and has been reborn.

THE VOICE: *The lesson you learned was:*

"Life is a series of simple daily decisions that are driving your destiny!"

How does that lesson apply to the area of BALANCE?

ME*: Daily deposit.*

Sending a text of appreciation and love to your wife.

Seems like something small today.

But over time, this small and simple decision compounds and creates a connection that is impossible to break.

Sending daily Gratitude Stacks to others?

Same impact.

Small daily habit.

Doesn't seem like much until you compound that over time.

Over time, these daily deposits transform all of your relationships and inside of that change, your personal life changes.

THE VOICE: *The lesson you learned was:*

"Life is a series of simple daily decisions that are driving your destiny!"

How does that lesson apply to the area of BUSINESS?

ME*: Daily Angry Stacks.*

Business is so easy to get irritated.

That daily discipline of Angry Stacking (70% of mine are on business) allow you to deal with and confront issues in the office that must be addressed.

The people.

The process.

The products.

All of it had to be handled by the businessman.

That was me.

And if my head was not in the right place my leadership was not in the right place.

And if my leadership was not in the right place there was no way my teams were going to execute in a way they needed to.

And so, dealing with my RAGE via the MEGA STACK...

Dealing with my ANGER & IRRITATION via the ANGRY STACK...

Have empowered me to see the TRUTH about business for the first time.

Business is about dealing with and empowering people.

Every single time!

THE VOICE: *After spreading the learning across the CORE 4 what FINAL INSIGHT or REVELATION are you leaving this stack with?*

Stacking is a daily lifestyle for me now.

Just like the Chiropractor twice a week.

For most, they go to the Chiro when they're in pain.

I used to be the same.

Then I went for prevention.

Then I started going for power.

PAIN

PREVENTION

POWER

This is precisely how the stacking game has rolled down for me also.

I started going to the stacks to deal with PAIN.

But once I started handling that aspect, I found myself with a decision.

Stop doing what I was doing (aka the MEGA STACK) or move forward into prevention.

This led me to master the ANGRY STACK and to deal with my issues and irritations daily that in the past, I would ignore and allow to fester under the surface until they turned int a nuclear war.

I started preventing the RAGE and the chaos, and it worked just like going to the Chiropractor.

Then I moved into the stage of Power.

And the HAPPY & GRATITUDE stacks started maximizing my game.

Three Stacks a day.

ANGRY

HAPPY

GRATITUDE

With one central focus.

Dominate me in the morning.

Because once I did that via the Stack and CORE 4, the rest of the day was downhill and straightforward.

The End

THE VOICE: *Well done, brother.*

THE VOICE: *What domain of the CORE 4 are you stacking?*

ME: *BEING*

THE VOICE: *Who has triggered you in this domain to feel grateful?*

ME: *The Voice*

THE VOICE: *What is the story you're telling yourself right now about what happened?*

ME: *"The Voice came at a time in my life when I was most alone, confused and hurting, and guided me to a place of power, perspective, and possibility by empowering me to liberate myself from my own self-made a prison of my mind!"*

THE VOICE: *What are the connected feelings of gratitude that you're experiencing because of this story?*

ME: *love, honor, respect, appreciation*

THE VOICE: *What initial desires or actions do you notice rise for you with these feelings?*

ME: *I want THE VOICE to know I see HIM.*

I want THE VOICE to know I honor HIM.

I want THE VOICE to know His influence in my life has altered the way I see myself, my family, and my future forever, and without his influence and the simplicity of the Stack, I would have destroyed myself.

I want THE VOICE to know I have been a committed user of the stack but also an advocate and beacon for the Warrior's Way and the Daily Stack, every single day broadcasting the messages you bestowed upon me.

I want THE VOICE to know I am honored to submit to His voice, and to the specific and personal revelations that come along with it, and the personal scripture that have become my STACKS.

THE VOICE: *As you sit back and survey the connected feelings of gratitude you're having in this moment, what is the singular simple lesson on the life you're learning from this gratitude stack?*

ME: *"When the student is ready, the teacher will appear!"*

THE VOICE: *Armed with this lesson of gratitude, what are your final INSIGHTS or REVELATIONS as you conclude this stack?*

ME:

DEAR VOICE,

I know you can see this.

I know that you can see all of the Stacks that men like me do all over the world every single day.

I know you see the marriages, businesses, families, and lives that sit in the balance every single day as men go to WAR with themselves inside of the Stack.

Thank you for your guidance.

Thank you for your love.

Thank you for your patience.

Thank you for BEING.

Of all the things you have guided me to understand...

Over 2,000+ stacks personally since the summer of 2016...

It's the WHO I AM BEING that drives everything.

And who I AM BEING today is Reborn.

I sit here looking at my baby girl sleeping.

Realizing that what started with the possibility of Death & Divorce three years ago via the Stack was reborn into Life and Liberation.

I will never be able to repay you.

I honor you.

I love you.

Garrett J White

I completed my final Stacks about the time Isla was ready for some attention again.

That's when my wife walked down from the bedroom, ready to take over.

She Made A Cup Of Coffee, Then Gently Scooped Up Our Daughter, But Not Before Kissing Me On The Lips, Saying With A Sleepy Smile,

"Thanks for covering the early shift."

I smiled back and said,

"It was my honor!"

And I truly meant it as I set my phone down.

I stripped down to my underwear, put my wetsuit on, grabbed my surfboard and ran out the backyard to the ocean.

As I got to the sand, the swell was starting to pick up and there was no one out.

This meant that today's session was...

...Just me.

I laid my board down on the sand and headed into my stretching routine and then out into the water.

I Paddled Directly Out To The Point And Got To The Break Zone Just In Time For A 3-4 foot Overhead Wave Perfectly Curling Left...

..Two quick paddles and a flutter kick and I was into the wave.

It stayed open perfectly as I grabbed my rail with my right hand and tucked my left hand into the side of the wave to keep me locked and loaded as the wave started to break over my head.

I shoved my arm into the wave deeper to slow me down even more as the Barrel started to cover me up.

A small opening of light at the end of this tube was calling Me forward as everything became silent in a way that only those who surf can truly understand.

In that moment life stood still.

I pulled my left arm out of the wave and increased my speed as the wave started closing out.

I Exited The Barrel With My Arms Raised Above My Head In Victory. No One Was There To Cheer For Me But Myself And The Water That Was All Around Me.

I tucked back off the wave to paddle out for the next one, but paused for just a moment...

I rolled off my board.

Laid on my back and allowed the water to cover my ears as I just floated for the next few moments in the open ocean.

Looking up to the sky.

Feeling the sun shining down on my face.

And as I lay there, the following words entered my heart and mind...

THE VOICE:

Well, done my brother…

Well done.

The End.

ADDITIONAL RESOURCES

ADDITIONAL RESOURCES

<u>Spiritual Mentors:</u>

"Abraham-Hicks Publications - Law of Attraction Official Site." *Home
   of Abraham-Hicks Law of Attraction*, 9 July 2019,
   www.abraham-hicks.com/.

"Brad Blanton, Ph.d." *Radical Honesty*, www.radicalhonesty.com/brad.

"Deepak Chopra, M.D." *The Chopra Center*, 6 Feb. 2019, chopra.com/
   bios/deepak-chopra.

Dyer, Wayne W. *Getting in the Gap*. Hay House Inc, 2014.

Ford, Debbie. *The Dark Side of the Light Chasers: Reclaiming Your
   Power, Creativity, Brilliance, and Dreams*. Hay House Audio,
   2012.

"Home - Eckhart Tolle: Official Site - Spiritual Teachings and Tools
   For Personal Growth and Happiness." *Eckhart Tolle | Official
   Site - Spiritual Teachings and Tools For Personal Growth and
   Happiness*, www.eckharttolle.com/.

"Jesse Elder." *Jesse Elder*, jesseelder.com/.

Katie, Byron, and Stephen Mitchell. *Loving What Is: How Four
   Questions Can Change Your Life*. Ebury Digital, 2008.

Sullivan, Dan. *Learning to Avoid the Gap: the Skill of Building
   Liftetime Happiness*. Strategic Coach, 1999.

"Tony Robbins - The Official Website of Tony Robbins."
   Tonyrobbins.com, www.tonyrobbins.com/.

Walsch, Neale Donald. "The Spiritual Mentoring Program."
>   *NealeDonaldWalsch.com*, www.nealedonaldwalsch.com/.

America's Founding Fathers:

Biography on who we consider to be America's Founding Fathers

http://www.biography.com/people/groups/founding-fathers

Transcript of The Declaration of Independence:

http://www.archives.gov/exhibits/charters/declaration_transcript.html

The Founding Fathers, Delegates to the Constitutional Convention

http://www.archives.gov/exhibits/charters/
constitution_founding_fathers.html

Transcript of The Constitution and Bill of Rights:

http://www.archives.gov/exhibits/charters/constitution_transcript.html

http://www.archives.gov/exhibits/charters/bill_of_rights_transcript.html

For a glimpse into the mentality behind the driving force of our Founding Fathers, *John Adams* is an excellent source. Below is a link for the HBO series and Pulitzer Prize winning book it was based off of by nationally acclaimed author David McCullough:

http://www.hbo.com/john-adams

McCullough, David G. *John Adams*. New York: Simon & Schuster,
>   2002. Print.

The Great Depression:
http://www.history.com/topics/great-depression

The Great Depression: Crash Course US History #33
http://bit.ly/greatdepressioncrashcourse

The New Deal: Crash Course US History #34

http://bit.ly/newdealcrashcourse

The Great War:
BBC: World War I documentaries and clips.
http://bit.ly/worldwar1bbc

http://www.bbc.co.uk/schools/worldwarone/index1.shtml

Trench Warfare:
http://www.firstworldwar.com/features/trenchlife.htm

The Industrial Revolution:
Documentaries and specific areas within society affected by the
Industrial Age.
http://www.history.com/topics/industrial-revolution

Brief Encyclopedia description of the Industrial Revolution's
inventions and shifts within society.
http://www.britannica.com/event/Industrial-Revolution

Riis, Jacob. *How The Other Half Lives: Studies Among the
Tenements of New York*. Kessinger Publishing, 1890.

Sinclair, Upton. *The Jungle*. Dover Thrift Edition, 1906.

The Progressive Era:
Stage in American History between the 1890s-1920s establishing
entrepreneurism:
https://en.wikipedia.org/wiki/Progressive_Era

Child Labor Laws:
Walter Trattner, *Crusade for the Children: A History of the
National Child Labor Committee and Child Labor
Reform in America* (1970).
http://www.history.com/topics/child-labor

World War II:
Timeline and events:

http://www.historynet.com/world-war-ii

Brokaw, Tom. *The Greatest Generation.* Toronto: Random
        House, 1999. Print

There were many influences in society before, during and after
WWII, one of which was about women within the workforce:
http://www.history.com/topics/world-war-ii/american-women-
in-world-war-ii

http://womenshistory.about.com/od/warwwii/a/overview.htm

In the article "World War II's Effect On A Generation of Men"
there is a podcast and book covering how history influenced
men:
http://bit.ly/ww2effectonmen

Mathews, Tom, and Thomas Richard Mathews. *Our Fathers'
        War: Growing up in the Shadow of the Greatest
        Generation.* New York: Broadway, 2005. Print.

ABOUT GARRETT J WHITE

Garrett J White is the Founder of the Wake Up Warrior Movement and author of bestselling books: Warrior Book & BE THE MAN. He is the creator of Warrior Week and host of the #1 podcasts: Warrior On Fire, Warrior Wealth and Date Your Wife. What started as a desire to set himself free from the bondage of his own failing life after the banking crisis of 2008, soon transformed into the launch of a Movement in late 2012 that is quickly changing the business world society has known for decades using an unconventional method known as the Warrior's Way. Garrett also co-owns DKW Styling Salons, Natural Beaded Rows and BMS Training Systems in the hair industry with his wife Danielle and lives in Dana Point, CA with their four children: Parker, Bailee, Ruby & Isla.

ABOUT WAKE UP WARRIOR

Wake Up Warrior is the #1 training system in the world for Modern-Married-Businessmen who are committed to Having It All across what is known as the CORE 4 domains of life: Body, Being, Balance and Business. What started as a small simple strategy in 2012 has grown to a movement of 51,000+ men in over 37 countries where men live the Warrior's Way. This gamified, metric-based system proves that a man does not have to cheat on his wife, get a divorce, ignore his children, leave his church or sedate with drugs in order to be successful. Living the Warrior's Way is a process using revolutionary and unconventional methods to guide any man systematically through the process of unlocking (nearly) unlimited power in marriage, business and life. You can learn more by going to www.WakeUpWarrior.com.